微纪元
MICRO ERA

CAO FEI
FANG DI
LU YANG
ZHANG PEILI

中国媒体艺术
Medienkunst aus China
Media Art from China

Nationalgalerie
Staatliche Museen zu Berlin

德中文化交流基金会
Gesellschaft für Deutsch-Chinesischen kulturellen Austausch e.V. (GeKA e.V.)

KERBER ART

Contents

Inhalt

THE group exhibition *Micro Era. Media Art from China* communicates—through artwork by Cao Fei, Fang Di, Lu Yang, and Zhang Peili—how relations between mind, body, and technology have changed over the past forty years, and not only in China. What emerges through the work of these artists—from *30x30* (1988), a performance that Zhang Peili did solely for the camera, without an audience, and that is considered to be the first video work in China, to the cineastic productions of Cao Fei, to Lu Yang's works designed in a digital anime style, to the documentary reflections of Fang Di—is a spectrum that provides an impression of the attitude towards life of several generations.

The title *Micro Era* cites the name of a short story written by Liu Cixin called 'The Micro-Era', 'Weijiyuan', '微纪元' (1999), from his book *The Wandering Earth*.[1] In it, Liu speculates about the cultural and ethical effects of a posthuman world without any historical awareness within the context of the cultural shift in China after 1989. 'The Micro-Era' describes a world without cares or suffering, inhabited solely by young people who will never grow up. They are actually micro-humans, whose size has been reduced genetically to roughly one trillionth the size of a normal human being. They are the survivors after the earth was set on fire by the heat of the sun. The paradisiacal present is based on a complete lack of memory of any past traumas or tragedies. The sole macro-human still alive, who has returned from a long journey in outer space, sacrifices the future of his species to this posthuman utopia of young people, with all their self-affirmation and dehumanized identity.

The list of artists reflects a dialogue that Cao Fei and Lu Yang personally selected: we asked the two artists invited by the Nationalgalerie to choose with whom they wanted to share the exhibition space. Cao Fei selected the young artist Fang Di, while Lu Yang invited her professor Zhang Peili. In the group exhibition that has thus come about, Cao Fei is showing her work *Asia One* (2018) and her documentary *11.11* (2018) for the first time in Germany. For Zhang Peili, the exhibition in Germany is the hitherto most extensive compilation of his works. With *Opposite Space* (1995), he presents a work that has previously been shown only one time. Lu Yang and Fang Di are having their first institutional appearance on such a scale.

1 Liu Cixin, 'The Micro-Era', in *The Wandering Earth* (London: Head of Zeus, 2013), pp. 235–72. Original title: '微紀元 (Weijiyuan)', in *Weijiyuan* (Shenyang, 2010), pp. 85–108.

ANNA-CATHARINA GEBBERS

Micro Era
Media Art from China

Micro Era
Medienkunst aus China

ANNA-CATHARINA GEBBERS

DIE Gruppenausstellung *Micro Era. Medienkunst aus China* vermittelt mit Werken von Cao Fei, Fang Di, Lu Yang und Zhang Peili, wie sich nicht nur in China das Verhältnis von Geist, Körper und Technologie in den letzten vierzig Jahren verändert hat. Ausgehend von *30x30* (1988), einer Performance, die Zhang Peili unter Ausschluss der Öffentlichkeit allein für die Kamera durchführte und die als erste Videoarbeit in China gilt, über die cineastischen Produktionen von Cao Fei und die im digitalen Anime-Stil gestalteten Werke von Lu Yang bis zu den dokumentarischen Reflexionen von Fang Di ergibt sich ein Spektrum, das einen Eindruck vom Lebensgefühl mehrerer Generationen vermittelt.

Der Titel *Micro Era* geht zurück auf die von Liu Cixin verfasste Kurzgeschichte „The Micro-Era", „Weijiyuan", „微纪元" (1999), aus seinem Band *The Wandering Earth*.[1] Liu spekuliert darin über die kulturellen und ethischen Auswirkungen einer postmenschlichen Welt ohne historisches Bewusstsein im Kontext des chinesischen Kulturwandels nach 1989. „Das Mikrozeitalter" schildert eine Welt ohne Sorgen und Leiden, in der es nur Jugendliche gibt, die niemals erwachsen werden. Tatsächlich handelt es sich um Mikromenschen, deren Größe genetisch auf ungefähr ein Billionstel der eines gewöhnlichen Menschen reduziert wurde. Sie sind die Überlebenden, nachdem die Erde von der Hitze der Sonne in Brand gesetzt worden war. Ihre paradiesische Gegenwart baut auf der völligen Vergessenheit aller vergangenen Traumata und Tragödien auf. Der einzige noch lebend von einer Langzeit-Weltraumreise zurückgekehrte Makromensch opfert die Zukunft seiner Gattung dieser posthumanen Utopie der Jugend mit all ihrer Selbstbejahung und entmenschlichten Identität.

Die Künstlerliste spiegelt einen von Cao Fei und Lu Yang selbst ausgewählten Dialog wider: Wir baten diese beiden von der Nationalgalerie eingeladenen Künstlerinnen, sich selbst auszusuchen, mit wem sie ihre Ausstellungsräume teilen wollten. Cao Fei wählte den jungen Künstler Fang Di, während Lu Yang ihren Professor Zhang Peili einlud. In der so entstandenen Gruppenausstellung zeigt Cao Fei erstmals in Deutschland ihre Arbeit *Asia One* (2018) und ihren Dokumentarfilm *11.11* (2018). Für Zhang Peili ist die Ausstellung die in Deutschland bislang größte Zusammenstellung

1 Liu Cixin, „The Micro-Era", in: *The Wandering Earth*, London 2013, S. 235–272. Originaltitel: „微紀元 (Weijiyuan)", in: *Weijiyuan*, Shenyang 2010, S. 85–108. Deutsche Übersetzung: „Das Mikrozeitalter", in: *Die wandernde Erde*, München 2019, S. 355–394.

The exhibition illustrates exemplarily how the classical concept of genre started dissolving, and not only in China. Artists such as Cao Fei and Lu Yang, as presented in *Micro Era*, create sequels to virtual worlds and games. Their works and those of Fang Di and Zhang Peili show how film and photography are connected with visual, work-oriented arts and the performing arts, and how it was not possible to clearly classify performance art or happenings within any genre since their emergence, and still is not today. The media art mentioned in the subtitle thus merely points to the fact that film, videos, holographs, the Internet, computers, games, and similar so-called new media are used as supports, mediators, or working material.

Micro Era takes up the group exhibition *living in time: 29 contemporary artists from China*,[2] which was presented in 2001 at the Nationalgalerie at Hamburger Bahnhof – Museum für Gegenwart – Berlin. This exhibition already included artwork by Cao Fei and Zhang Peili and was also conceived by a team of Chinese-German curators, including Pi Li. The exhibition highlighted how contemporary artists from China have reacted to the economic, political, ideological, and technical changes in China since the 1980s. *Micro Era* continues this approach in 2019.

The process of developing the exhibition was already accompanied by a broad spectrum of media in written and visual digital exchange, video conferences, and several meetings in Berlin, Beijing, and Hong Kong. I would therefore like to thank first and foremost the artists, Cao Fei, Fang Di, Lu Yang, and Zhang Peili, as well as my co-curators Victor Wang and Yang Beichen and our curatorial advisor Pi Li for the highly productive, constructive, and harmonious collaboration. Our curatorial work was enthusiastically supported by Alexander Wilmschen and Lu Yang's artistic-curatorial assistant Ida Yang.

The exhibition illustrates exemplarily how the classical concept of genre started dissolving, and not only in China.

We are most grateful to the director of the Nationalgalerie, Udo Kittelmann, who secured us space for this work. Our collective thanks also go to the Governing Mayor of the City of Berlin, Michael Müller, and the Lotto-Stiftung Berlin for their generous support, to the GeKA e. V. for taking the initiative, and to Angelika Jaros for the valuable and in this constellation indispensable organizational project coordination. Maren Eichhorn, Jörg Völlnagel, Fabian Fröhlich, Fiona Geuß, Claudia Ehgartner, and many other staff members at the Staatliche Museen assisted us with great commitment. For the patience involved in the graphic design of the exhibition and this catalogue, we thank the StudioKrimm. We are grateful to everyone for their trust and assistance in connection with this exhibition project.

2 *living in time: 29 contemporary artists from China*, with works by Cao Fei, Chang Yung Ho / Atelier FCJZ, Chen Shaoxiong, Ding Yi, Feng Mengbo, Geng Jiangyi, Gu Dexin, Hu Jieming, Li Yongbing, Liu Qinghe, Lu Chunsheng, Lu Hao, Ou Ning, Qiu Zhenzhong, Shi Hui, Shi Yong, Song Dong, Wang Gongxin, Wang Jianwei, Xu Zhen, Yang Fudong, Yang Yong, Yang Zhenzhong, Yin Xiuzhen, Yu Hong, Zhang Peili, Zheng Guogu, Zhao Lin / Zhou Tiehai, Zhu Jia; curators: Hou Hanru, Fan Di'an, Gabriele Knapstein; project assistants: Nicole Hartje, Pi Li, Franciska Zólyom. Nationalgalerie at the Hamburger Bahnhof – Museum für Gegenwart – Berlin, 2001.

seiner Werke. Mit *Opposite Space* (1995) zeigt er ein Werk, das zuvor erst ein Mal zu sehen war. Lu Yang und Fang Di haben ihren ersten institutionellen Auftritt dieser Größenordnung überhaupt.

Exemplarisch lässt sich in der Ausstellung nachvollziehen, wie sich nicht nur in China der klassische Gattungsbegriff aufzulösen begann. Künstler*innen wie die in *Micro Era* vertretenen Cao Fei und Lu Yang erschaffen Sequels virtueller Welten und Games. Ihre und die Werke von Fang Di und Zhang Peili zeigen, wie sich Film und Fotografie mit bildenden werkorientierten Künsten und der darstellenden Kunst verbinden, wie sich Performance oder Happening schon seit ihrer Entstehung und bis heute nicht eindeutig einer Gattung zuordnen lassen. Die im Untertitel genannte Medienkunst ist insofern lediglich ein Hinweis darauf, dass Film, Videos, Holografien, Internet, Computer, Spiele und ähnliche sogenannte Neue Medien als Träger, Vermittler oder Arbeitsmaterial zum Einsatz kommen.

> Exemplarisch lässt sich in der Ausstellung nachvollziehen, wie sich nicht nur in China der klassische Gattungsbegriff aufzulösen begann.

Micro Era knüpft an die Gruppenausstellung *living in time. 29 zeitgenössische Künstler aus China*[2] an, die 2001 in der Nationalgalerie im Hamburger Bahnhof – Museum für Gegenwart – Berlin präsentiert wurde. Bereits diese Ausstellung zeigte Werke von Cao Fei wie Zhang Peili und wurde ebenfalls von einem chinesisch-deutschen Kurator*innenteam erdacht, zu dem auch Pi Li gehörte. Die Ausstellung zeigte, wie zeitgenössische Künstler*innen aus China auf den ökonomischen, politischen, ideologischen, aber auch technologischen Wandel in China seit den 1980er-Jahren reagiert haben. Diesen Ansatz setzt *Micro Era* im Jahr 2019 fort.

Bereits den Entwicklungsprozess der Ausstellung begleitete eine ganze Bandbreite von Medien in schriftlichem und visuellem digitalem Austausch, Videokonferenzen und mehreren Treffen in Berlin, Peking und Hongkong. Danken möchte ich daher zuallererst und vor allem den Künstler*innen Cao Fei, Fang Di, Lu Yang und Zhang Peili sowie meinen Co-Kuratoren Victor Wang und Yang Beichen und unserem kuratorischen Berater Pi Li für die höchst produktive, konstruktive und harmonische Zusammenarbeit. Unsere kuratorische Arbeit wurde tatkräftig assistiert durch Alexander Wilmschen und Lu Yangs künstlerisch-kuratorische Assistentin Ida Yang.

Unser größter Dank gilt dem Direktor der Nationalgalerie Udo Kittelmann, der uns den Raum für diese Arbeit gesichert hat. Und unser gemeinsamer Dank geht an den Regierenden Bürgermeister der Stadt Berlin Michael Müller und an die Lotto-Stiftung für ihre großzügige Unterstützung, an den GeKA e. V. für die Initiative und an Angelika Jaros für die wertvolle und in dieser Konstellation unabdingbare organisatorische Projektkoordination. Mit großem Einsatz standen uns Maren Eichhorn, Jörg Völlnagel, Fabian Fröhlich, Fiona Geuß, Claudia Ehgartner und viele weitere Mitarbeiter*innen der Staatlichen Museen zur Seite. Für die Geduld bei der grafischen Gestaltung der Ausstellung und dieses Katalogs danken wir dem StudioKrimm. Ihnen allen danken wir für ihr Vertrauen und ihre Hilfe bei diesem Ausstellungsprojekt.

2 *living in time. 29 zeitgenössische Künstler aus China.* Mit Werken von Cao Fei, Chang Yung Ho/Atelier FCJZ, Chen Shaoxiong, Ding Yi, Feng Mengbo, Geng Jiangyi, Gu Dexin, Hu Jieming, Li Yongbing, Liu Qinghe, Lu Chunsheng, Lu Hao, Ou Ning, Qiu Zhenzhong, Shi Hui, Shi Yong, Song Dong, Wang Gongxin, Wang Jianwei, Xu Zhen, Yang Fudong, Yang Yong, Yang Zhenzhong, Yin Xiuzhen, Yu Hong, Zhang Peili, Zheng Guogu, Zhao Lin/Zhou Tiehai, Zhu Jia. Kurator*innen: Hou Hanru, Fan Di'an, Gabriele Knapstein; Projektassistenz: Nicole Hartje, Pi Li, Franciska Zólyom. Nationalgalerie im Hamburger Bahnhof – Museum für Gegenwart – Berlin, 2001.

PI LI 皮力

The Evolution of Video Art in China

VIDEO art, though an exotic genre of art, is not merely a consequence of following the trail of Western society. The emergence of video art in China, or its acceptance by Chinese artists, only happened due to certain cultural conditions. Therefore, before we get into the topic of Chinese contemporary video art, I believe that it is necessary and meaningful to review the process of how video art appeared in China. If in the past the artists had sensed the danger of art being controlled by politics, then the cynical realism and political pop at that time would make young artists feel that framed paintings, driven by commercial interests, were imposed by Western postcolonialism. Art controlled either by mainstream politics or by the art market is based on the outdated art medium and on creative methodology (realism-utilitarianism). Against such a backdrop, the Chinese artists began to introduce and experiment with video art. Young artists desired to find a new art medium which would not be commercialized by Western galleries and which also poses a strong contrast to the official art. The medium would not only allow the existence of personalized feelings and languages but also be easy to use, disseminate, and communicate. Under such circumstances, video art became their choice.

The medium would not only allow the existence of personalized feelings and languages but also be easy to use, disseminate, and communicate.

In terms of young artists, the time it takes to perceive video art leads to a deeper experience than with any traditional medium. The experience gives the works a stretching force which enables them to surpass the literal description, that is, video, which, unlike realistic paintings, is fully interpreted in words. It requires audiences' real experience over a certain period of time.

Die Entwicklung der Videokunst in China

PI LI 皮力

VIDEOkunst, obwohl ein eher exotisches Kunstgenre, ist keine reine Folgeerscheinung auf den Spuren der westlichen Gesellschaft. Ihr Auftreten in China beziehungsweise ihre Akzeptanz durch chinesische Künstler*innen fand erst unter bestimmten kulturellen Voraussetzungen statt. Bevor wir zum eigentlichen Thema der zeitgenössischen chinesischen Videokunst kommen, ist es daher notwendig und sinnvoll zunächst die Entstehung von Videokunst in China zu betrachten. Während Künstler*innen in der Vergangenheit die Gefahr verspürt hatten, dass Kunst politisch kontrolliert werden könnte, so entwickelte sich mit dem zynischen Realismus und politischen Pop unter jungen Künstler*innen der Eindruck, dass ihre kommerziell verwertbaren gerahmten Gemälde eine vom westlichen Postkolonialismus aufgezwungene Kunstform darstellten. Sowohl die politisch gelenkte Kunst als auch der Kunstmarkt basierten auf einem veralteten Kunstmedium und überholten kreativen Methoden, die sich am realistisch-utilitaristischen Kunstbegriff orientierten. Vor diesem Hintergrund begannen Chinas Künstler*innen mit Videokunst zu experimentieren. Sie wollten ein neues Kunstmedium finden, das nicht schon durch westliche Galerien kommerzialisiert worden war und das gleichzeitig einen starken Kontrast zur offiziellen Kunst bilden sollte. Das Medium sollte nicht nur die Existenz individueller Gefühle und Sprache zulassen, sondern auch einfach zu nutzen, zu verbreiten und zu kommunizieren sein. Unter diesen Voraussetzungen fiel ihre Wahl auf die Videokunst.

Das Medium sollte nicht nur die Existenz individueller Gefühle und Sprache zulassen, sondern auch einfach zu nutzen, zu verbreiten und zu kommunizieren sein.

Meanwhile, the interaction of the video installation invites physical involvement during the reception process. In 1996, China held its first exhibition of video art called *Phenomenon and Image* (现象和影像). In Chinese, the title has more meanings than just 'phenomenon and image'. Video means 'reflection' (象) and image indicates 'response' (像). Young artists chose video as a medium because video art embodies 'reflection', which is rather deeper and closer to the nature of art than traditional paintings. The curator of the exhibition, Qiu Zhijie (邱志杰), who is also a video artist, wrote in the preface, 'the falsehood of historical determinism is to simply consider the human being as a perceptive object, while man not only perceives and senses, but also imagines and takes it into action.'[1] Here is the equation:

Traditional media = reaction = virtual individual = perception = unilateral video = reflection = real individual = perception, imagination, action = interactive

In 1989, the German artist Ernst Mitzka[2] was invited to the China Academy of Art in Hangzhou to give lectures. He brought 8 hours of video art material with him, including work by Gary Hill, Bill Viola, and Matthew Barney. Works of these artists inspired two generations of artists like Zhang Peili (张培力) and Qiu Zhijie (邱志杰)[3] to access the complete video art information and realize the possibility of this medium, whereas they chose different ways. Zhang Peili is known as one of the earliest experimentalists not only of Chinese contemporary art, but also of video art: in 1988, he completed his first video work (on view in the exhibition *Micro Era. Media Art from China*).[4] Generally speaking, Chinese artists in the 1980s were mostly concerned with the 'grand narration' of society and culture, which made them apply the language style of logic and conceptualism. In short, Zhang's early work was greatly influenced by Gary Hill and the style of Fluxus artists in their early works. Such orientation was even more distinctive in the works of his famous series *Uncertain Pleasure* (不确定的快感, *Uncertain Pleasure I* from 1996 is also on view in *Micro Era*). They were going all out to distinguish video art from mass TV programs. Therefore, he denied the existence of any traditional measures, sound effects, or any figuration conventions of TV appearing in his works. Zhang's style influenced many artists, for example, Zhu Jia (朱加), who tied a video camera onto a wheel to facilitate shots, or Kan Xuan (阚萱)

Such differences between the West and China may lie in the different resources: the rebellion towards the system in the West; the focus on the media itself in China.

1 Qiu Zhijie, Foreword, in *1996 Xianxiang/yingxiang: yishu yu lishi yishi (1996 Phenomena/Image: Art and the Historical Consciousness)*, ed. Qiu Zhijie, self-published: Beijing, 1996, page unknown. Exhibition: *Phenomena/Image–'96 Video Art Exhibition*, 現象影像 –'96 錄像藝術展, curated by Qiu Zhijie, 邱志傑, Wu Meichun, 吳美純, with: Chen Shaoping, 陳少平, Chen Shaoxiong, 陳劭雄, Gao Shiming, 高世名, Gao Shiqiang, 高世強, Geng Jianyi, 耿建翌, Li Yongbin, 李永斌, Lu Lei, 陸磊, Qian Weikang, 錢喂康, Qiu Zhijie, 邱志傑, Tong Biao, 佟飈, Wang Gongxin, 王功新, Yan Lei, 顏磊, Yang Zhenzhong, 楊振中, Zhang Peili, 張培力, Zhu Jia, 朱加, The Gallery of the China Academy of Art, 中國 美術學院畫廊, Hangzhou, China, 14–19 September 1996.

2 Video artist Ernst Mitzka spoke at the China Academy of Fine Arts on invitation by his colleague and fellow professor at the Hamburg Academy of Fine Arts, the painter K.P. Brehmer. Mitzka screened the entire program of Kunstkanal (Art Channel), a television program created as part of the arts festival celebrating the 2,000th anniversary of the city of Bonn. Aired in late September 1989, each episode contained original experimentation with visual design, screen text, motion graphics, and other electronic effects, as well as video works like Bill Viola's *Anthems* (1983) and Peter Campus's *Three Transitions* (1973).

3 Zhang Peili was born 1957 in Hangzhou, China; Qiu Zhijie was born 1969 in Zhangzhou, China.

4 *30×30* (1988), Single-channel video (PAL), colour, sound, 32'9".

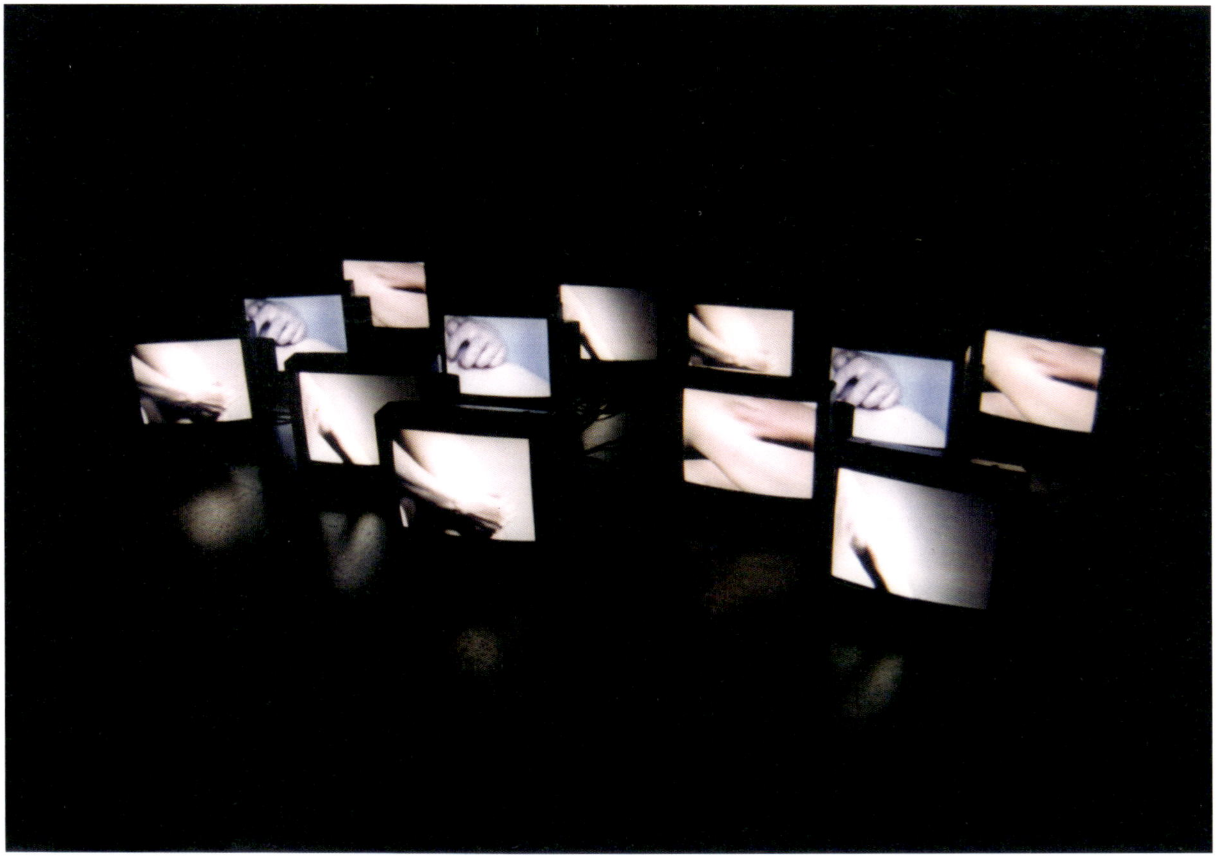

Zhang Peili
Uncertain Pleasure II, 1996
Installationsansicht / Installation view, the 1st Fukuoka Asian Art Trienniale 1999, Fukuoka Asian Art Museum, Japan
Sechs-Kanal-zwölf-Monitor-Videoinstallation (PAL), Farbe, ohne Ton / Six-channel, twelve-screen video installation (PAL), colour, silent, 30'

Aus der Sicht der Nachwuchskünstler*innen führt die Zeit, die man für die Wahrnehmung von Videokunst im Vergleich zu traditionellen Bildmedien benötigt, zu einer tieferen Erfahrung. Diese Erfahrung verleiht den Arbeiten eine Intensität, die über die wörtliche Beschreibung hinausgeht, sodass sich Video anders als realistische Gemälde nicht vollständig mit Worten erklären lässt. Es erfordert die reale Erfahrung des Publikums innerhalb eines bestimmten Zeitraums. Währenddessen kommt es in der Interaktion mit der Videoinstallation innerhalb des Rezeptionsprozesses zu einem physischen Involviertsein. 1996 wurde in China zum ersten Mal Videokunst ausgestellt. Der Titel der Ausstellung kann mit *Phenomenon and Image* (现象和影像) übersetzt werden, ist im Chinesischen aber vieldeutiger. Video bedeutet Reflexion (象), und Bild (像) bezeichnet Reaktion. Der Grund, warum junge Künstler*innen Videokunst zu ihrem Medium wählten, liegt darin, dass sie die Reflexion geradezu verkörpert und dem Wesen von Kunst tiefer und näher kommt als traditionelle Gemälde. Der Kurator Qiu Zhijie (邱志杰), selbst Videokünstler, schrieb im Vorwort des Ausstellungskatalogs: „Der Irrglaube des historischen Determinismus besteht darin, den Menschen einfach als Wahrnehmungsobjekt zu begreifen, während er nicht nur wahrnimmt und empfindet, sondern auch imaginiert und tätig ist."[1] Daraus ergibt sich folgende Gleichung:

1 Qiu Zhijie, Vorwort, in: *1996 Xianxiang/yingxiang: yishu yu lishi yishi (1996 Phenomena/ Image: Art and the Historical Consciousness)*, hg. v. Qiu Zhijie, Selbstverlag: Peking 1996, Seite unbekannt. Ausstellung: *Phenomena / Image–'96 Video Art Exhibition* 現象影像 —'96 錄像藝術展, kuratiert von Qiu Zhijie 邱志傑, Wu Meichun 吳美純, mit: Chen Shaoping 陳少平, Chen Shaoxiong 陳劭 雄, Gao Shiming 高世名, Gao Shiqiang 高世強, Geng Jianyi 耿建翌, Li Yongbin 李永斌, Lu Lei 陸磊, Qian Weikang 錢喂康, Qiu Zhijie 邱志傑, Tong Biao 佟飈, Wang Gongxin 王功新, Yan Lei 顏磊, Yang Zhenzhong 楊振中, Zhang Peili 張培力, Zhu Jia 朱加, The Gallery of China Academy of Art 中國美術學院畫廊, Hangzhou, China, 14.–19.9.1996.

and Yang Zhenzhong (杨振忠), who repeated daily life in their works. What was similar yet different from Zhang is one artist, Wang Gongxin (王功新), who resided in New York for a decade and was greatly influenced by Bill Viola. The magnification of trivial details from everyday life resulted in unconventional experiences. Such means undoubtedly generated many works with strong visual effects. Such differences between the West and China may lie in the different resources: the rebellion towards the system in the West; the focus on the media itself in China. It is perhaps due to the different origins of Chinese and foreign video art.

As a result, younger Chinese artists consider these works to be 'standard video art' or 'insipid tradition'. The possibilities presented by video technology and, in turn, how it embodies aesthetic values have been focused on by artists, as represented by Qiu Zhijie. For him, the route that Zhang followed was to treat Western video art as sort of classical, while he ignored the opportunities that the new, inexpensive equipment and techniques have brought. For Qiu, the reason why he found early video art meaningless is the anti-system sentiment, along with financial and technical reasons. As a result, in the second video art exhibition in 1997, the curator Wu Meichun (吴美纯) wrote: 'what we are facing is not what we can do by means of video art, but rather, what the video art is. It is too early to define video art. The so-called "standard video" is destined to be weary, although still in its process of formation. Born as a medium, it is challenging, powerful, but inexpensive; private and personal, but easy to duplicate and spread; it is intuitive but full of imagination.'[5] Under the instruction of such thoughts, video art in the last decade of the twentieth century in China started to develop in three directions: documentary, narrative, and interaction.

Documentary

In the mid-1990s, the movie circle in China launched a large-scale campaign of the New Documentary Movement. Directors represented by Wu Wenguang (吴文光) emphasize the absence of the photographer during photo shoots and try to exhibit the real state of the objective revealed. The movement is regarded as resistance to the grand narration of the governmental TV programs since the founding of the People's Republic of China. Such orientation leads to no improvement in the documentary language and method. To be strict, what they created is 'real documentary' rather than 'new documentary', though this movement interflowed with video art in the art circle, combining a 'new documentary art' beyond documentary. Wang Jianwei is a unique pioneer in this respect. In his

5 Wu Meichun, 'Curator's Thoughts', in *Demonstration of Video Art '97 ('97 luxiang yishu guanmozhan)*, ed. Wu Meichun, self-published, Beijing, 1997, page unknown. Exhibition: *Demonstration of Video Art '97 China ('97 Zhongguo luxiang yishu guanmozhan)*, curated by Wu Meichun, Art Gallery of the Central Academy of Fine Arts, Beijing, China.

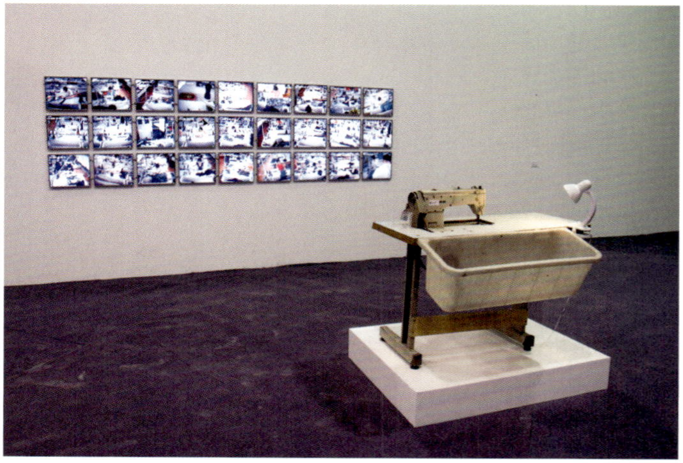

Zhang Peili
480 Minutes, 2008
Nähmaschine, 30-Kanal-Videoinstallation, Farbe, ohne Ton / Sewing machine, 30-channel video installation, colour, silent, 480'

Traditionelle Medien = Reaktion = virtuelle Person = Wahrnehmung = vom Video ausgehend = Reflexion = reale Person = Wahrnehmung, Vorstellung, Handlung = interaktiv.

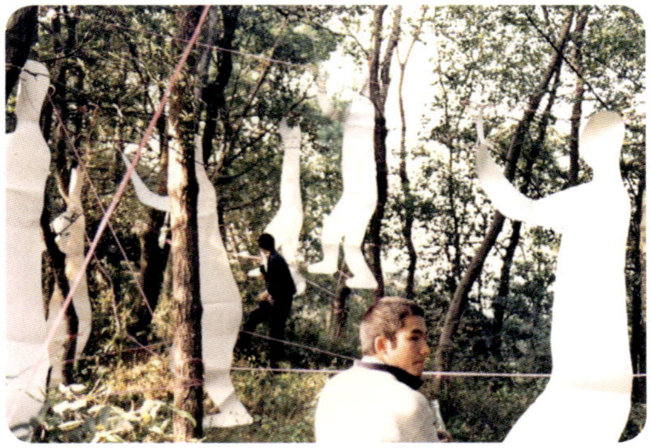

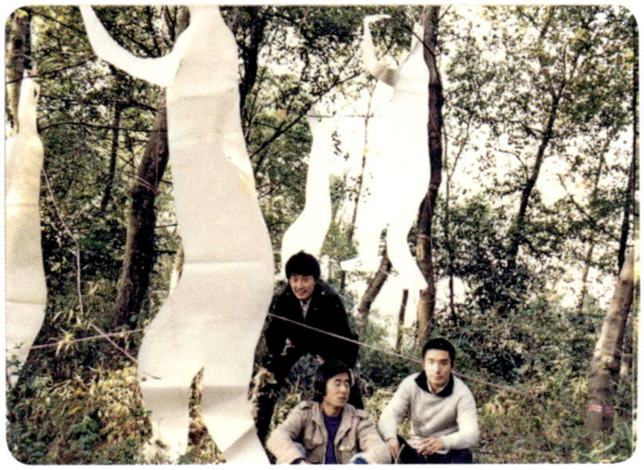

Zhang Peili
Walkers in Green Space,
Installationsansicht / Installation view, Hangzhou, 1986,
Weißes Papier, Höhe jeweils 300 cm, insgesamt zehn Teile / white paper, 300 cm (height) each, 10 pieces in total

1989 lud die Kunsthochschule in Hangzhou den deutschen Künstler Ernst Mitzka[2] ein, eine Reihe von Vorlesungen zu halten. Er brachte acht Stunden Videomaterial mit, darunter Werke von Gary Hill, Bill Viola und Matthew Barney. Diese Arbeiten regten Künstler*innen zweier Generationen wie Zhang Peili (张培力) und Qiu Zhijie (邱志杰)[3] dazu an, sich mit Videokunst auseinanderzusetzen und die Möglichkeiten des Mediums zu erkunden, wobei sie unterschiedliche Wege einschlugen. Zhang Peili gilt als einer der frühen Experimentatoren zeitgenössischer chinesischer Kunst und Videokunst. Seine erste Videoarbeit, die auch in der Ausstellung *Micro Era. Medienkunst aus China* zu sehen ist, stammt von 1988.[4] Allgemein betrachtet waren die meisten chinesischen Künstler*innen in den 1980er-Jahren mit der „großen Erzählung" ihrer Kultur und Gesellschaft beschäftigt, wofür sie sich einen von Logik und Konzeptualismus geprägten Stil aneigneten. Zhangs frühe Arbeiten waren, kurz gesagt, sehr von Garry Hill und den frühen Werken der Fluxus-Künstler*innen beeinflusst. Besonders deutlich ist dies in seiner berühmten Serie *Uncertain Pleasure* (不确定的快感; *Uncertain Pleasure I* von 1996 ist ebenfalls in der Ausstellung *Micro Era* zu sehen). Allen ging es damals in erster Linie darum, Videokunst von Massenfernsehen zu unterscheiden. Zhang verweigerte in seinen Arbeiten infolgedessen den Einsatz jeglicher traditioneller Mittel wie Soundeffekte oder Darstellungskonventionen des Fernsehens. Zhangs Stil beeinflusste zahlreiche Künstler*innen, wie Zhu Jia (朱加), der für seine Aufnahmen eine Videokamera auf ein Rad band, oder Kan Xuan (阚萱) und Yang Zhenzhong (杨振忠), deren Arbeiten eine Wiederholung des alltäglichen Lebens zeigen. Wang Gongxin (王功新), der ein Jahrzehnt in New York lebte und stark von Bill Viola beeinflusst war, arbeitete ähnlich, wobei sich seine Werke jedoch von Zhangs unterscheiden.

Die Fokussierung trivialer Details aus dem Alltagsleben führte zu unkonventionellen Erfahrungen. Die Mittel brachten zweifellos eine Reihe stark visuell wirkender Arbeiten hervor. Möglicherweise gehen die Unterschiede zwischen dem Westen und China auf die verschiedenen Ursprünge der Videokunst zurück: der Rebellion gegen das System im Westen und der Fokussierung auf die Medien selbst in China.

Infolgedessen erachten die jüngeren chinesischen Künstler*innen diese frühen Arbeiten

2 Der Videokünstler Ernst Mitzka hielt an der China Academy of Fine Art auf Einladung seines Künstlerfreundes und Kollegen an der Hamburger Akademie der Bildenden Künste, des Malers K.P. Brehmer, einen Vortrag. Mitzka zeigte das gesamte Programm des *Kunstkanals*, einer Fernsehsendung, die im Rahmen des Kunstfestivals zum zweitausendjährigen Jubiläum der Stadt Bonn entstanden war. Die acht verschiedenen Episoden, die Ende September 1989 ausgestrahlt wurden, zeigten Experimente mit visuellen Designformaten, Bildschirmtext, Bewegtgrafiken und elektronischen Effekten sowie Videoarbeiten wie etwa von Bill Violas *Anthems* (1983) und Peter Campus' *Three Transitions* (1973).

3 Zhang Peili wurde 1957 in Hangzhou geboren, Qiu Zhijie 1969 in Zhangzhou.

4 *30×30* (1988), 1-Kanal-Video (PAL), Farbe, Ton, 32'9".

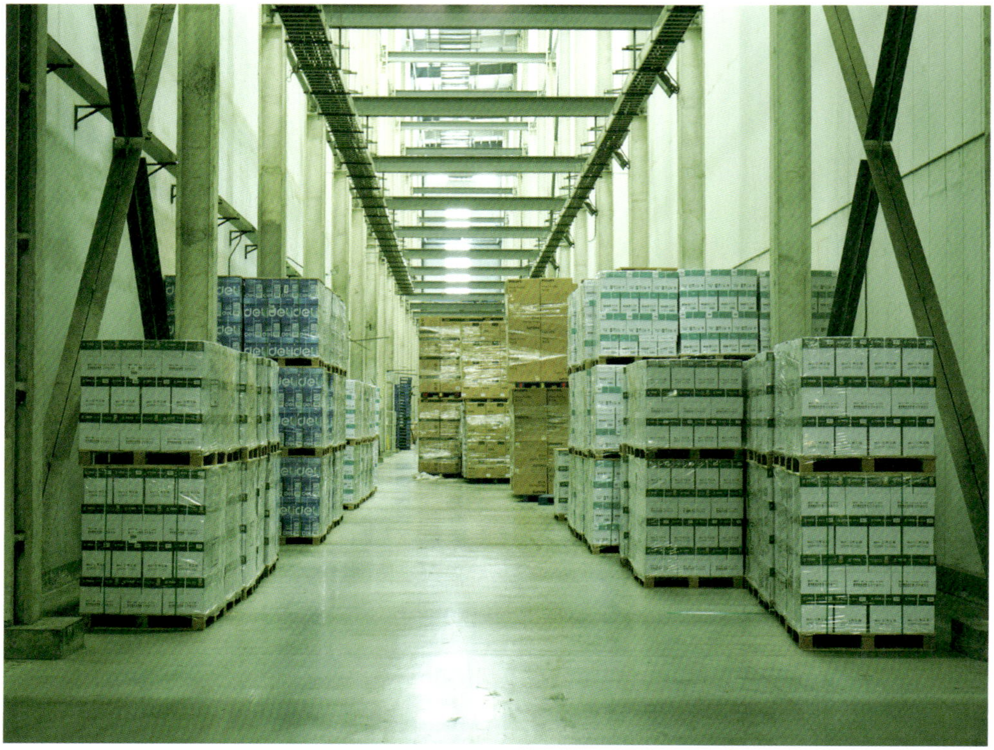

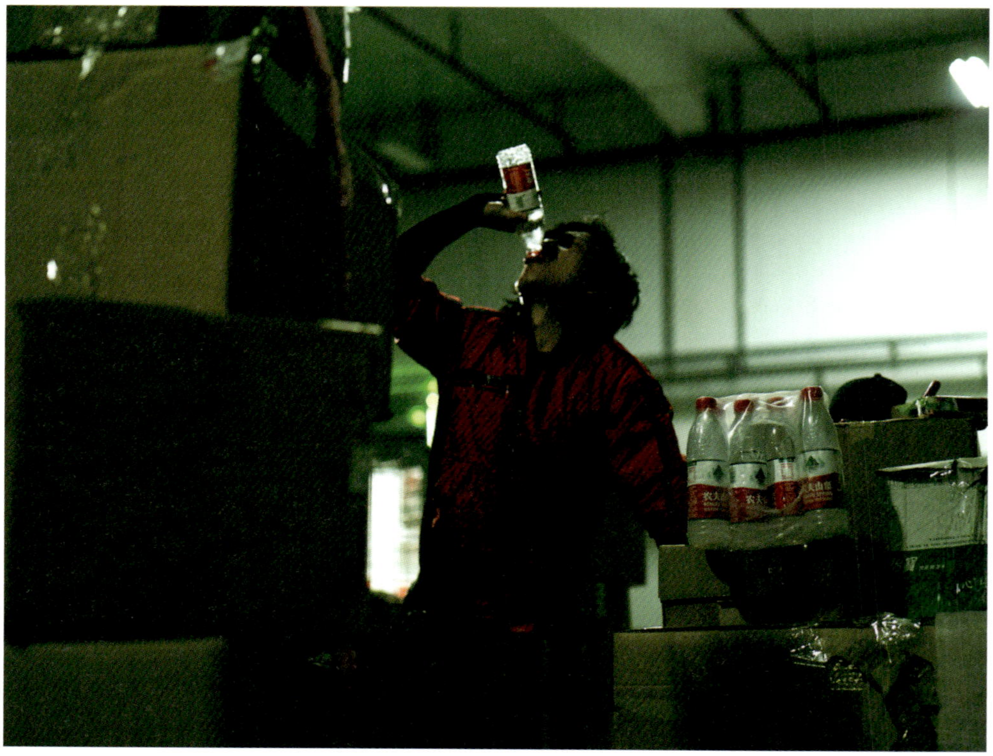

als „durchschnittlich“ oder „schal gewordene Tradition“. Videokünstler wie Qiu Zhijie haben sich intensiv mit den Möglichkeiten der Videotechnik und ihren ästhetischen Werten auseinandergesetzt. Qiu sieht in Zhangs künstlerischer Laufbahn eine Huldigung westlicher Videokunst, während er die Chancen durch die neue preiswerte Ausrüstung und Technik ignorierte. Die frühe Videokunst hält Qiu in ihrem Glauben an das Antiestablishment sowie aus finanziellen und technischen Gründen für bedeutungslos. So schrieb die Kuratorin Wu Meichun (吴美纯) anlässlich der zweiten Videokunstausstellung 1997: „Wir stehen nicht vor der Frage, was wir mit Videokunst anfangen können, sondern vielmehr was Videokunst ist. Für eine Definition ist es noch zu früh. Allerdings scheint sich die bisherige Videokunst bereits erschöpft zu haben, obwohl sie noch im Prozess des Entstehens ist. Als Medium ist Video anspruchsvoll und leistungsstark, aber preiswert; es ist individuell und dennoch leicht zu kopieren und zu verbreiten; es ist intuitiv und zugleich imaginativ.“[5] Unter dem Eindruck solcher Überlegungen hat sich die Videokunst in den 1990er-Jahren in China in drei Richtungen entwickelt: als dokumentarische, narrative und interaktive Videokunst.

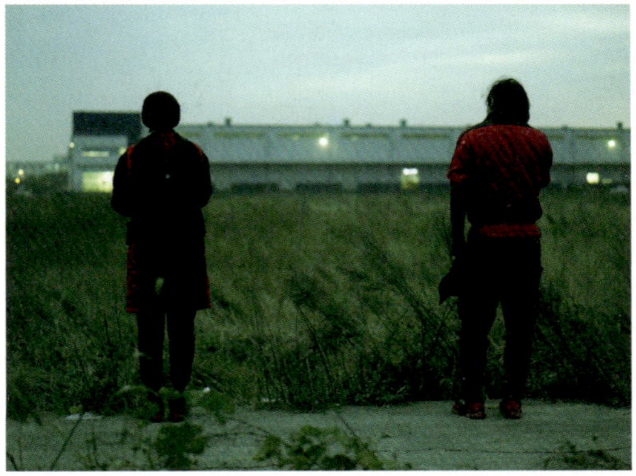

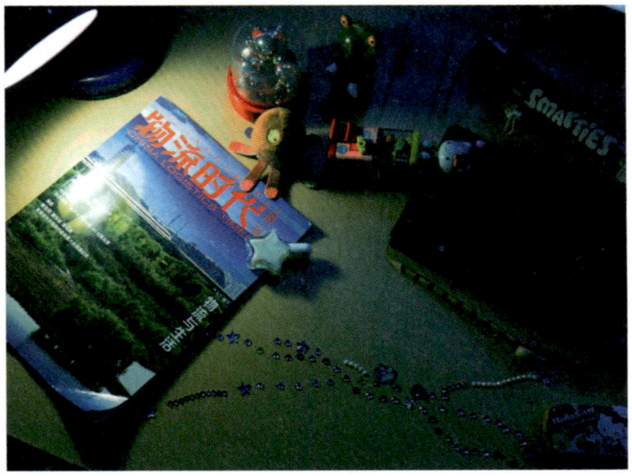

Cao Fei
Asia One, 2018
Ein-Kanal-Videoinstallation, Farbe, Ton / Single-channel video installation, colour, sound, 63'20"

Künstlerischer Dokumentarfilm

Mitte der 1990er-Jahre entstand in der Filmszene in China die breite Strömung „Neue Dokumentarfilmbewegung“. Die von Wu Wenguang (吴文光) repräsentierten Regisseure betonten die Abwesenheit des Fotografen respektive der Fotografin während der Aufnahmen und versuchen den wirklichen Zustand des dargestellten Objekts zu zeigen. Die Neue Dokumentarfilmbewegung wird als Widerstandsinitiative gegen die „großen Narrative“ in den Programmen des Regierungsfernsehens seit der Gründung der Volksrepublik China gewertet. Diese Ausrichtung führte aber zu keiner Verbesserung der dokumentarischen Bildsprache und Methode. Streng genommen brachte die Bewegung eher einen „reinen Dokumentarfilm“ statt eines neuen Dokumentarfilms hervor – auch wenn sie sich innerhalb der Kunstszene mit der Videokunst vermischt hat, um als eine neue Dokumentarfilmkunst über das Genre des Dokumentarfilms hinauszugehen. Wang Jianwei ist in dieser Hinsicht der einzige Pionier. In *Living Elsewhere* (生活在别处) folgt er den Lebensspuren von vier Bauern, die in einer noch im Bau befindlichen Villa leben, und deckt die ursprüngliche Funktion des unfertigen Gebäudes auf. Wang hat in seinen Arbeiten den ‚unprofessionellen‘ Dokumentarfilmstil entwickelt; manchmal stehen die Bilder für acht Minuten, um die Phänomene ergründen zu können und nicht einfach abzufilmen.“

5 Wu Meichun, „Curator's Thoughts“, in: *Demonstration of Video Art '97 ('97 luxiang yishu guanmozhan)*, hg. von Wu Meichun, Selbstverlag, Peking 1997, Seite unbekannt. Ausstellung: *Demonstration of Video Art '97 China ('97 Zhongguo luxiang yishu guanmozhan)*, kuratiert von Wu Meichun, Art Gallery of the Central Academy of Fine Arts, Peking, China.

Living Elsewhere (生活在别处), he traces the life of four farmers in a villa under construction and discloses the villa's original function. Among his works, Wang created a very 'nonprofessional' documentary, in which some of the images stand still for 8 minutes, which for him is necessary, since his purpose is to study the phenomena rather than to simply record.

Narrative

As the reflection of standard video art, narration appeared also to be seen as an element. Video techniques enabled video art to share many achievements with movie aesthetics—with disposal measures adopted by classical movies being applicable to video at all times. Moreover, the time disposal in the video has more flexibility thanks to the help of digital measures: various digital stunts, which created various relationships of temporal dimensions and greatly enriched the traditional movie language. The involvement of three-dimensional animation makes it possible for every whim to become a visual reality. All of this created many possibilities for younger artists. Representative artists in this field include Yang Fudong (杨福东) and Jiang Zhi (蒋志), among others. These artists have received more influence from movie aesthetics than from the video art tradition. Moreover, they are seeking more chances to shoot film. From them, we can see a possibility of applying video to conduct personal writings.

Interaction

Interaction is actually derived from a questioning of video art. Will video art finally be devoured by movie aesthetics and insipid tradition? Will digital technology bring new aesthetic values, aside from better image quality and convenience? With these questions, video art installation matters, as a 'right time, right place' art. That is to say, besides the attribution of video installation and video itself, this form of art also includes the uniqueness of the installation as more than the sum of the two. Telecasting of multilayer monitors or various reflected images distributed in predesigned structures have formed a three-dimensional dramatic structure. Chinese video art has developed into two distinguished installation forms, which focus on knowledge and experience respectively.

Video installations which focus on knowledge always appear in a specific scene. The image generates some semantic connection with property, while at the same time producing meaning. The filming tools can be used to highlight the topic of a work. For example, *baby talk* (婴语) by Wang Gongxin (王功新) and *Screen* (屏风)

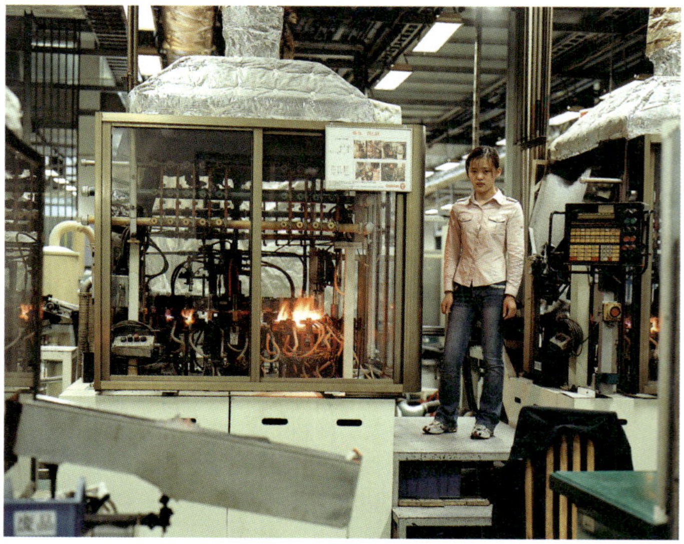

Cao Fei
Whose Utopia, 2006,
Ein-Kanal-Video, Farbe,
Ton / One-channel video,
colour, sound, 20'

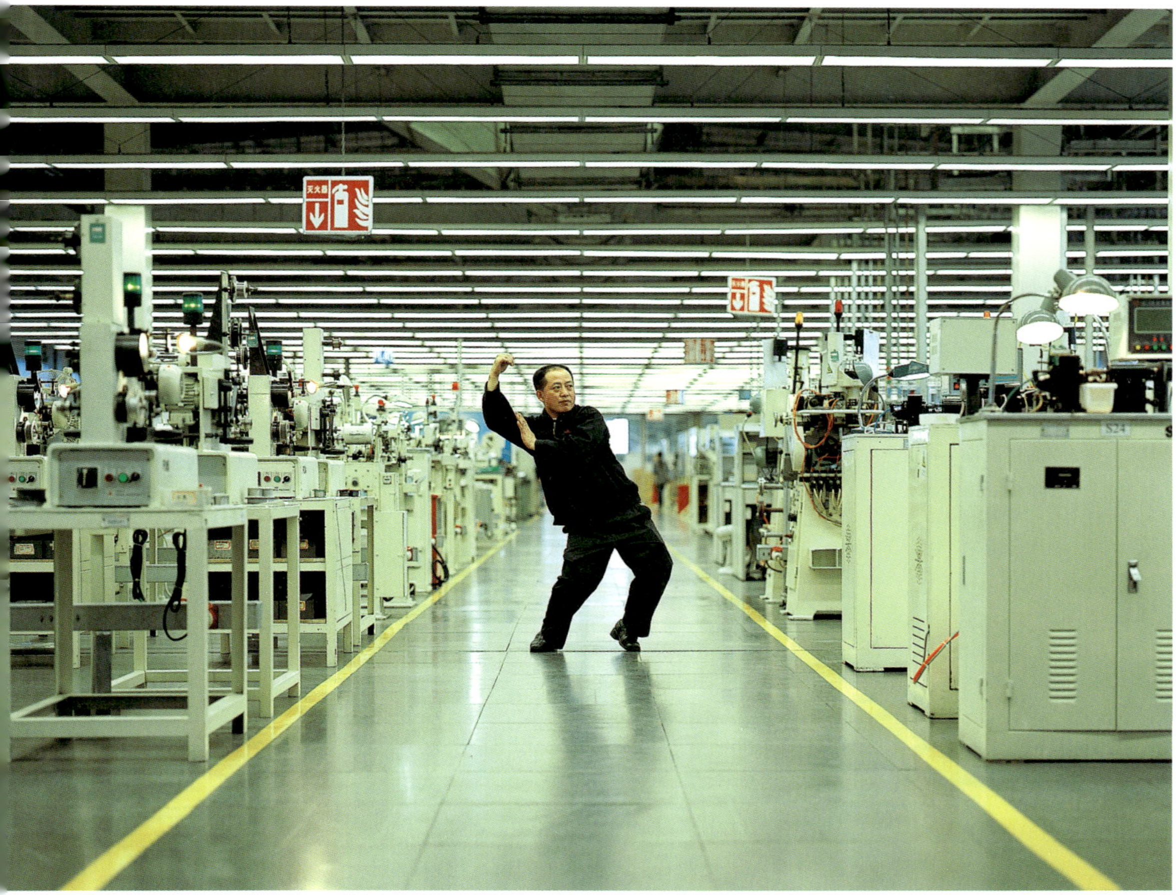

Narrative Videokunst

Die Narration ist ein klassisches Element der Videokunst. Ihre vielen technischen Möglichkeiten teilt sie mit der Filmästhetik. Alle in klassischen Filmen zur Verfügung stehenden Mittel sind immer auch auf die Videokunst übertragbar. Darüber hinaus erweist sich die Zeiteinteilung im Video aufgrund digitaler Messeinheiten als flexibler: Die unterschiedlichsten digitalen Tricks erzeugen neue Beziehungen in den Zeitdimensionen und haben die traditionelle Filmsprache erheblich bereichert. Dreidimensionale Animation lässt jeden Einfall zu einer visuellen Realität werden. Für jüngere Künstler*innen bieten sich hier zahlreiche Möglichkeiten. Repräsentativ in diesem Bereich sind unter anderen Yang Fudong (杨福东) und Jiang Zhi (蒋志). Diese Künstler sind mehr von der Filmästhetik als von der Videokunst beeinflusst und drehen auch Filme. Das Medium Video setzen sie dabei ein, um eher persönliche Werke zu schaffen.

Cao Fei
Whose Utopia, 2006,
Ein-Kanal-Video, Farbe,
Ton / One-channel video,
colour, sound, 20'

by Wang Jianwei (汪建伟). In *baby talk*, the facial expressions of families teasing a baby were projected onto the bed. The milk flows out from the mouth of the image and then is backed from other points, in turn, to formulate a sort of circulation. In *Screen*, Wang discussed the relationship between the secret and its revelation under the 'cultural shield'. This work is more like a visual version of the 'archaeology knowledge' by Michel Foucault. The indication provided by the two works keeps swinging between vague and clear. The visual, audio, and kinaesthesia experience on site sometimes transcends the original enactment of the author to foster complex and profuse imagination. Video installations that are focused on experience sometimes calculate the trace of the audiences' physical movement in the interior structure of the installation, such as in *the present tense* (现在进行时) by Qiu Zhijie and *Sight Adjustor* (视力矫正器) by Chen Shaoxiong (陈绍雄). Such works are based on ergonomics, awaiting the audiences' approach from a certain location and route. Audiences' bodies were predesigned as a factor that will influence the installation composition and scene itself on site. The phenomena established by the bodies of passers-by is not exterior knowledge, but inner experience being evoked.

Interaction has been the priority for video installations. Artists try to ascertain the possibility of video art through the pursuit of interaction. But sometimes there is risk, which means that the more you seek interaction as a temporary relief, the more you suspect the spaces provided by the video art, which results in disaster. Therefore, many artists have begun to seek other interactive modes besides video installation. Artists who were focused on experience began to abandon video art and in turn seek the possibilities provided by new technology. More technical and interactive multimedia art appeared around this period. At the same time, those focused on knowledge were trying to seek a connection to the spacial context and social interaction by overcoming media boundaries. In 1999, Wu Ershan (乌尔善)—together with installation artists, jazz singers, and modern dancers—held the event *Evolution@JAZZ* (进化爵士). If Wu Ershan's involvement was not spontaneous but by accident, then that of Wang Jianwei (汪建伟) could be seen as active. He invited video artists, puppeteers, and performance artists to complete the play derived from *Screen*. In these works, the overall stage was a magnificent interactive work of synchronized video, installation, and performance.

But sometimes there is risk, which means that the more you seek interaction as a temporary relief, the more you suspect the spaces provided by the video art, which results in disaster.

Through the development of video art in China, we can see that a new era is approaching. Western video art originated from artists' rebellion towards the system, while in China video art derived from artists' interest in media. The professionalization of video art was strengthened in Western society due to its acceptance in the art world since 1968. In the West, video art was protected from movies, TV, and photography and then brought into galleries, which led to a combination of video and installation. During

Interaktive Videokunst

Interaktion geht eigentlich auf neue Fragestellungen an die Videokunst zurück. Wird die Videokunst letztendlich von der Filmästhetik und einer schal gewordenen Tradition verschlungen? Bringt die Digitaltechnik, außer einer besseren Bildqualität und mehr Komfort, auch neue ästhetische Werte? Vor diesem Hintergrund wurde die Videoinstallation bedeutend und sie kam genau zum richtigen Zeitpunkt. Als Kunstform ist sie mehr als die Summe von Installation und Video. Übereinandergestapelte Monitore oder verschiedene im Raum verteilte reflektierte Bilder schaffen eine dreidimensionale dramatische Struktur. Die chinesische Videokunst hat zwei Installationsrichtungen entwickelt: Während die eine um das Wissen kreist, zielt die andere auf Erfahrungen.

Bisweilen besteht durch das Streben nach Interaktion jedoch die Gefahr, dass die durch Videokunst eröffneten Räume selbst fragwürdig werden, was schließlich in einem Desaster endet.

Videoinstallationen, die auf das Wissen abzielen, treten immer auf bestimmte Weise in Erscheinung. Das Videobild ist semantisch mit einer Eigenschaft verbunden und gleichzeitig erzeugen die Bilder Bedeutung. Die filmischen Mittel werden häufig so eingesetzt, dass sie das Thema der Arbeit betonen. Zum Beispiel bei *baby talk* (婴语) von Wang Gongxin (王功新) und *Screen* (屏风) von Wang Jianwei (汪建伟). In *baby talk* werden die Gesichtsausdrücke von Familienmitgliedern, die ein Baby necken, auf das Bett projiziert. Die Milch fließt aus dem abgebildeten Mund und wird an anderer Stelle wieder aufgefangen, sodass eine Art Zirkulation entsteht. In *Screen* diskutiert Wang aus kulturspezifischer Perspektive das Verhältnis zwischen einem Geheimnis und seiner Preisgabe, eine Art Visualisierung der *Archäologie des Wissens* von Michel Foucault. Beide Arbeiten pendeln zwischen Mehrdeutigkeit und Klarheit. Die visuelle, auditive und kinästhetische Erfahrung transzendiert hin und wieder die ursprüngliche Intention des Autors und wird zu einer komplexen und verschwenderischen Imagination. Auf Erfahrung zielende Videoinstallationen beziehen manchmal die physische Bewegung des Publikums in die innere Struktur der Installation mit ein, wie in *the present tense* (现在进行时) von Qiu Zhijie und *Sight Adjustor* (视力矫正器) von Chen Shaoxiong (陈绍雄). Diese auf Ergonomik basierenden Arbeiten erwarten die Annäherung des Publikums von einem bestimmten Ort aus und auf einem bestimmten Weg. Die Körper des Publikums werden als beeinflussender Faktor in die Komposition der Installation und Szene einbezogen. Das durch die vorbeigehenden Körper erzeugte Phänomen ist kein äußeres Wissen, sondern evoziertes inneres Erleben.

Interaktion findet meist bei Videoinstallationen statt. Künstler*innen erproben die Möglichkeiten der Videokunst durch den Einsatz von Interaktion. Bisweilen besteht durch das Streben nach Interaktion jedoch die Gefahr, dass die durch Videokunst eröffneten Räume selbst fragwürdig werden, was schließlich in einem Desaster endet. Viele Künstler*innen haben deshalb begonnen, sich mit anderen interaktiven

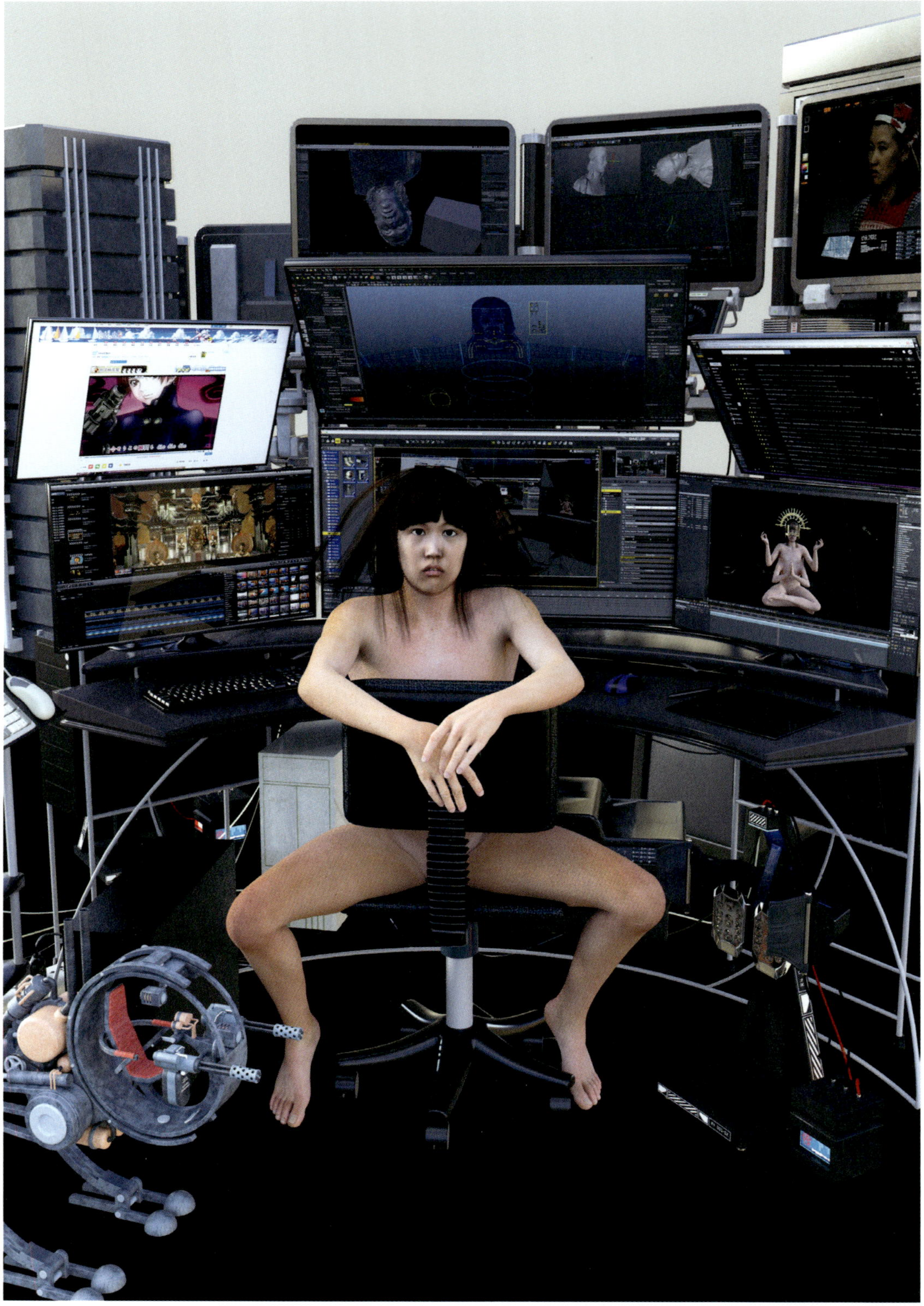

Formen auseinanderzusetzen. Künstler*innen, deren Thema die Erfahrung war, wandten sich vom Video ab und neuen Technologien zu. In dieser Zeit entstand eine eher technische und interaktive Multimediakunst. Zugleich positionierten sich auch die Künstler*innen neu, die sich mit dem Wissen beschäftigt hatten, indem sie mit den strengen Medienkategorisierungen brachen. 1999 entstand so Wu Ershans (乌尔善) *Evolution@JAZZ* (进化爵士), eine interdisziplinäre Performance gemeinsam mit Installationskünstler*innen, Jazzsänger*innen und Modern-Dance-Tänzer*innen. Während Wu Ershans Beteiligung an dem Projekt eher zufällig zustande kam, kann das Vorgehen von Wang Jianwei (汪建伟) als planvoll gelten. Er lud Video- und Performancekünstler*innen sowie Puppenspieler*innen zur Mitarbeit an dem Stück ein, das auf *Screen* zurückgeht. Die ganze Bühne war eine großartige interaktive Arbeit aus aufeinander abgestimmtem Video, Installation und Performance.

Entsprang die westliche Videokunst ursprünglich aus der Rebellion gegen das System, so stand in China das Interesse an den Medien im Vordergrund.

An der Entwicklung der Videokunst in China lässt sich die Entstehung einer neuen Epoche ablesen. Entsprang die westliche Videokunst ursprünglich aus der Rebellion gegen das System, so stand in China das Interesse an den Medien im Vordergrund. Die Professionalisierung der Videokunst wurde im Westen seit 1968 durch ihre Aufnahme in die Kunstwelt gefördert. Sie wurde von Film, Fernsehen und Fotografie dezidiert unterschieden und kam dann in die Galerien, wo sie sich zur Videoinstallation weiterentwickelte. Im Verlauf dieses Prozesses wandte sich die Videokunst von der reinen Kritik an der Informationskultur hin zu einer Kombination sozialen Denkens, was im Gegenzug zu einer Aufwertung der Videokunst führte.

Videokunst geht jedoch über Medienkritik hinaus. Individuell und manuell hergestellte zeitgenössische Kunst kann mit kommerziellen Informationsmedien weder in einen substanziellen Dialog treten noch kann sie sie zügeln. Betrachten wir die Videokunstpraxis im Westen vor 1969, so wird deutlich, dass das Verhältnis zwischen Videokunst und Massenmedien dem einer robusten Fliege und einer Fliegenklatsche gleicht. Im letzten Jahrzehnt des 20. Jahrhunderts begannen chinesische Künstler*innen, wie auch andere Künstler*innen weltweit, allmählich zu realisieren, dass sie ihre eigenen Bereiche und Methoden jenseits der Massenmedien finden müssen.

Folglich haben im neuen Millennium die konzeptionellen Änderungen neue Eigenschaften der Videokunst in China hervorgebracht, wie sich an den Werken Cao Feis (曹斐) und Yang Fudongs (杨福东) zeigen lässt. Kaum dass sie Anfang des 21. Jahrhunderts die Bühne betraten, unterschieden sie sich schon deutlich von ihren Vorgänger*innen. Cao Fei stammt aus der stark kommerzialisierten Stadt Guangzhou. Ihre Arbeiten sind in der Popkultur und der visuellen Kultur verankert. Zudem kombiniert sie gezielt Dokumentationen und fiktionale Erzählungen. Das Video *Whose Utopia* (谁的乌托邦) zum Beispiel handelt von Industriearbeitern, die nach

Lu Yang
Poster aus / from
LuYang Delusional Mandala
2015

this process, video art turned from criticism of informational culture to the combination of social thoughts, which in turn results in the validity of video art itself. It is the duty of video art to criticize the informational culture, but that is not all. Personalized manual contemporary art cannot dialogize commercialized informational media substantially, nor can it rein it in. Judging by video art practice in the West before 1968, we will see clearly that the relationship between video art and mass media is like that of a strong fly and a fly flap. In the last decade of the twentieth century, Chinese artists, as other artists worldwide, gradually realized that they can only find their own territories and techniques beyond the scope of mass media.

Lu Yang
Electromagnetic Brainology Brain Control Messenger, 2017
Zwei-Kanal-Video, Farbe, Ton / Two-channel video, colour, sound, 10'8"

Consequently, well into the new millennium, these conceptual changes have led to several new characteristics of video art in China, which are represented by some artists, for instance Cao Fei (曹斐) and Yang Fudong (杨福东). They had just entered the stage at the very beginning of the twenty-first century, but were obviously distinguished from their predecessors. Cao Fei comes from a highly commercialized city, Guangzhou. Her works are visually connected with pop and visual culture. Moreover, purposefully, she pursues a combination of both documentary and fictional narrative. For example, the piece *Whose Utopia* (谁的乌托邦), a short film focused on the industrial workers who immigrated to Shenzhen—which, by being mixed with documentary recording and performance, created a new form of narrative that sticks to reality while keeping some distance from it. Such narrative style is highlighted in her later works, which thereby shape her unique style.

For Yang Fudong, films and the film industry are what spark his interest consistently. Yang's work *A Strange Paradise* (陌生天堂) shows his preference towards the texture especially presented by cinema films in his early years. Another work, *The 7 Intellectuals in the Bamboo Forest* (竹林七贤), rediscovered a tradition among China's films of the 1930s. In the latter, the records of work from the filming site and the refined film were released in the exhibition hall, spontaneously. Until very recently, with a sort of ambition, Yang transformed the exhibition hall into the filming site, which allowed the 'filming process' to become the subject being viewed besides the filming work itself.

To simply generalize the changes of China's video art at the turn of the new millennium, there is an emphasis on viewing the technological revolution generated by the soaring new media, especially during the 1990s. At the same time, these artists, who are facing the artwork being commercialized rapidly around the world, are trying to create a new trend—by means of video art works—towards decommercializing the works, that is to say, by creating a brand-new media that can avoid being commercialized. Thus, video art works have become a particularly unique means of communication. Besides the characters mentioned above, after the year 2000, the

To simply generalize the changes of China's video art at the turn of the new millennium, there is an emphasis on viewing the technological revolution generated by the soaring new media, especially during the 1990s.

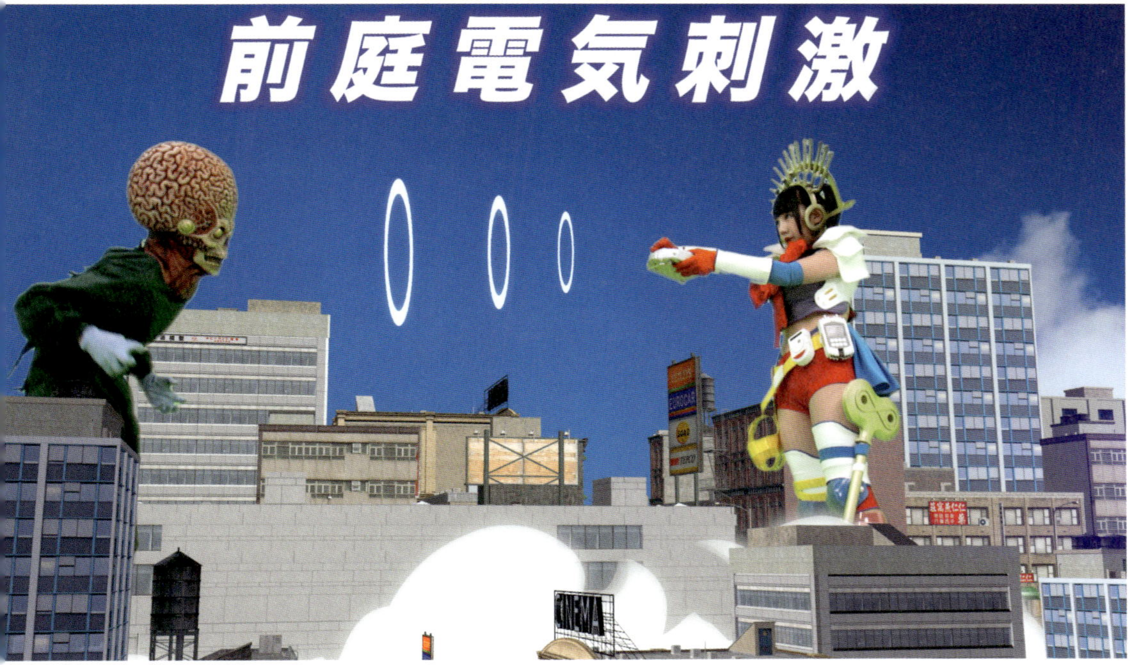
前庭電気刺激

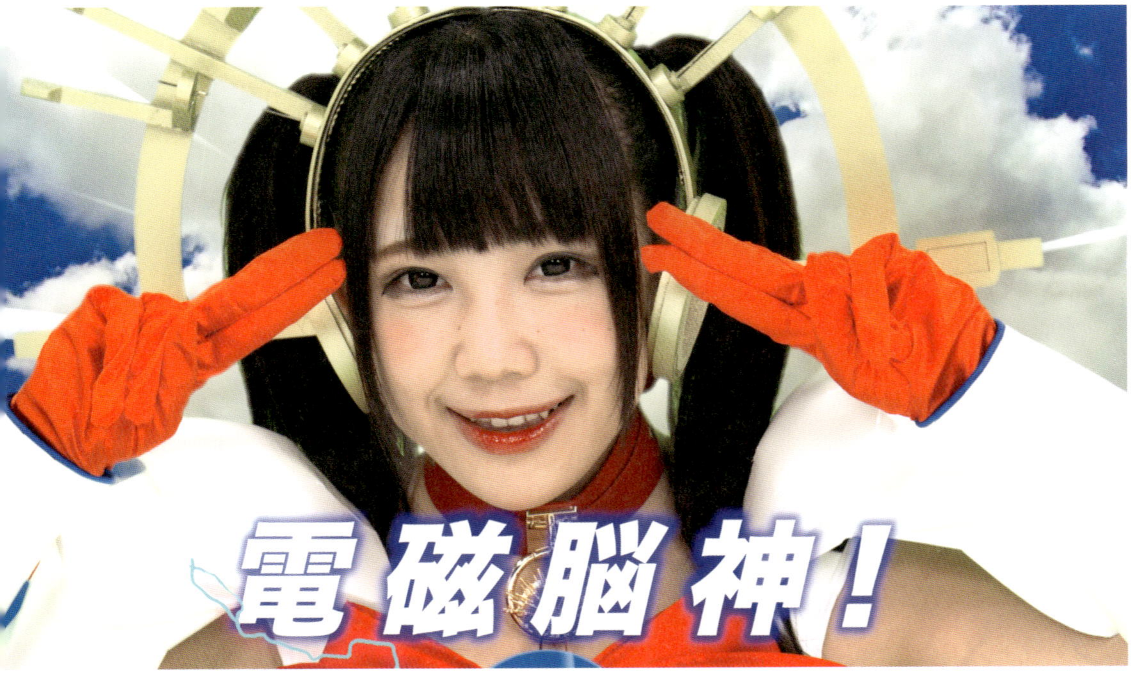
電磁脳神！

connection between artists and pop culture has been far more complicated. As of 1999, China enjoyed a soaring economy after joining the World Trade Organization. In this respect, pop culture, commercial culture, and the mechanism behind these two cultures have provided the filmic language with an enormous richness that has been noticed by artists. Significantly, because of the thriving economy and the development of the Internet, there is little difference between Chinese artists and those from the West in terms of how they accept the information, the technique they adopt, and the funding resources. More significant is how, with increasingly intense globalization and the popularity of social media, a Chinese artist's living experience is no longer as extraordinarily distinguished as it was in the past. For example, the work of Lu Yang (陆扬), which is based on the subculture of a new generation, is no longer labelled with 'Made in China', but with the proposition of globalization and visual experience. Thus, based such a context, those even younger artists started acquiring new techniques and working formats to produce more sophisticated and larger-scale video art works.

The worldwide financial crisis followed close on the heels of the Olympic Games held in Beijing in the year 2008. Since then, an age witnessing the unprecedented crisis of globalization is here. One of the related phenomena is an anti-globalization force emphasized by all sorts of movements: the Occupy Wall Street movement, the Anti-WTO movement, Trumpism, the Yellow Vest movement, the Sunflower movement, and the Umbrella movement. Another phenomenon, the continuous ban on some social sites like Google and Facebook in China, can be seen as a corresponding reaction to the crisis of globalization. At the same time, China's political and cultural environment has changed rapidly, which was accompanied by the constitutional reform of the president's term. All kinds of phenomena in this age—for example, the soaring social sites, the crisis of globalization, the popularity of populism, the sudden rise of neo-authoritarianism in China, the 'chilling effect' throughout mainstream media—are of mutual cause-effect, which indicate the advent of the Post-Truth Era. This signifies the break-up of the monopolistic authoritative information mechanism, while more and more personal points of view are assembled. The anxiety of the Post-Truth Era increasingly equates to the globalized living experience, which seems to embody more possibilities for the artists.

The anxiety of the Post-Truth Era increasingly equates to the globalized living experience, which seems to embody more possibilities for the artists.

These possibilities are evident in some works. One such case is the works of Fang Di (方迪), which is a reflection of a mixture of anti-colonialism history in Asia and Africa and the blended reality under the 'one silk road'. *The Beijing Ballroom Project* (北京舞厅) by Hao Jingban (郝敬班) is a second case, which is a rearrangement on the rise and fall of ballroom dancing throughout the twentieth century—a work combining records, archives, a field-trip study, and image writing to create the mingled clips which are composed

Shenzhen eingewandert sind. In einem Mix aus dokumentarischer Aufzeichnung und Performance kreiert sie eine neue Form der Erzählung, die in der Realität verhaftet ist und zugleich Distanz zu ihr hält. Diesen unverwechselbaren Erzählstil baut sie in ihren späteren Arbeiten noch aus.

Für Yang Fudong stehen Filme und die Filmindustrie im Mittelpunkt seines Interesses. In der Arbeit *A Strange Paradise* (陌生天堂) zeigt sich seine Vorliebe für die Struktur alter Kinofilme. In *The 7 Intellectuals in the Bamboo Forest* (竹林七贤) entdeckt er eine Tradition chinesischer Filme aus den 1930er-Jahren neu. Im letztgenannten Werk wurden die Aufnahmen vom Drehort und der bearbeitete Film spontan in der Ausstellungshalle gezeigt. Bis vor Kurzem war es Yangs Bestreben, den Ausstellungsraum selbst in einen Drehort zu verwandeln, was es ihm erlaubte, neben dem Film auch den Prozess des Filmens zum Gegenstand des Betrachtens zu machen.

Allgemein lässt sich über die Veränderungen in Chinas Videokunst zu Beginn des Millenniums sagen, dass der Akzent auf der digitalen Revolution liegt, die während der 1990er-Jahre mit dem Aufkommen der neuen Medien eingesetzt hat. Gleichzeitig versuchen Künstler*innen angesichts der rapiden weltweiten Kommerzialisierung der Kunst einen neuen Trend in der Videokunst zu setzen, hin zu ihrer Entkommerzialisierung, um damit ein ganz neues Medium zu schaffen, das nicht kommerzialisiert werden kann. Auf diese Weise ist Videokunst zu einem besonderen Kommunikationsinstrument geworden. Hinzu kommt, dass die Beziehung zwischen Künstler*innen und Popkultur nach 2000 sehr viel komplexer geworden ist. Ab 1999 erlebte China mit seinem Beitritt zur Welthandelsorganisation eine Wirtschaftsblüte. Insofern haben Pop- und Handelskultur und die Mechanismen hinter diesen beiden Kulturen die filmische Sprache enorm bereichert, was von den Künstler*innen aufgenommen wurde. Durch die starke Wirtschaft und die Entwicklung des Internets gibt es bezeichnenderweise zwischen chinesischen und westlichen Künstler*innen kaum Unterschiede in der Art, wie sie Informationen aufnehmen, Technik anwenden und Fördermittel einwerben. Noch bedeutender ist, dass mit der zunehmenden Globalisierung und Verbreitung sozialer Medien die Lebenserfahrung chinesischer Künstler*innen sich nicht mehr so sehr von der westlicher Künstler*innen unterscheidet, wie es in der Vergangenheit der Fall war. So werden die Arbeiten von Lu Yang (陆扬), die zur Subkultur einer neuen Generation gehört, nicht mehr als „Made in China“ gelabelt, sondern unter den Themen Globalisierung und Visual Experience. Dementsprechend haben sich auch jüngere Künstler*innen neue Techniken und Arbeitsformate erarbeitet, um anspruchsvollere und groß angelegte Videoarbeiten zu verwirklichen.

Allgemein lässt sich über die Veränderungen in Chinas Videokunst zu Beginn des Millenniums sagen, dass der Akzent auf der digitalen Revolution liegt, die während der 1990er-Jahre mit dem Aufkommen der neuen Medien eingesetzt hat.

Die weltweite Finanzkrise folgte unmittelbar auf die Olympischen Spiele in Peking 2008. Seitdem hat eine noch nie dagewesene Globalisierungskrise

of historical and social fragments. The work of Shen Xin (沈莘) is the third case, which is also a combination of performance on stage, documentary, and archives, aiming to blur the border between reality and illusion, while nevertheless purposely referring to both the stretching force and the contradictions between two fields: one field is identity and power, while the other field is the development of globalization and science. The works made by these artists represent a specific way of thinking by contemporary artists. In other words, since we are in an era—a globalization time when the intellectual experience, mode of production, and technique are increasingly of no difference—we should raise such questions as: What, then, is the point of video art creation? For today's artists, neither national identity nor the 'Made in China' label counts any more, but the values of works rooted in the personal experience and the local experience do. Globalization means mobilization and migration, while the personal experience and the local experience carry the meaning of 'gravity'—a force of rooting and immobilization, which is particularly true in terms of video art within a globalization context.

For today's artists, neither national identity nor the 'Made in China' label counts any more, but the values of works rooted in the personal experience and the local experience do.

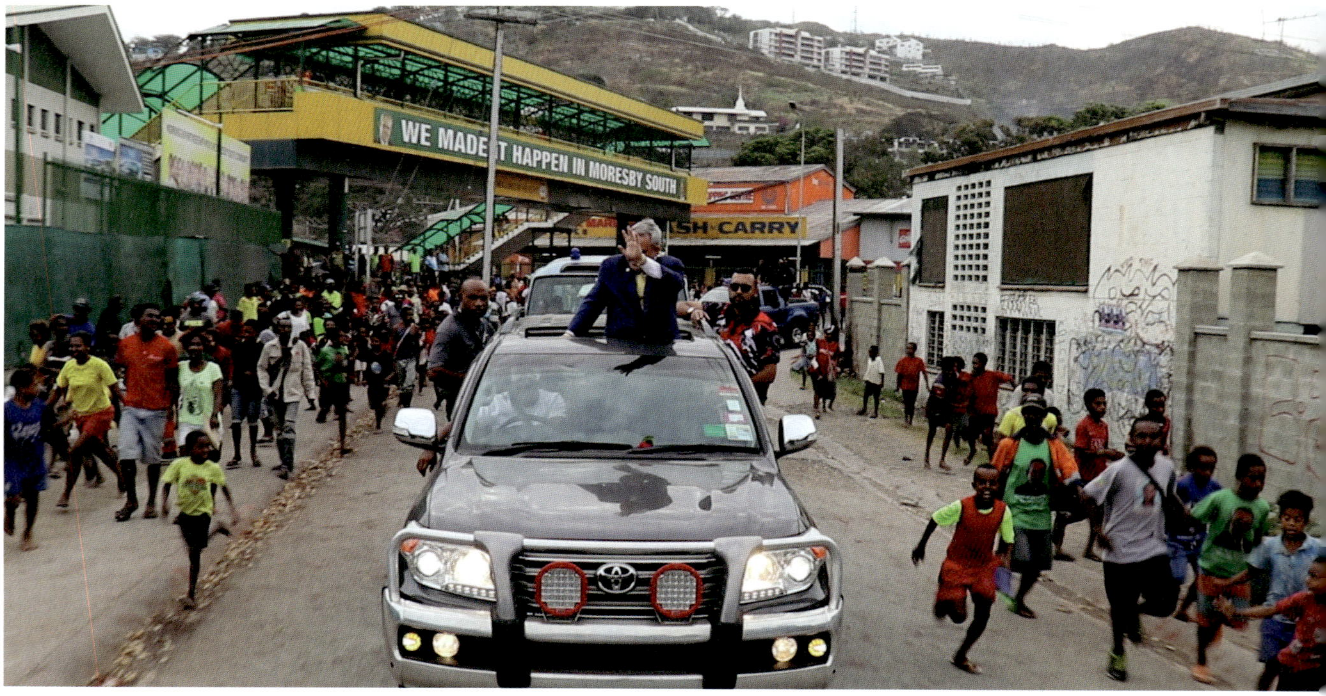

Fang Di
Minister, 2019,
Ein-Kanal-Videoinstallation, Farbe, Ton / Single-channel video installation, colour, sound, 60'

eingesetzt. Eins der damit verbundenen Phänomene sind Antiglobalisierungskräfte, die sich in verschiedenen Bewegungen ausdrücken: der Occupy Wall Street, der Anti-WTO-Bewegung, dem Trumpismus, den Gelbwesten, der Sonnenblumen- und der Regenschirm-Bewegung. Ein weiteres Phänomen, die dauerhafte Sperrung sozialer Netzwerke wie Google und Facebook in China, kann als korrespondierende Reaktion auf die Globalisierungskrise gewertet werden. Gleichzeitig haben sich Chinas politische und kulturelle Rahmenbedingungen rasant geändert, begleitet von einer Verfassungsreform der Amtszeit des Präsidenten. Alle Arten von Epochenphänomenen – wie die Verbreitung sozialer Netzwerke, die Globalisierungskrise, der Populismus, der plötzliche Aufstieg neoautoritärer Kräfte in China, der „Chilling effect" durch die Massenmedien – sind das Resultat von Ursache und Wirkung und kündigen die Ankunft des postfaktischen Zeitalters an. Es kennzeichnet die Auflösung der monopolistisch-autoritativen Informationsmechanismen, während sich mehr und mehr persönliche Standpunkte ansammeln. Das Unbehagen im postfaktischen Zeitalter entspricht zunehmend der globalisierten Lebenserfahrung, die für Künstler*innen mehr Möglichkeiten bereitzuhalten scheint.

Das Unbehagen im postfaktischen Zeitalter entspricht zunehmend der globalisierten Lebenserfahrung, die für Künstler*innen mehr Möglichkeiten bereitzuhalten scheint.

Dies zeigt sich zum Beispiel in den Werken von Fang Di (方迪), die eine Mischung aus Reflexionen über die antikolonialistische Geschichte Asiens und Afrikas darstellen und mit der Realität von Chinas Neuer Seidenstraße verschnitten werden. Das *Beijing Ballroom Project* (北京舞厅) von Hao Jingban (郝敬班) ist ein weiteres Beispiel: Die Arbeit erzählt vom Aufstieg und Niedergang des chinesischen Tanzhauses während des 20. Jahrhunderts und kombiniert Musikaufnahmen, Archivmaterial, eine Feldstudie und beschriftete Bilder zu Clips, die sich aus historischen und sozialen Fragmenten zusammensetzen. Auch Shen Xin (沈莘), das dritte Beispiel, arbeitet mit einer Kombination aus Performance auf der Bühne, Dokumentation und Archivbildern, um die Grenzen zwischen Realität und Illusion zu verwischen. Ihre Arbeiten spielen auf die Dehnkräfte und Gegensätze zwischen zwei Feldern an. Dabei steht das eine Feld für Identität und Macht, während das andere die Entwicklung der Globalisierung und Wissenschaft darstellt. Die Arbeiten dieser Künstler*innen repräsentieren eine spezifische Denkweise in der zeitgenössischen Kunst. Mit anderen Worten, da wir uns in einer globalisierten Zeit befinden, in der intellektuelle Erfahrung, Produktionsweise und Technik zunehmend keinen Unterschied machen, sollten wir die Frage stellen, worum es der Videokunst eigentlich geht. Für die heutigen Künstler*innen zählen weder nationale Identität noch das Label „Made in China", sondern die Relevanz ihrer Werke, die in persönlicher und lokaler Erfahrung wurzeln. Globalisierung bedeutet Mobilisation und Migration, während individuelle und lokale Erfahrung den Stellenwert der „Schwerkraft" befördern, eine Wurzel schlagende und unbewegliche Kraft, die in besonderem Maße auf die Videokunst im Kontext der Globalisierung zutrifft.

Artists

Künstler*innen

Cao Fei 曹斐
Fang Di 方迪
Lu Yang 陆扬
Zhang Peili 张培力

Cao Fei 曹斐

Humans and Machines, Hand in Hand

In greyish-blue light, eight slender figures enter a deserted plant of enormous size with measured steps. They do not hurry in the process of capturing every detail, entering the interior rooms, wandering through tattered belt conveyors, or climbing carefully stacked mountains of palettes, picking up individual objects, examining them curiously, and tossing them aside again. Their surprise when looking at the objects leads one to surmise: they are looking at remnants of the present time that are incomprehensible to them in a perhaps not too distant future. They leave the plant over a field, bored or perhaps like the living dead from the films of George A. Romero,[1] as main protagonists in a dehumanized or post-human scenario to come.

The setting that follows also points, despite the great familiarity, more to a future picture of day-to-day working life. It apparently deals with the same plant. But, here, the plant is still in operation. The whirring sounds of the first images give way to a rhythmical, more musical soundtrack. The camera also flies through endless towers of shelves and captures conveyor belts rolling at a Fordistically steady tempo. The halls are deserted—apart from a cute robot with artificial intelligence accompanying one young female and one young male worker, whose different tasks they nonetheless never bring together. In spite of the workers' isolation, the robot and surveillance systems do not allow for any private sphere.

We find ourselves in the gigantic, automated logistics centre 'Asia One Unmanned Warehouse' and in the year 2021. Surrounded by a melancholy loneliness, the protagonists function in processes that are continuously repeated. At some point, the images and sounds become independent, without it becoming entirely clear whether it is a hallucination and, if yes, whose: synthetic disco music rings out; dancers whose

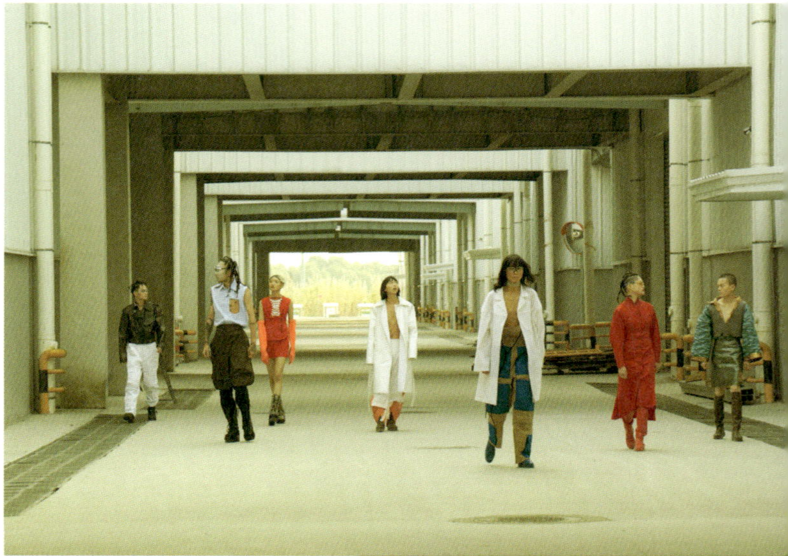

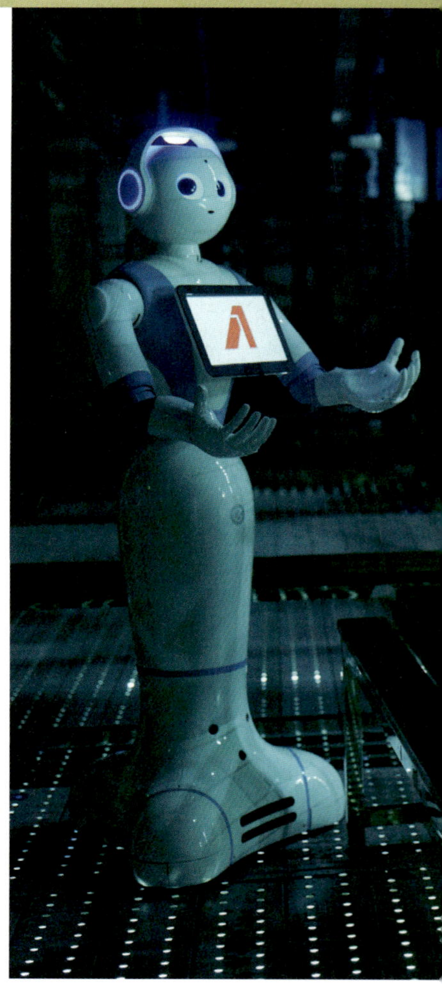

Seite / Pages 30–49

Asia One, 2018
Ein-Kanal-Videoinstallation, Farbe, Ton / Single-channel video installation, colour, sound, 63'20"

1 See George A. Romero, *Night of the Living Dead*, USA, 1968, or *Zombie*, USA, 1978.

Mensch und Maschine, Hand in Hand

Cao Fei 曹斐

1 Vgl. George A. Romero, *Die Nacht der lebenden Toten*, USA 1968, oder *Zombie*, USA 1978.

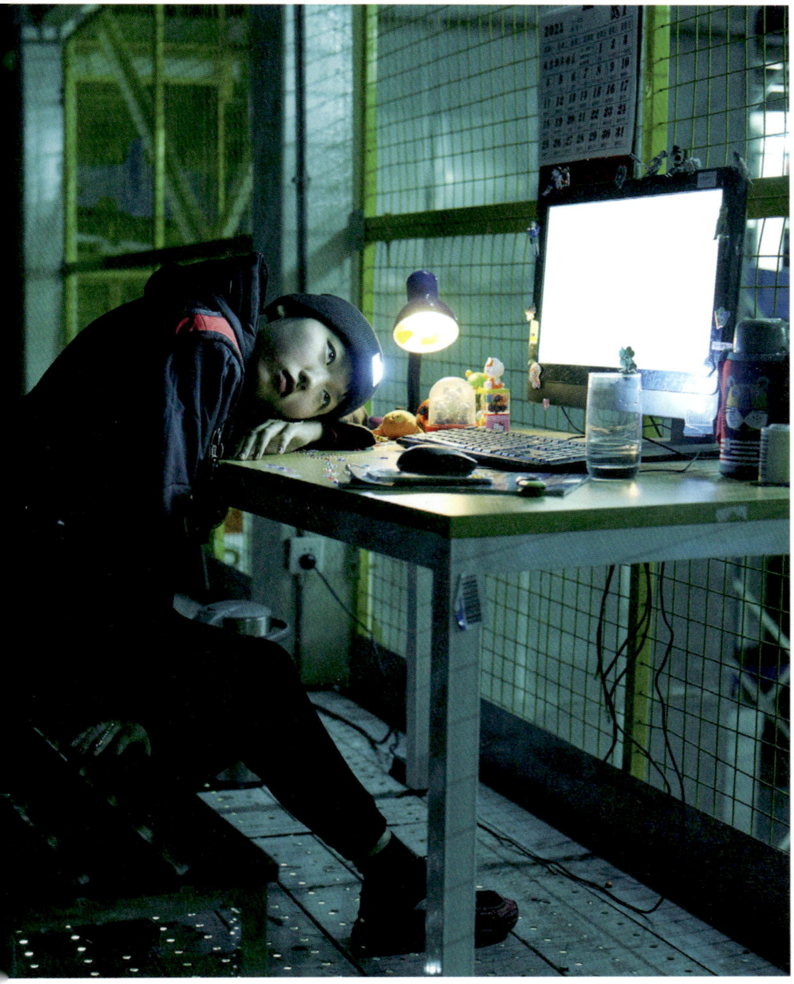

Acht schlanke Gestalten betreten gemessenen Schrittes im graublauen Licht eines dunstigen Himmels eine stillgelegte Betriebsanlage gigantischen Ausmaßes. Sie haben keine Eile, während sie jedes Detail erfassen, die Innenräume betreten, über zerfledderte Fließbänder streunen oder auf sorgfältig gestapelte Palettengebirge steigen, einzelne Objekte neugierig untersuchend aufheben und wieder wegwerfen. Ihr Befremden beim Anblick der Gegenstände lässt es ahnen: Sie betrachten in einer womöglich nicht allzu fernen Zukunft Rückstände der aktuellen Gegenwart, die ihnen nicht mehr verständlich sind. Über eine Wiese verlassen sie das Gelände irgendwann, gelangweilt oder aber wie die lebenden Toten aus den Filmen von George A. Romero[1], als Hauptdarsteller eines bevorstehenden entmenschlichten, eines posthumanen Szenarios.

Auch das Setting, das sich anschließt, weist trotz größerer Vertrautheit eher auf ein kommendes Bild des Arbeitsalltags hin. Offenbar handelt es sich um dieselbe Anlage. Hier ist sie jedoch noch in Betrieb. Die flirrenden Töne der ersten Bilder weichen einer rhythmischen, musikalischeren Soundspur. Dazu fliegt die Kamera durch endlose Regaltürme und fängt in fordistisch gleichmäßigem Tempo rollende Fließbänder ein. Die Hallen sind menschenleer – bis auf eine von einem niedlichen Roboter mit Künstlicher Intelligenz begleitete junge Arbeiterin und einen jungen Arbeiter, deren unterschiedliche Aufgaben sie nie zusammenführen. Doch trotz ihrer Einsamkeit erlauben ihnen die Roboter und Überwachungssysteme keinerlei Privatsphäre.

Wir befinden uns im gigantischen automatisierten Logistikzentrum „Asia One Unmanned Warehouse" und schreiben das Jahr 2021. Von einer melancholischen Einsamkeit umweht, funktionieren die Protagonisten in sich permanent wiederholenden Prozessen. Irgendwann

choreographies call to mind the model opera *On the Docks*[2] from the Cultural Revolution appear on the conveyor belts under a banner with the words 'Man and Machine, Hand in Hand'; here, their movements mirror the biopolitics of the machine-like and evade it at the same time; an inflatable octopus embraces the machinery with its tentacles or lies on the floor like the cut-off head of Medusa; errors interrupt the routines of the factory and break into the imagination of the protagonists in the form of burst-open packages or by means of the deliberate confusion of the AI robot. And following their initially hesitant glances, the young woman and the young man develop feelings for each other. Despite the monotonous day-to-day working life, they have apparently become caught up in emotional entanglements amidst the unmanned character of intelligent production, the human and the nonhuman. Meditative concentration becomes a revolt against the routines of day-to-day working life.

Cao Fei is presenting her work *Asia One* (2018) for the first time in Germany in the group exhibition *Micro Era*. The fact that the images of the future are based on surreal and at the same time very real signs in contemporary society is shown by the documentary film *11.11* (2018), presented in parallel to *Asia One*, which portrays the present with a different thematic focus and in a different visual language. The combination of the two films makes one think of Jean-Luc Godard's deconstructivist *Histoire(s) du cinéma*[3] (1988–98) and is a reminder that there are details in the present about which Henri Bergson stated that they possibly elude most contemporaries, but might retrospectively become the decisive characteristics of an epoch for people of the future.[4] Cao Fei invites us to recognize the signs of the world to come and to grasp a moment in which traditional cinematic narrative styles and the excessive visual worlds of mediatized society are overlaid, but in which the demarcations between human and post-human society have already been made.

The documentary film *11.11* shows the work overload in the logistics industry before and after the Double Eleven Shopping Day[5] in China. JD.com is one of the biggest e-commerce companies in China. While *Asia One* does without words, apart from the song text, in *11.11* we hear the pace-setting calls of the foremen of the logistics company, the laudatory platitudes of the marketing staff, but also the reports of drivers. The advertising clips from corporate communications create a scenario based on drones and robots, which largely does without human personnel in production, while human beings are able to dedicate themselves to consumption. Between advertising films with a futuristic aesthetic and documentary insights into the squalid districts of couriers, a narrative about a more or less promising future unfurls:

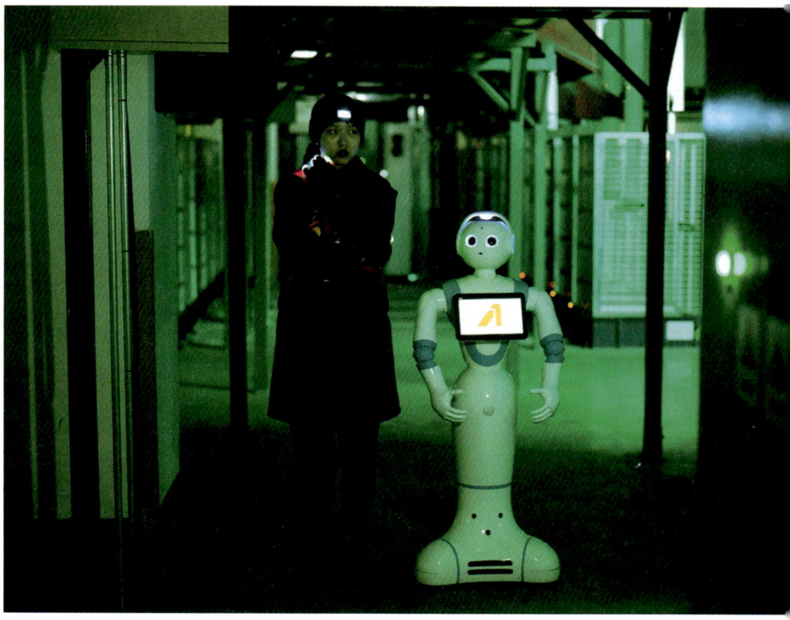

2 *On the Docks* (Chin. 海港 *Haigang*), directed by Xie Jin, is one of the eight so-called 'original' model operas created during the Cultural Revolution (1966–76) under the influence of the Communist Party of China (CPC), which encompass political Beijing operas, ballets, symphonies, and piano pieces.

3 Jean-Luc Godard, *Histoire(s) du cinéma – Geschichte(n) des Kinos*, with an essay by Klaus Theweleit in the German language version, 264 min., colour and black-and-white, Berlin, 2009.

4 See Henri Bergson, *Time and Free Will*, trans. F. L. Pogson (London: George Allen & Unwin, 1950).

5 Chinese equivalent of Black Friday.

verselbstständigen sich die Bilder und Töne, ohne dass ganz klar wird, ob es sich um eine Halluzination handelt und wenn ja, von wem: Synthiediscomusik ertönt; auf den Fließbändern tauchen unter einem Banner mit den Worten „Mensch und Maschine, Hand in Hand" Tänzer*innen auf, deren Choreografien an die Modelloper *On the Docks*[2] der kulturellen Revolution erinnern; hier spiegeln ihre Bewegungen die Biopolitik des Maschinellen und entziehen sich ihr zugleich; ein aufblasbarer Oktopus umarmt mit seinen Fangarmen die Anlagen oder liegt wie ein abgeschlagenes Medusenhaupt am Boden; Fehler brechen in Form von aufgeplatzten Paketen oder durch mutwillige Irritation des KI-Roboters in die Routinen der Fabrik und in die Imagination der Protagonisten ein. Und nach ersten zaghaften Blicken entwickeln die junge Frau und der junge Mann allmählich Gefühle füreinander. Im eintönigen Arbeitsalltag haben sie sich augenscheinlich in emotionalen Verstrickungen zwischen dem Unbemannten der intelligentisierten Produktion, dem Menschlichen und dem Nichtmenschlichen verfangen. Aus meditativer Hingabe wird ein Aufbegehren gegen die Routinen des Arbeitsalltags.

Cao Fei präsentiert ihre Arbeit *Asia One* (2018) in der Gruppenausstellung *Micro Era* erstmals in Deutschland. Dass die Zukunftsbilder auf den surrealen und zugleich sehr realen Zeichen in der aktuellen Gesellschaft basieren, zeigt die parallel zu *Asia One* gezeigte Dokumentation *11.11* (2018), die mit einem anderen thematischen Schwerpunkt und in einer anderen visuellen Sprache die Gegenwart schildert. Die Zusammenstellung beider Filme lässt an Jean-Luc Godards dekonstruktivistische(n) *Histoire(s) du cinéma*[3] (1988–1998) denken und erinnert daran, dass es in der Gegenwart Details gibt, von denen Henri Bergson sagte, sie entgingen womöglich den meisten Zeitgenossen, könnten aber für die Zukünftigen retrospektiv zum Entscheidenden einer Epoche werden:[4] Cao Fei lädt uns ein, die Zeichen einer kommenden Welt zu erkennen und einen Moment zu erfassen, in dem sich traditionelle filmische Erzählweisen und die überbordenden Bildwelten der Mediengesellschaft überlagern, aber auch die Weichen zwischen humaner und posthumaner Gesellschaft gestellt werden.

Der Dokumentarfilm *11.11* zeigt die Arbeitsüberlastung des Logistiksektors vor und nach dem Double Eleven Shopping Day[5] in China. JD.com ist einer der größten E-Commerce-Unternehmen in China. Während *Asia One* bis auf die Songtexte ohne Worte auskommt, hören wir in *11.11* die taktgebenden Rufe der Vorarbeiter des Logistikunternehmens, die anpreisenden Floskeln der Marketingmitarbeiter, aber auch die Berichte der Fahrer. Die Werbeclips der Unternehmenskommunikation entwerfen ein auf Drohnen und Robotern basierendes Szenario, das weitgehend ohne menschliches Personal in der Produktion auskommt, während sich die Menschen dem Konsum hingeben können. Zwischen Werbefilmbildern in futuristischer Ästhetik und dokumentarischen Einblicken in die elenden Quartiere der Kuriere entspinnt sich eine Narration über eine mehr oder weniger verheißungsvolle Zukunft:

Beginnend mit der Warensortierung im gigantischen Sortierzentrum von JD.com am Stadtrand von Peking und Bildern aus der nationalen Kommandozentrale zum Double Eleven am Hauptsitz von JD.com folgt die Kamera den Paketen zu den zahlreichen Lieferpunkten. Die an den Online-Einkaufsterminals arbeitenden Kuriere bringen die Waren ebenso in Pekings

2 *Am Hafen* (chin. 海港 *Haigang*), Regie: Xie Jin, ist eine der acht sogenannten Original-Modellopern, die in der Kulturrevolution (1966–1976) unter dem Einfluss der Kommunistischen Partei Chinas (KPCh) entstanden und politische Peking-Opern, Ballette, Sinfonien und Klavierstücke umfassen.

3 Jean-Luc Godard, *Histoire(s) du cinéma – Geschichte(n) des Kinos*, mit einem Essay von Klaus Theweleit in der dt. Sprachfassung, 264 Min., Farbe/schwarz-weiß, Berlin, 2009.

4 Vgl. Henri Bergson, *Zeit und Freiheit*, übers. von Paul Fohr, Berlin, 2006.

5 Chinesisches Äquivalent zum Black Friday.

Starting with the sorting of goods in JD.com's gigantic sorting centre on the periphery of the city of Beijing and with pictures of the national command centre for Double Eleven Day at the headquarters of JD.com, the camera follows packages to the numerous delivery points. The couriers working at the online shopping terminal deliver goods to Beijing's glittering commercial office tower districts and also to traditional hutong districts and residential buildings with narrow hallways. In the meantime, we learn more about the life dreams and living conditions of the drivers from rural regions, who work hard for sixteen to eighteen hours a day to support their families and strive to give their children a better future with their small salaries. The film sketches a landscape of consumption fuelled by a high-performing Internet economy.[6]

Asia One, like the documentary film *11.11*, was also created at original locations. This reflects Cao Fei's general interest in industrialization and urbanization, not only in China today. Cao was born in 1978 and thus after the Cultural Revolution. Her work reflects the rapid and productive changes that she has experienced in China during her lifetime and the central paradoxes that can also be felt outside of the People's Republic. It also touches on the individual isolation resulting from technological economic development, consumerism, globalization, and the dissociative effect of increasingly 'real' virtual worlds.

Cao Fei embeds the films in an installation in which the logos of JD.com and elements of the plant appear. Her films extend the metaphor of the rhythmic pattern of the images resulting from the Fordist 'compulsive order' and bring their protagonists, exhausted by *Modern Times* like in Charlie Chaplin's eponymous film,[7] to dance. In the same spirit, she also transfers the escapism that makes the cinema so attractive to her characters. Cao thus compresses the cinema to its quintessence and simultaneously has aspects of the real flow into it, without striving to simulate a filmic representation of life. One might think of the term *acinema*,[8] which Jean-François Lyotard coined in the 1970s, as well as of his later characterization of a 'sovereign film', which inscribes elements of acinema within the 'representative-narrative form'.[9]

Cao's critical reflection on the biopolitics of the moving image also operates with, via, and through imagery, while simultaneously relating the context of neo-capitalism as well as the affective feedback loop in which contemporary recipients-producers of images live—never moralizing, but displaying subtle humour. *Asia One* shows that music, dance, and poetry survive even in uncertain, frightening times—and that precisely this, in turn, makes the survival of the humane possible. — Anna-Catharina Gebbers

6 The film informs us that JD.com generated total sales of 120 million renminbi (RMB) solely on the Double Eleven Day documented.

7 Charlie Chaplin, *Modern Times*, black-and-white, silent, USA, 1936.

8 Jean-François Lyotard, 'Acinema' (1973), trans. Paisley N. Livingston, in Andrew Benjamin (ed.), *The Lyotard Reader* (Oxford: Blackwell, 1989), pp. 169–80. Lyotard formulated his aesthetic program acinema for a film emancipated from the accepted conventions of narrative cinema. Lyotard diagnoses film as ultimately being subject to the compulsive order of capitalist commodity logic: 'Writing with movements—cinematography—is conceived and practised as an incessant organizing of movements following the rules of representation for spatial localization, those of narration for the instantiation of language, and those of the form "film music" for the soundtrack' (p. 170). The acinema that Lyotard calls for is supposed to circumvent these rules by slowing down moving images, immobilizing them as still images, and thus facilitating a 'fascinating paralysis'. Or, conversely, by consistently accelerating an 'excess of movement' that no longer allows any 'synthesis of identification' by means of cognition.

9 See Jean-François Lyotard, 'The Idea of a Sovereign Film' (1995), in Graham Jones and Ashley Woodward (eds.), *Acinemas: Lyotard's Philosophy of Film* (Edinburgh: Edinburgh University Press, 2017), pp. 62–72, esp. p. 63.

kommerzielle glitzernde Büroturmquartiere wie in traditionelle Hutong-Bezirke und Wohnblöcke mit engen Hausfluren. Derweil erfahren wir mehr über die Lebensträume und die Existenzumstände dieser hart 16 bis 18 Stunden arbeitenden, aus ländlichen Gegenden stammenden Fahrer, die mit ihrem schmalen Gehalt ihre Familien unterstützen und ihren Kindern eine bessere Zukunft bieten wollen. Der Film skizziert die Landschaft eines Konsums, der von einer leistungsstarken Internetwirtschaft angetrieben wird.[6]

Wie der Dokumentarfilm *11.11* ist auch *Asia One* an Originalschauplätzen entstanden. Dies spiegelt Cao Feis generelles Interesse an der Industrialisierung und Urbanisierung nicht nur im heutigen China. Cao wurde 1978 und damit nach der Kulturrevolution geboren. Ihre Arbeit reflektiert die schnellen und produktiven Veränderungen, die sie in China während ihres Lebens erlebt hat und die zentralen Paradoxien, die auch jenseits der Volksrepublik spürbar sind, so wie die individuelle Isolation, welche aus technologischer, wirtschaftlicher Entwicklung, Konsumismus, Globalisierung und der dissoziativen Wirkung zunehmend „realer“ virtueller Welten resultiert.

Cao Fei bettet die Filme in eine Installation ein, in der Logos von JD.com und Elemente der Betriebsanlage auftauchen. Ihre Filme erweitern die Metapher der Rhythmisierung der Bilder durch den fordistischen „Ordnungszwang“ und bringen ihre wie in Charlie Chaplins gleichnamigem Film von den *Modernen Zeiten*[7] ermatteten Protagonist*innen zum Tanzen. In gleichem Sinne überträgt sie auch den die Attraktivität des Kinos ausmachenden Eskapismus auf ihre Figuren. Cao verdichtet das Kino so auf seine Quintessenzen und lässt gleichzeitig Aspekte des Realen einfließen, ohne eine filmische Repräsentation des Lebens vortäuschen zu wollen. Man mag an den von Jean-François Lyotard in den 1970er-Jahren geprägten Begriff des *acinéma*[8] und seine spätere Charakterisierung des „souveränen Films“ denken, der Elemente des acinéma in die „erzählend-darstellende Form“ integriert.[9]

Caos kritische Reflexion der Biopolitik des bewegten Bildes agiert mit, über, durch die Bilder und erzählt zugleich vom Kontext des Neokapitalismus sowie der affektiven Feedbackschleifen, in dem heutige Bild-Rezipienten-Produzenten leben. Nie belehrend, sondern mit subtilem Humor. *Asia One* zeigt, dass auch in unsicheren, beängstigenden Zeiten immer Musik, Tanz und Poesie überleben – und dass genau dies wiederum das Überleben des Humanen ermöglicht. — Anna-Catharina Gebbers

6 Der Film informiert uns, dass JD.com allein am dokumentierten Double-Eleven-Tag einen Gesamtumsatz von 120 Millionen Renminbi (RMB) erzielte.

7 Charlie Chaplin, *Modern Times* (dt. *Moderne Zeiten*), 87 Min., schwarz-weiß, ohne Ton, USA 1936.

8 Jean-François Lyotard, „L'acinéma“ (1973), in: *Essays zu einer affirmativen Ästhetik*, Berlin 1982, S. 25–43. Lyotard formulierte sein ästhetisches Programm *acinéma* für einen von den gängigen Konventionen des Erzählkinos emanzipierten Film. Lyotard diagnostiziert dem Film einen letztlich der kapitalistischen Warenlogik geschuldeten „Ordnungszwang“: „Mit Bewegungen zu schreiben, kinematographieren, wird als stete Organisierung von Bewegung aufgefaßt und dementsprechend gehandhabt. Es gibt Regeln der Repräsentation für die Lokalisierung im Raum, Regeln der Narration für die Strukturierung der Sprache, Regeln des Genres ‚Filmmusik‘ für die Tonspur“ (S. 26). Das von Lyotard geforderte *acinéma* soll diese Regeln unterlaufen, indem es die Laufbilder entschleunigt, immobilisiert bis hin zum Standbild und so eine „faszinierende Paralyse“ ermöglicht. Oder aber im Gegenteil durch konsequente Beschleunigung einen „Bewegungsexzess“ erzeugen, der keine „Synthesen der Identifizierung“ durch die Wahrnehmung mehr zulässt.

9 Vgl. ders., „Idee eines souveränen Films“ (1995), in: *Das Elend der Philosophie*, Wien 2004, S. 181–191.

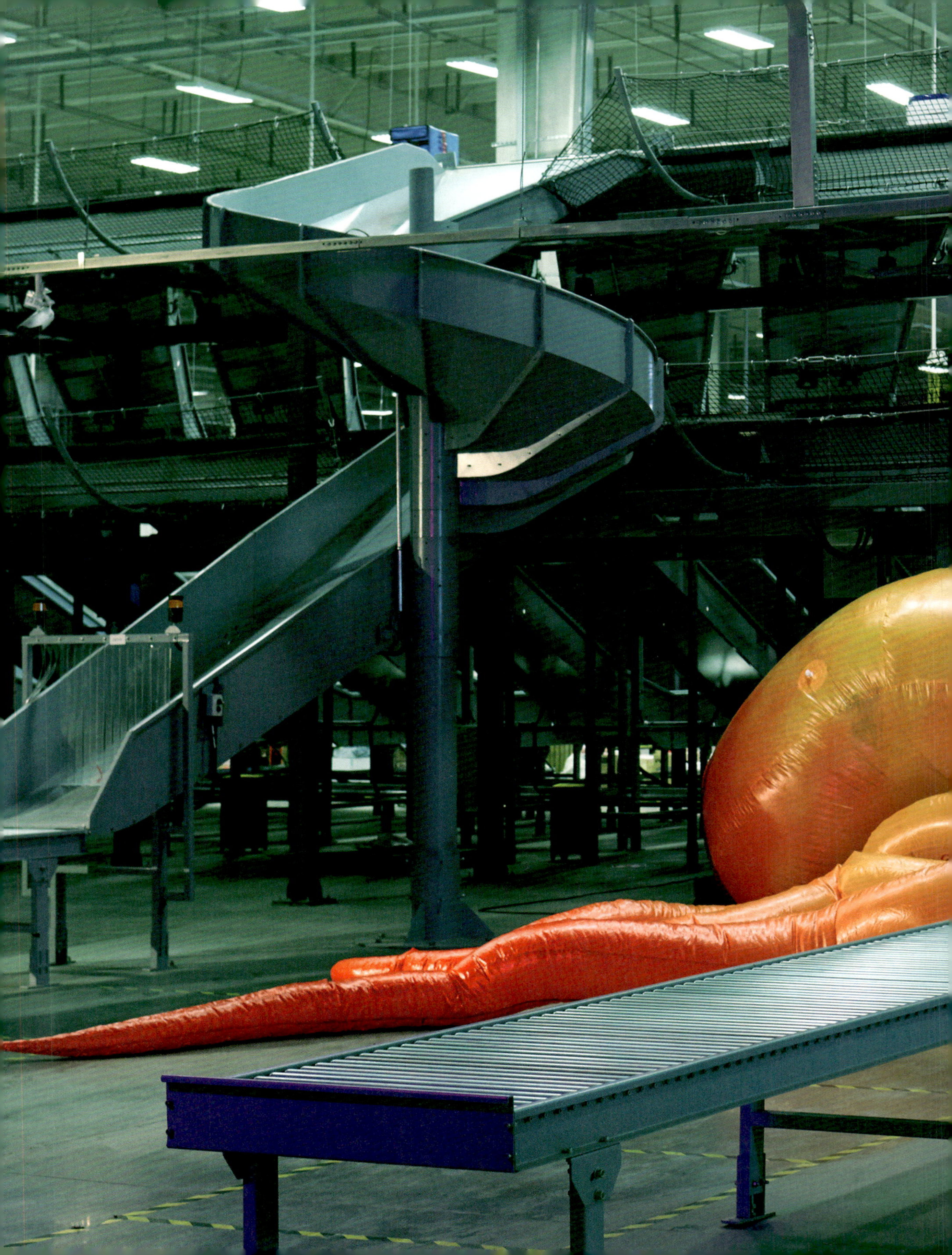

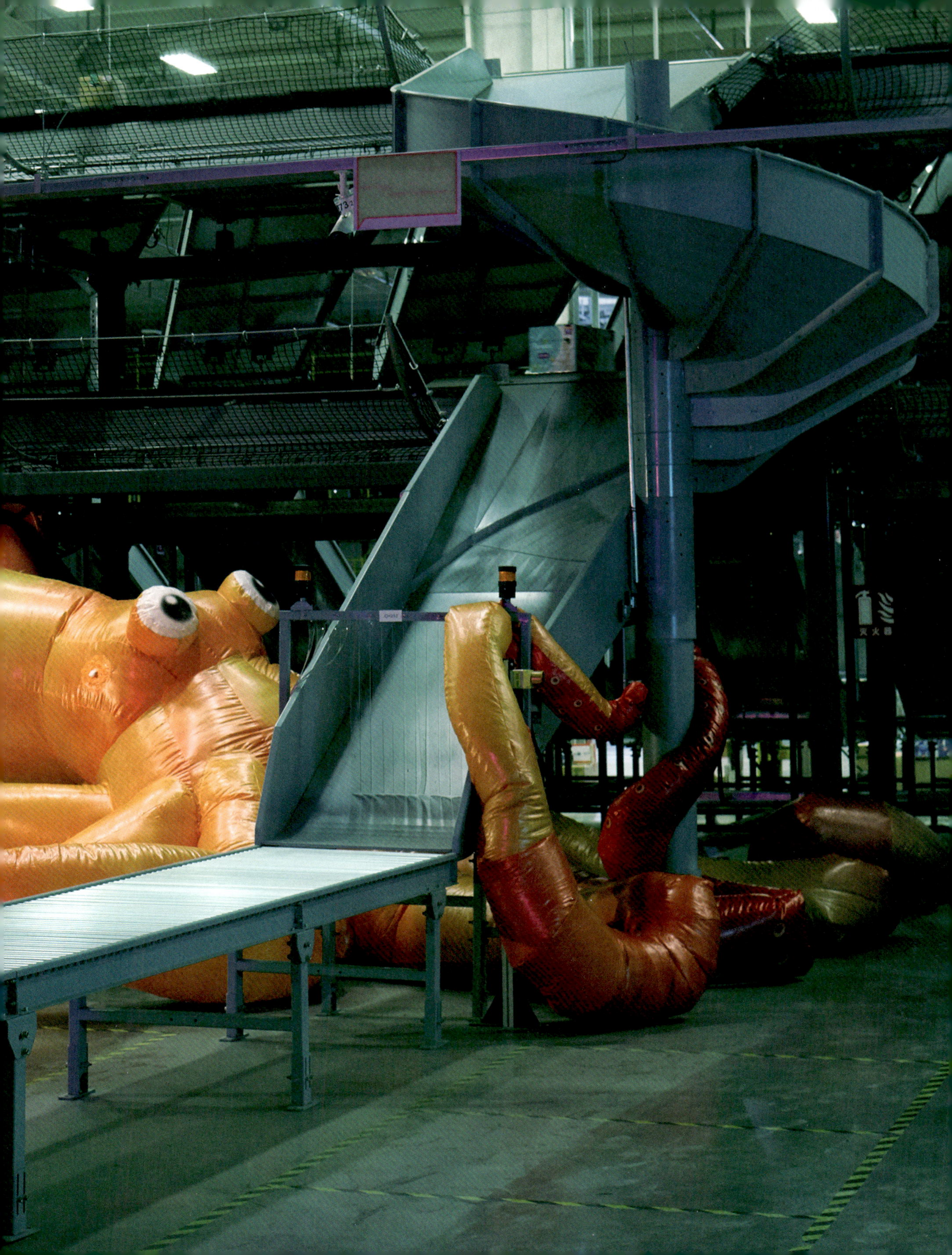

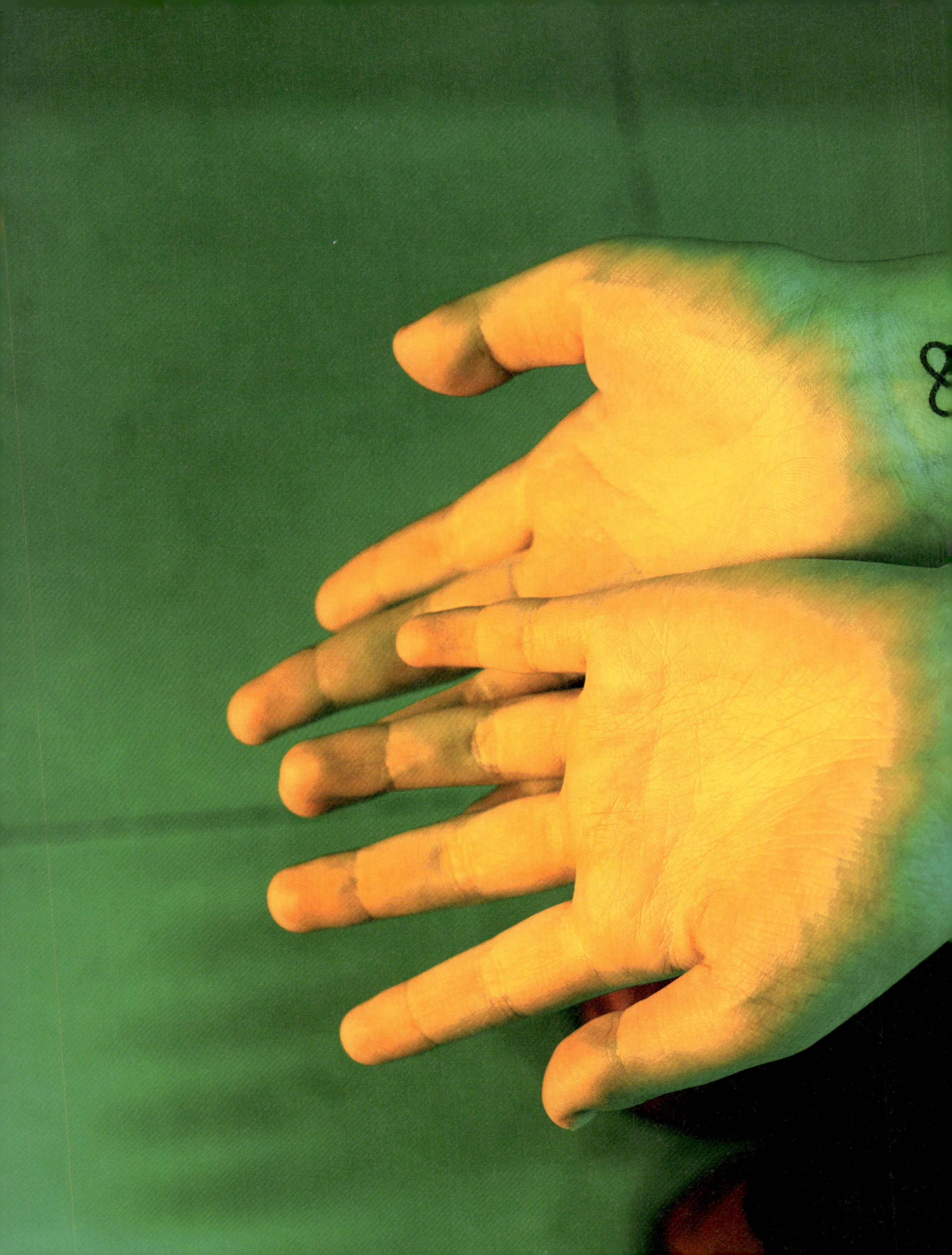

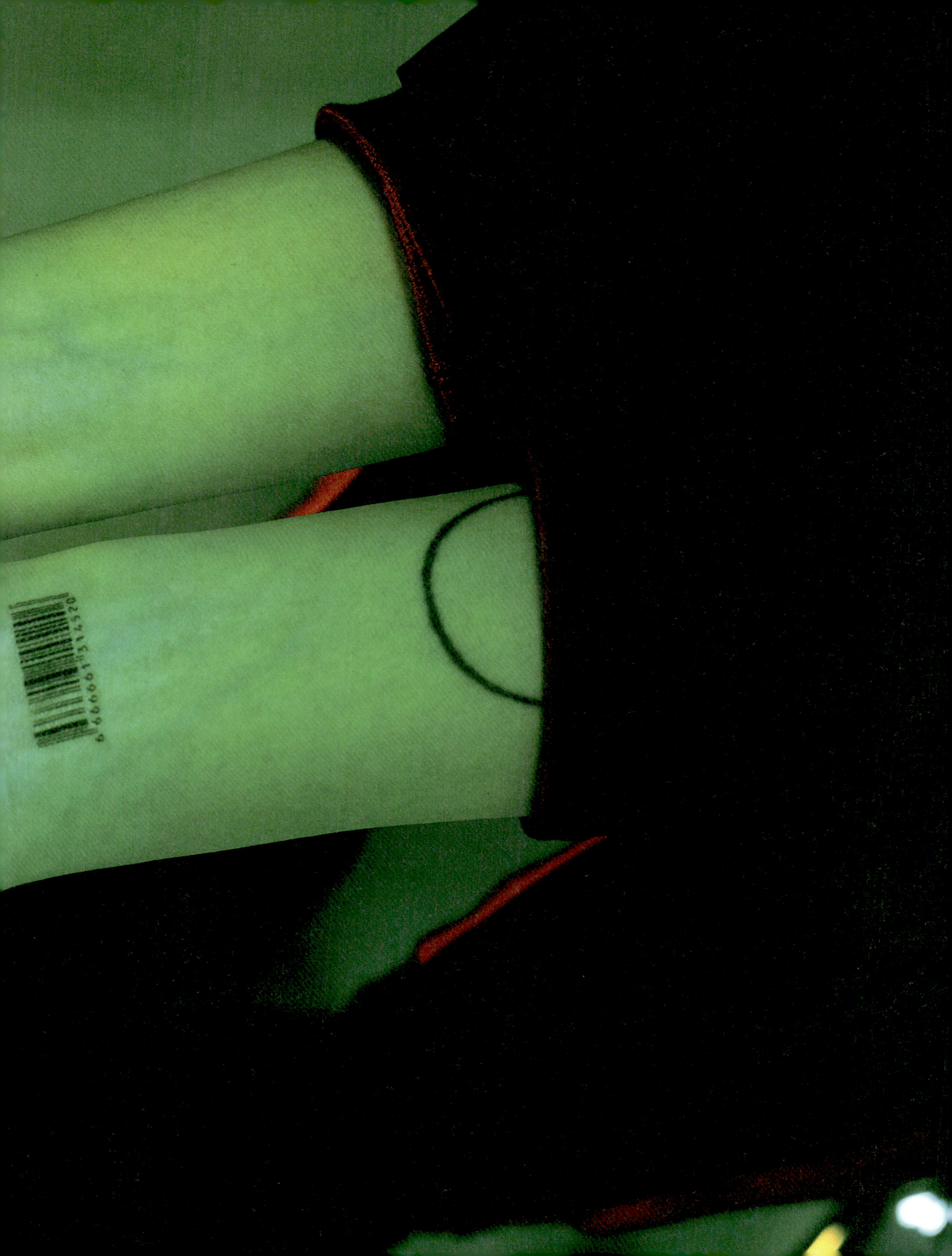

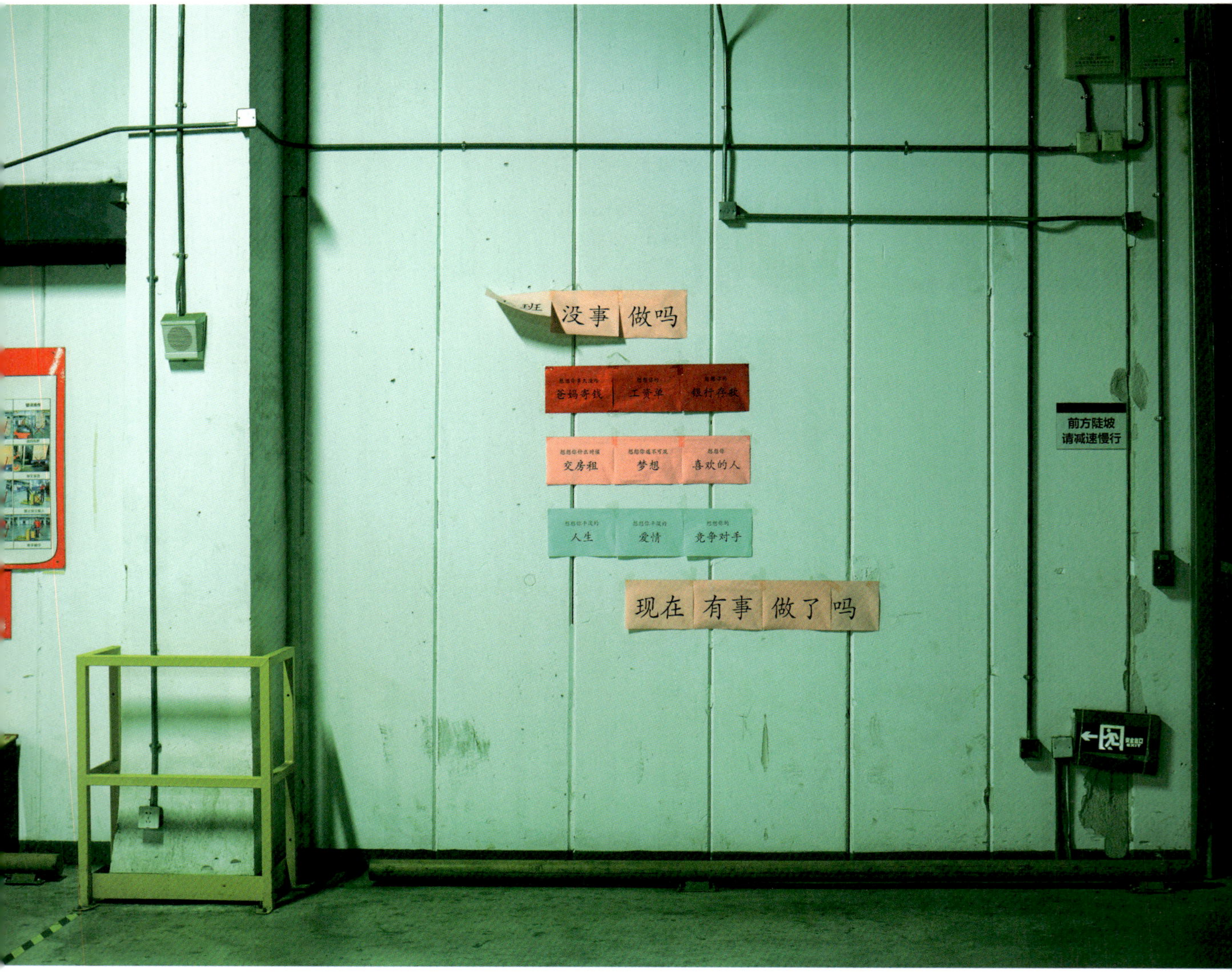
没事 做吗
爸妈寄钱
工资单
银行存款
交房租
梦想
喜欢的人
人生
爱情
竞争对手
现在 有事 做了 吗
前方陡坡
请减速慢行

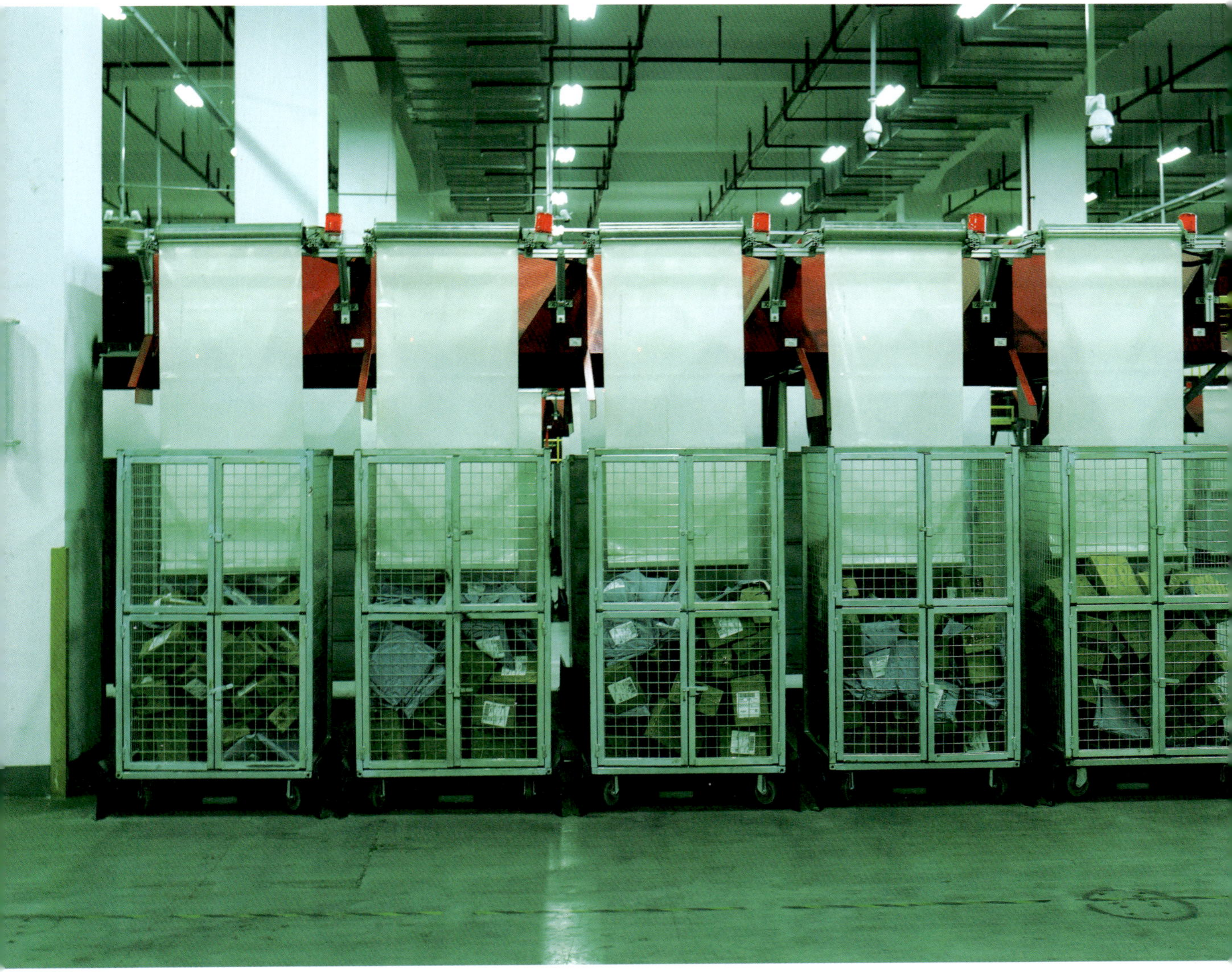

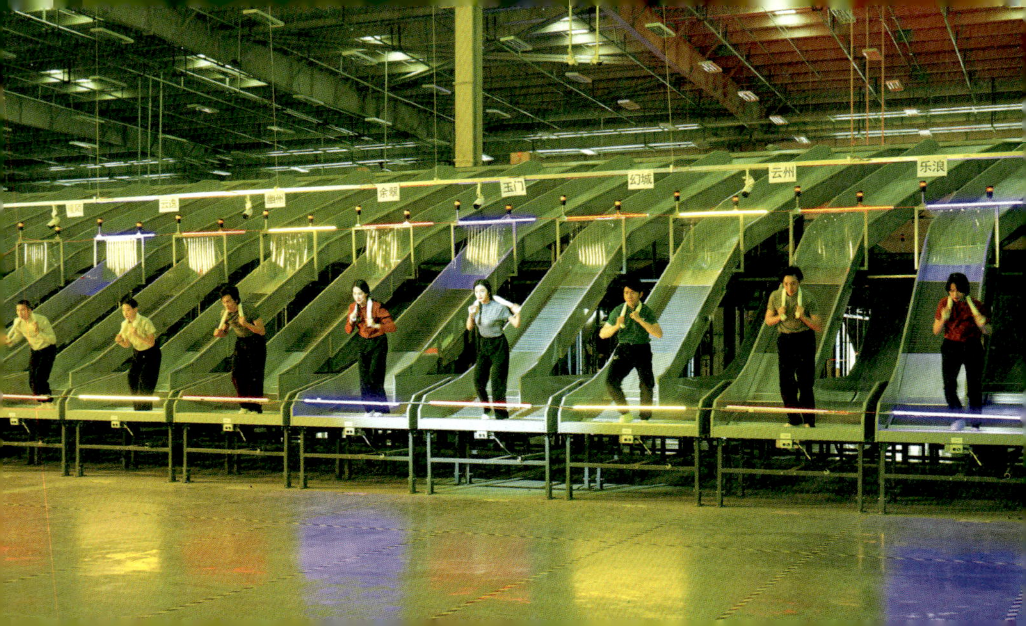
幽州
余粮
玉门
幻城
云州
乐浪

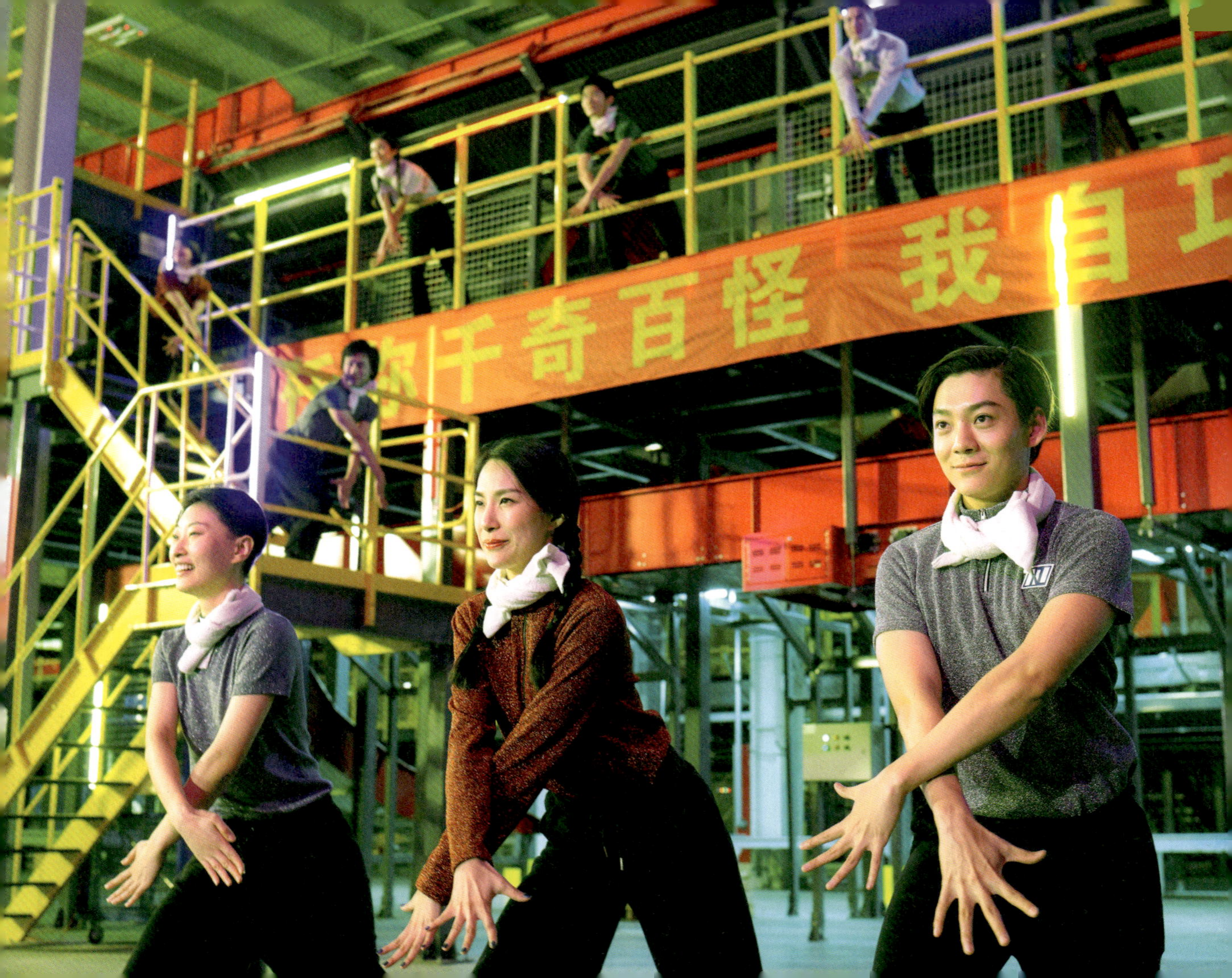
千奇百怪 我 自

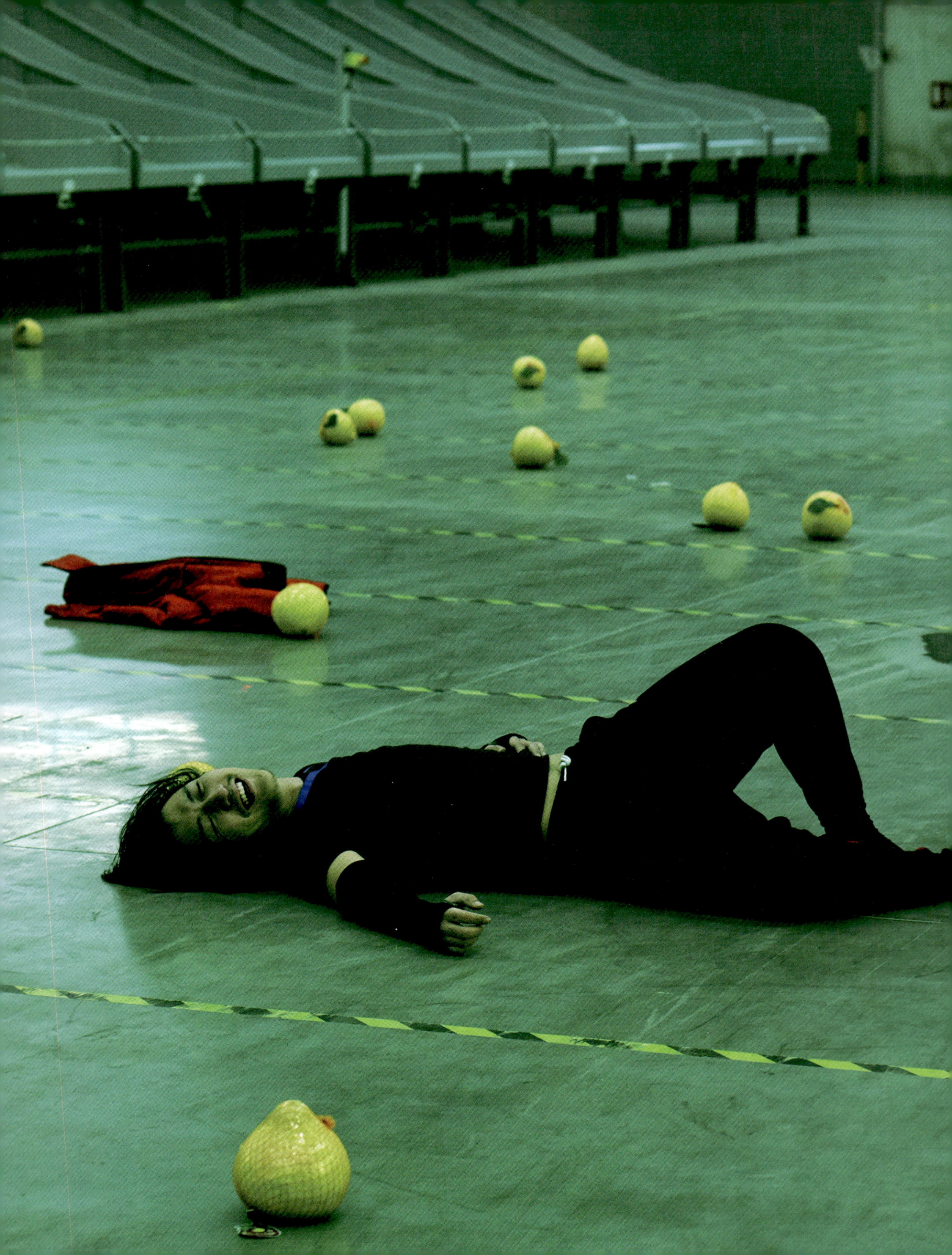

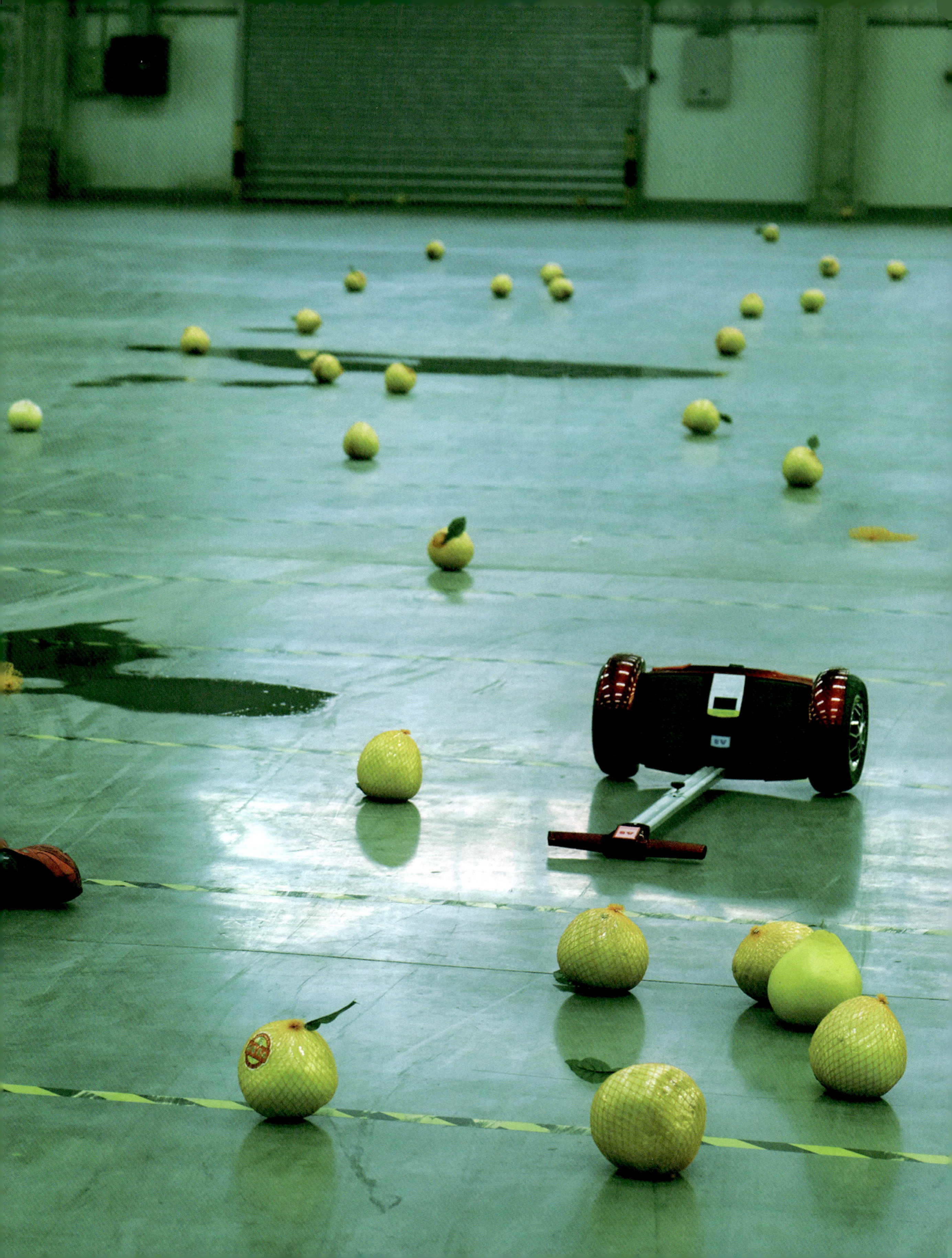

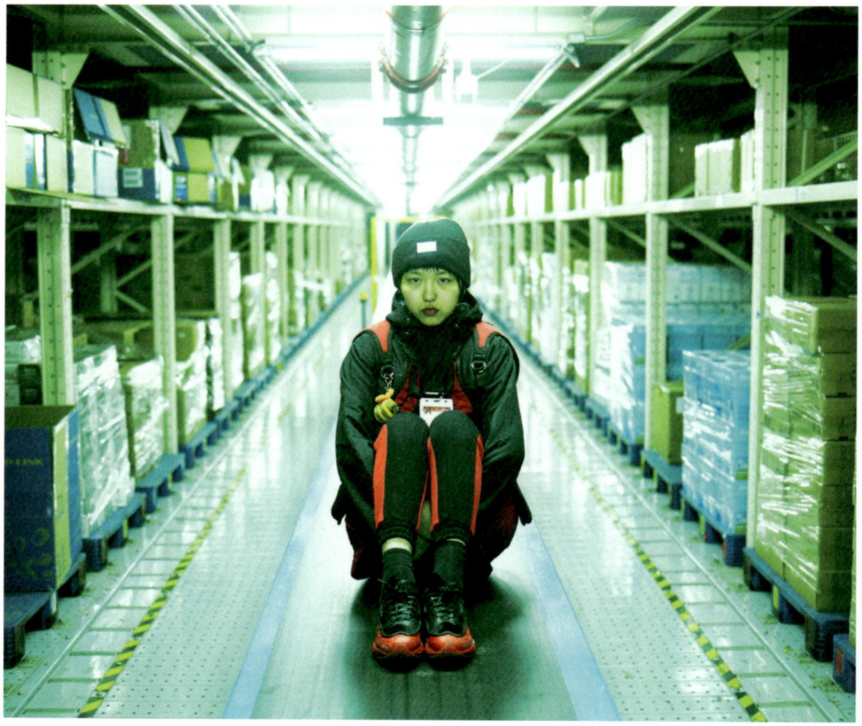

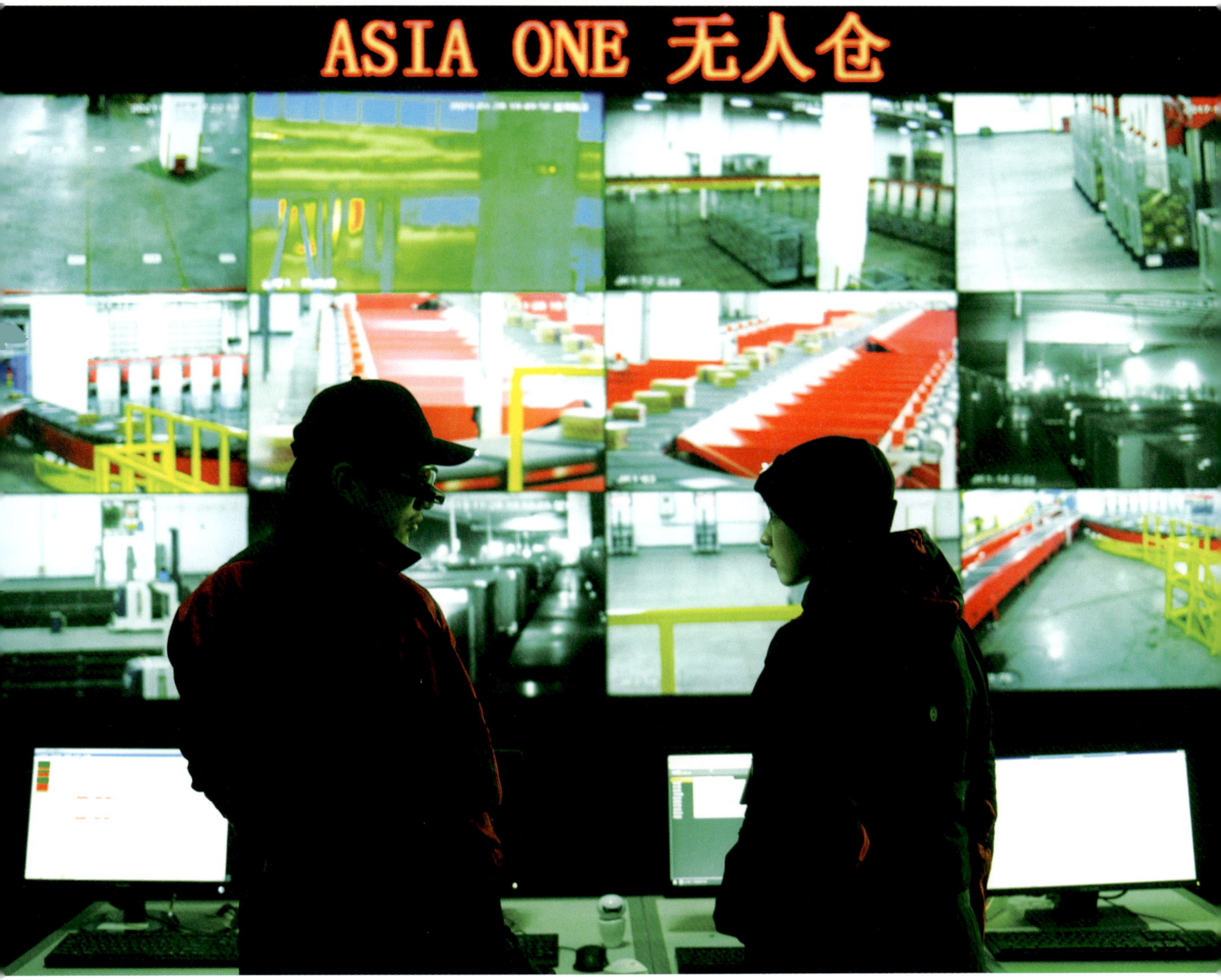
ASIA ONE 无人仓

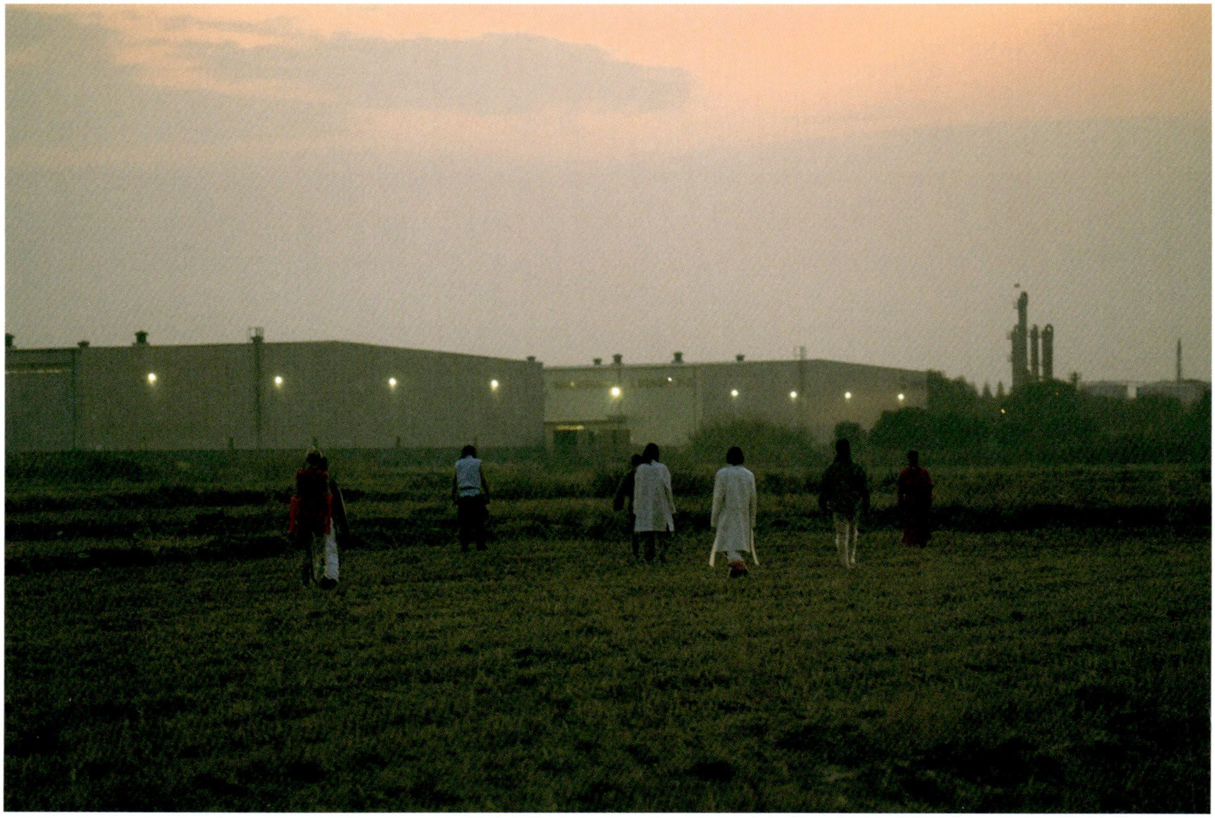

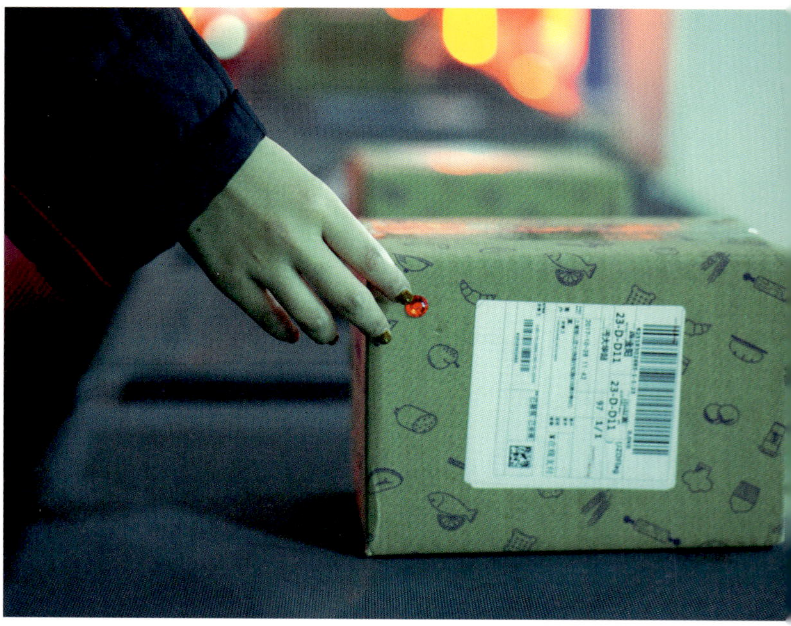

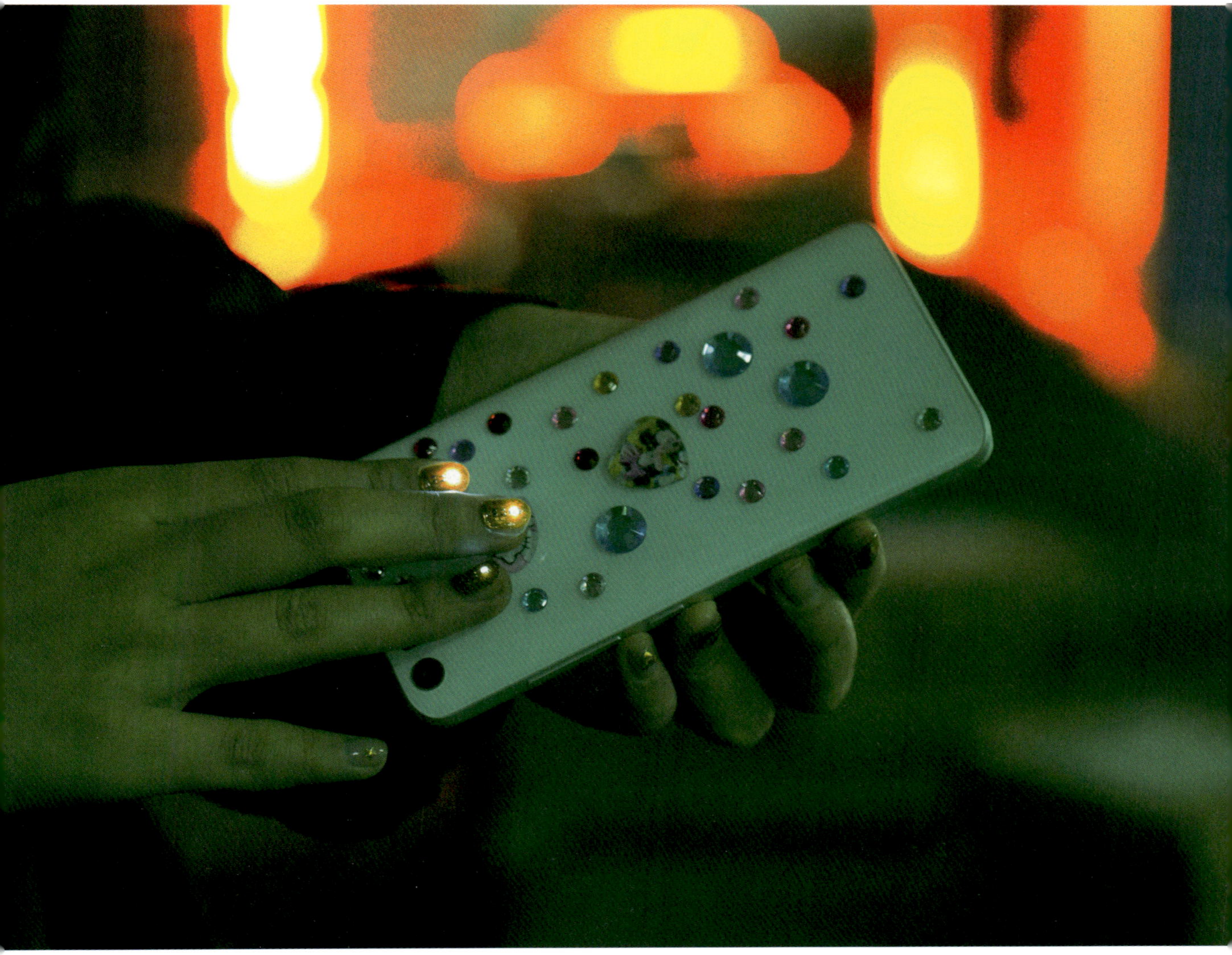

Seite / Pages 30–49

Asia One, 2018
Ein-Kanal-Videoinstallation, Farbe,
Ton / Single-channel video installation,
colour, sound, 63'20"

Seite / Pages 50–63

Minister, 2019
Ein-Kanal-Videoinstallation, Farbe, Ton / Single-channel video installation, colour, sound, 60'

Fang Di has a photo he took with the current Chinese president, Xi Jinping. In the Chinese-speaking world, this is, undoubtedly, an outstanding achievement, and, for some people, it might even be interpreted as vouching in some way for his past, his present, and his future. Sometimes, when a friend asks, Fang Di will take out his phone and show them the photo, but he has never shared it on any social-networking platform. Perhaps he thinks the sharing of such an honour should be conducted with due solemnity, as it involves two aspects of his identity which are hard to reconcile: not only is Fang Di an employee of a state-owned enterprise who has been stationed in Papua New Guinea long term to oversee infrastructure projects, but he is also an artist. This contradiction makes the conclusion that is supposed to be drawn from the photo of him with President Xi more complex and manifold, and this is also why it seems so 'contemporary'.

Fang Di has shared with me lots of his experiences working overseas. On first hearing them, these stories had an almost legendary quality to them, from the colonial history to the deeply entrenched corruption now pervasive in Papua New Guinea, from the mysterious culture of the tribal villages to more mundane political networking, from strange people to strange plants. It is hard to distinguish from his narrative whether he is talking as an artist or as a project manager for a state-owned enterprise, but what is for certain is that none of his colleagues know about his other identity. Just like his colleagues, he shuttles between Shenzhen and Port Moresby, but the majority of his time is spent whiling away the long boring nights on that hot and humid island in the South Pacific. I have no idea how he is able to hide that he is an artist, or what kind of cover or pretence he might employ to do so. As well as the stories he told, I'm also curious about his

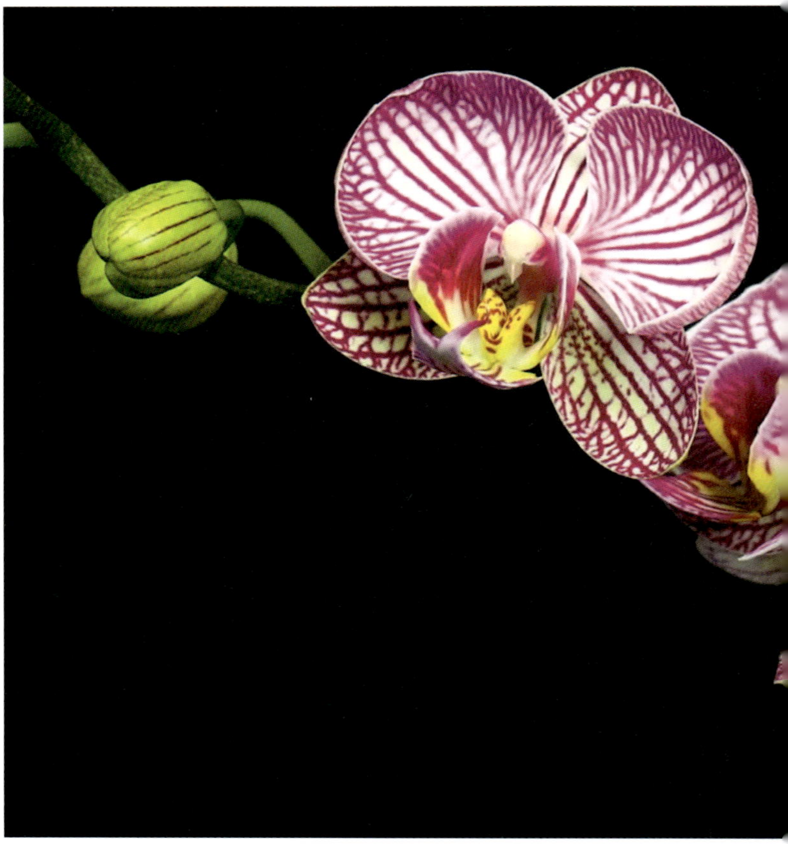

Fang Di 方迪

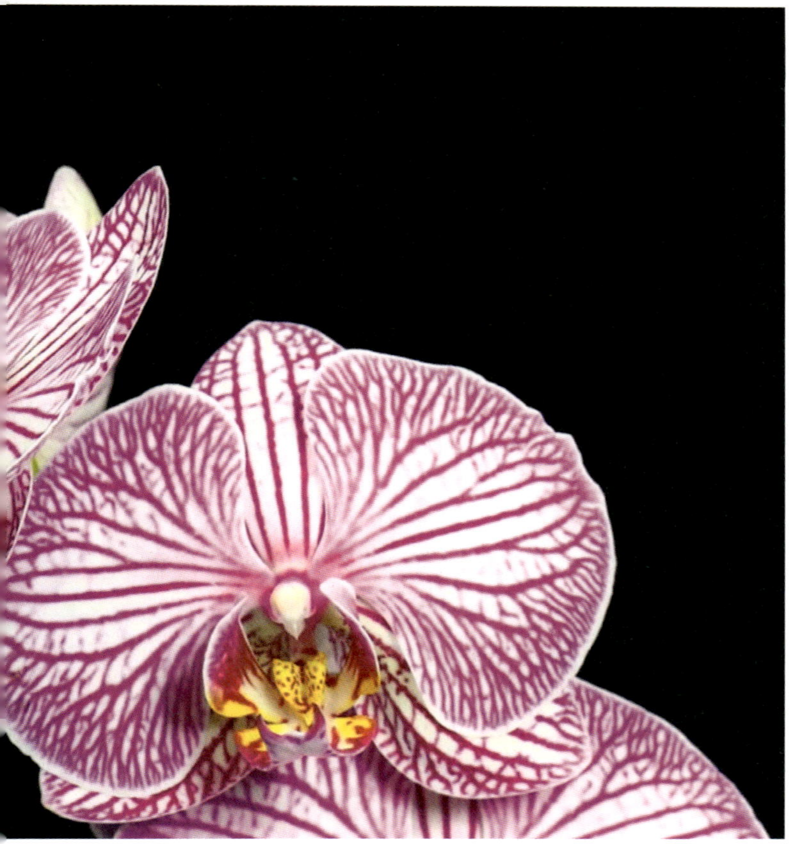

Fang Di ist im Besitz eines Fotos, das ihn mit dem derzeitigen chinesischen Staatspräsidenten Xi Jinping zeigt. In der chinesischsprachigen Welt stellt dies ohne Zweifel ein besonderes Verdienst dar und manche könnten es ihm sogar als Zeugnis für seine Vergangenheit, Gegenwart und Zukunft auslegen. Ab und zu, wenn Freunde danach fragen, holt Fang Di sein Mobiltelefon hervor und zeigt es ihnen, auf den Plattformen sozialer Netzwerke hat er das Foto aber noch nie geteilt. Vielleicht weil er der Meinung ist, dass das Teilen einer solchen Auszeichnung mit dem nötigen Ernst vor sich gehen sollte – betrifft es doch zwei Aspekte seiner Identität, die nur schwer miteinander zu vereinbaren sind: seine Tätigkeit als Angestellter eines Staatsunternehmens, das in Papua-Neuguinea langfristige Infrastrukturprojekte betreut, und seine Arbeit als Künstler. Dieser Widerspruch macht die Schlussfolgerung, die sich vermeintlich aus dem Foto mit Präsident Xi ziehen lässt, noch komplexer und vielschichtiger, aber auch außerordentlich „zeitgemäß".

Fang Di hat mir viel von seinen Arbeitserfahrungen in Übersee erzählt. Wenn man sie zum ersten Mal hört, haftet diesen Berichten eine fast legendäre Qualität an, angefangen bei der Kolonialgeschichte und der tief verankerten heute omnipräsenten Korruption in Papua-Neuguinea über die rätselhaften dörflichen Stammeskulturen, das tagespolitische Netzwerken bis hin zu außergewöhnlichen Menschen und seltsamen Pflanzen. Ob er als Künstler oder Projektmanager eines Staatsunternehmens spricht, ist dabei kaum zu unterscheiden, aber fest steht, dass keine/r seiner Kolleg*innen von seiner anderen Identität weiß. Genau wie sie pendelt er zwischen Shenzhen und Port Moresby, aber die meiste Zeit verbringt er damit, die langen, langweiligen Nächte auf dieser heißen und feuchten Insel im Südpazifik verstreichen zu lassen.

everyday work, and what his colleagues would feel if one day they were to discover that they have been living for so long with an artist in their midst. He has clearly found some sort of turning gate by which he can switch between these two identities, endlessly shifting back and forth between two different fields, like a smuggler carrying his burden in secret.

I once joked with him, saying, 'No other artist in China understands the Belt and Road Initiative quite like you.' This national project, which esteems economic ties and exchange above all else, couldn't be more concrete for Fang Di. For him, it is about how he can communicate with the inefficient bureaucracy of the Papua New Guinean government in order to secure the documents he needs for a project to go ahead, and so forth. Beneath this, however, so many different perspectives lie. Reaping the benefit of China's advanced technology and rich experience in basic infrastructure projects, Papua New Guinea has become the place to which all of the advanced experience that China has gained in the forty years since China's 'Reform and Opening Up' is exported. These advances have gradually replaced what was left behind by the former colonial rulers. China is seen, however, as a new model for modernity. Fang Di's company is based in Shenzhen (which is also his hometown), China's biggest special economic zone, brimming with brand-new skyscrapers and new migrants, with a top-notch IT industry and a very fashionable economy. In other words, the Chinese model has seen its greatest success there. Like Dubai, Shenzhen fits with Keller Easterling's notion of 'extrastatecraft'; it is an 'advocate for globalization' and 'an excellent carrier for economically developed, political quarantine, and corporate externalizing'.[1] There, neoliberalism and socialism have made a strategic pact and reached a new ideological 'consensus'

1 Keller Easterling, *Extrastatecraft: The Power of Infrastructure Space* (London: Verso, 2014), p. 121.

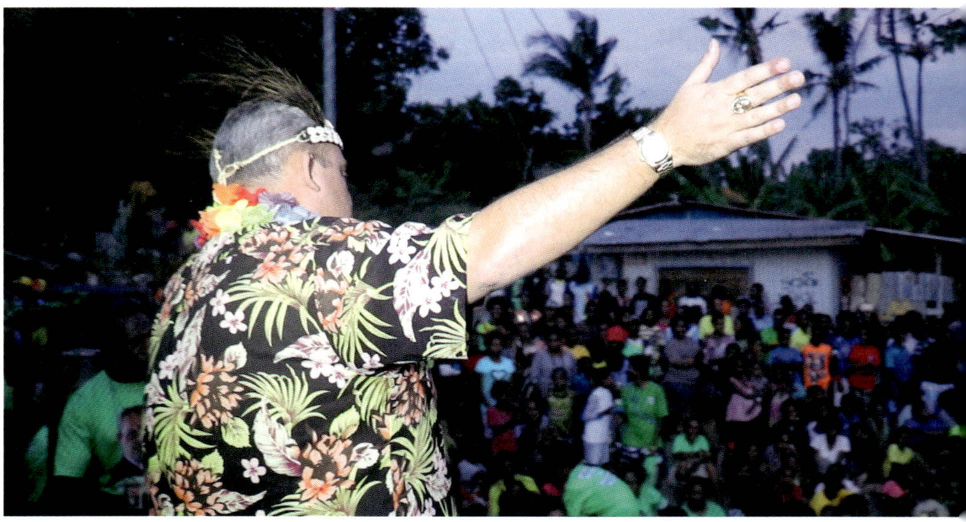

Ich habe keine Ahnung, wie er es anstellt zu verbergen, dass er ein Künstler ist, oder welcher Art Tarnung oder Täuschung er sich zu diesem Zweck bedienen könnte. Ebenso wie seine Geschichten interessiert mich sein Alltag und was seine Kolleg*innen wohl davon halten würden, eines Tages zu entdecken, dass sie seit so langer Zeit mit einem Künstler in ihrer Mitte leben. Ganz sicher hat er eine Art Drehtür gefunden, mit deren Hilfe er sich zwischen diesen beiden Identitäten bewegen kann, permanent hin- und herwechselnd zwischen zwei verschiedenen Bereichen wie ein Schmuggler, der heimlich seine Last trägt.

Einmal sagte ich im Scherz zu ihm: „Kein anderer Künstler in China versteht die Belt-and-Road-Initiative besser als du." Dieses nationale Projekt, das Wirtschaftsbeziehungen und Handel über alles stellt, könnte für Fang Di nicht greifbarer sein. Dabei geht es für ihn darum, wie er mit der ineffizienten Regierungsbürokratie Papua-Neuguineas kommunizieren kann, um an Dokumente zu gelangen, die er für den Fortgang eines Projekts braucht, usw. Aber dahinter verbergen sich noch viele andere Aspekte. In dem Maße, wie Papua-Neuguinea von Chinas fortschrittlicher Technologie und reicher Erfahrung bei Basisinfrastrukturprojekten profitierte, wurde es zu einem Ort, in den China all seine gesammelten Kenntnisse aus vierzig Jahren Reform- und Öffnungspolitik exportiert hat.

Diese Fortschritte haben sukzessive ersetzt, was die früheren Kolonialherrscher hinterlassen haben. China wird insbesondere als neues Modernitätsmodell wahrgenommen. Fang Dis Unternehmen hat seinen Sitz in Shenzhen (seiner Heimatstadt), der größten Sonderwirtschaftszone Chinas, voll mit neuen Wolkenkratzern, Migrant*innen, ausgestattet mit einer erstklassigen IT-Industrie und einer sehr modernen Ökonomie. Mit anderen Worten: Das chinesische Modell hat hier seinen größten Erfolg erzielt. Wie auf Dubai trifft der von Keller Easterling geprägte Begriff der „Extrastatecraft" auch auf Shenzhen zu, die sich als „Verfechterin der Globalisierung" versteht und eine „ausgezeichnete Trägersubstanz für wirtschaftliche Entwicklung, politische Isolierung und korporative Externalisierung"[1] bietet. Neoliberalismus und Sozialismus sind hier einen strategischen Pakt eingegangen, der in einen neuen, von Kapital und Technologie geführten ideologischen „Konsens" namens „Reformbeschleunigung" mündete. Aber was bedeutet das für einen zeitgenössischen Künstler? Mit welcher Art von Realität hat es ein Künstler, der die Arbeit für ein Staatsunternehmen als „Tarnung" benutzt, im Makrokontext der Belt-and-Road-Initiative zu tun?

Die Realität ist hier zweifelsohne so facettenreich wie ein moderner Film mit verschiedenen Handlungssträngen. In seiner jüngsten Arbeit *Minister* (2019) versucht Fang Di, seine Tarnung als Intervention für eine neue Erzählung von Globalisierung einzusetzen. Die Videoarbeit thematisiert Papua-Neuguineas Infrastrukturminister Justin Tkatchenko, einen Politiker mit komplexem Werdegang. Durch seine Arbeit lernte der Künstler ihn allmählich besser kennen und entwickelte ein Interesse für die Legenden über seine Vergangenheit: In Australien mit osteuropäischen Wurzeln geboren, verschafft sich Tkatchenko mit seinem Gartenbauunternehmen Zutritt zum papua-neuguineischen Markt, später wird er ein bekannter Moderator von Fernseh- und Radioprogrammen, was ihm den Weg in die Politik ebnet, und schließlich steigt er zu einem der mächtigsten Politiker des Landes auf und nimmt eine aktive Rolle als Player in Chinas Belt-and-Road-Initiative

1 Keller Easterling, *Extrastatecraft: The Power of Infrastructure Space*, London 2014, S. 121.

called 'reform accelerationism' led by capital and technology. But what does this mean to a contemporary artist? In the macro-context of the Belt and Road Initiative, what kind of reality does an artist using the 'cover' of working at a state-owned enterprise need to deal with?

Reality here is, without doubt, multifaceted, like a modern film which revolves around several different threads. In his latest piece *Minister* (2019), Fang Di tries to use his 'cover' to intervene in this new narrative of globalization. The video work takes Papua New Guinea's lands minister, Justin Tkatchenko, as its subject, a Papua New Guinean politician with a complicated background. The artist has gradually become more familiar with him due to his work and has developed an interest in the legends of his past: born in Australia with Eastern European heritage, Tkatchenko broke into the Papua New Guinean market with his horticulture business, later becoming a household name as the presenter of TV and radio programs, opening up a path to politics, and finally becoming one of the most powerful politicians in the country and a proactive player in China's Belt and Road Initiative. What is interesting here is that all of this comes back to a plant—specifically, the orchid. This beautiful and bizarre-looking flower is one of Papua New Guinea's unique natural resources, and orchids are the reason that Tkatchenko came to this country in the first place. To some extent, orchids served as the 'cover' for this future politician—offsetting the postcolonial aspects of the entire story and making people less likely to associate him with a return to 'white rulers'.

I was, therefore, unable to avoid making another association, with the book *The Orchid Thief* (2000) and the film adaptation of the book, *Adaptation* (2002). Similar to the latter, *Minister* is clearly an attempt to adapt a clichéd script. Throughout the entire video piece, Fang Di attempts, using a large collection of archival footage and interviews, to recreate Tkatchenko's personal history and this South Pacific country's development over the last thirty years, reaching for some deep-seated historical truth. This is, no doubt, a risky task. As an outsider, the artist needed to find an appropriate approach with respect to the protagonist's friends and observers of Papua New Guinea; and as a participant in an aid project, Fang Di really had no way to distance himself from the entire development story, as his perspective is embedded in the narrative. His perspective is an artistic one, and also a Chinese one, which undoubtedly adds a layer to the piece as a text, like a hidden form of interference, a perspective granted by the Belt and Road Initiative, which creates a montage of this island nation's people, its history, and its natural environment. — Yang Beichen 杨北辰

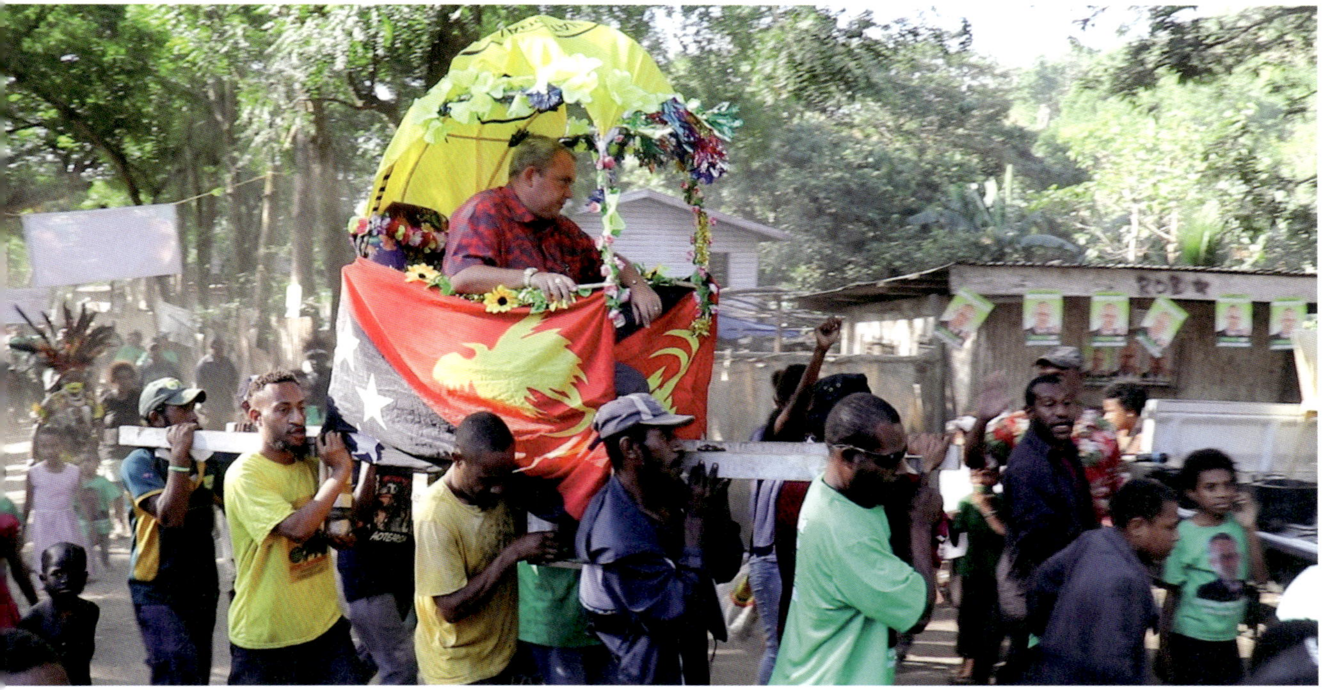

ein. Interessant daran ist, dass alles auf eine Pflanze zurückzuführen ist – genauer die Orchidee. Diese schöne und bizarr anmutende Blume gehört zu Papua-Neuguineas einzigartigen natürlichen Ressourcen, und Orchideen waren in erster Linie der Grund, warum Tkatchenko ins Land kam. In gewisser Weise fungierten Orchideen als Tarnung für den zukünftigen Politiker, indem sie die postkolonialen Aspekte der ganzen Angelegenheit kompensierten und die lokale Bevölkerung ihn weniger mit der Rückkehr „weißer Machthaber“ in Verbindung brachte.

Für mich drängt sich aus diesem Grund die Assoziation mit dem Buch *Der Orchideendieb* (2000) und seiner Filmadaption *Adaption* (2002) auf. Ebenso wie der Film stellt *Minister* eindeutig den Versuch dar, ein klischeehaftes Drehbuch zu adaptieren. In der Videoarbeit rekonstruiert Fang Di anhand einer umfangreichen Sammlung von archivarischem Filmmaterial und Interviews Tkatchenkos persönliche Geschichte und die der Entwicklung des südpazifischen Landes während der letzten dreißig Jahre, um so zu tiefer verwurzelten historischen Wahrheiten vorzudringen. Das ist ohne Frage ein riskantes Unterfangen. Als Außenstehender musste der Künstler eine angemessene Position zwischen respektvollem Abstand und gleichzeitiger Nähe gegenüber den Freunden des Protagonisten auf Papua-Neuguinea und dem Betrachter finden; und als Beteiligter eines Hilfsprojekts hatte Fang Di tatsächlich keine Möglichkeit, sich selbst vom gesamten Verlauf der Geschichte zu distanzieren, da seine Perspektive in die Erzählung eingebettet ist. Es ist eine künstlerische und zugleich eine chinesische Perspektive, die der Arbeit zweifellos eine Ebene hinzufügt, ebenso wie die versteckte Form der Einmischung, die durch die Perspektive der Belt-and-Road-Initiative einfließt und sich zu einer Bildmontage über die Bevölkerung des Inselstaats, ihre Geschichte und ihren natürlichen Lebensraum zusammensetzt. — Yang Beichen 杨北辰

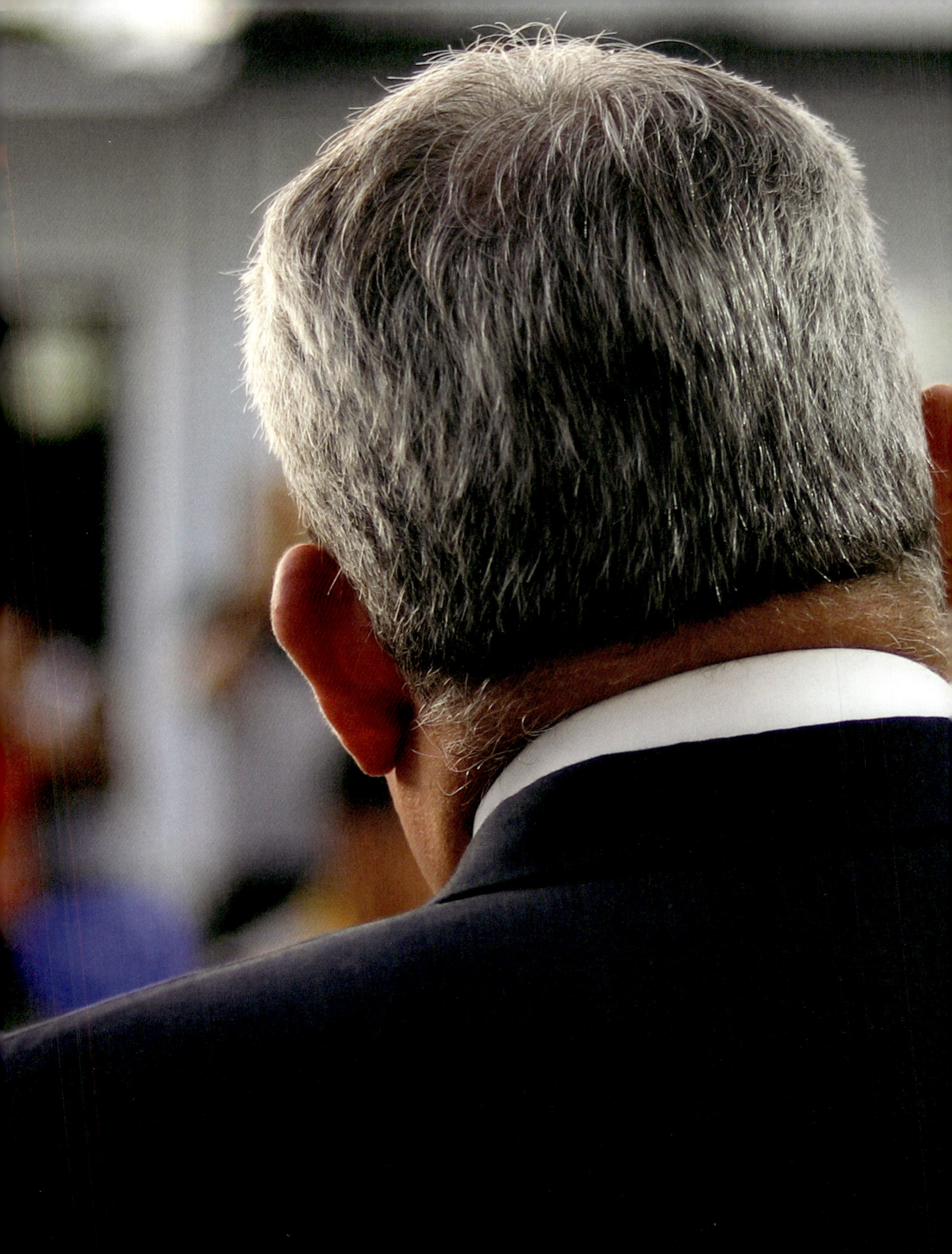

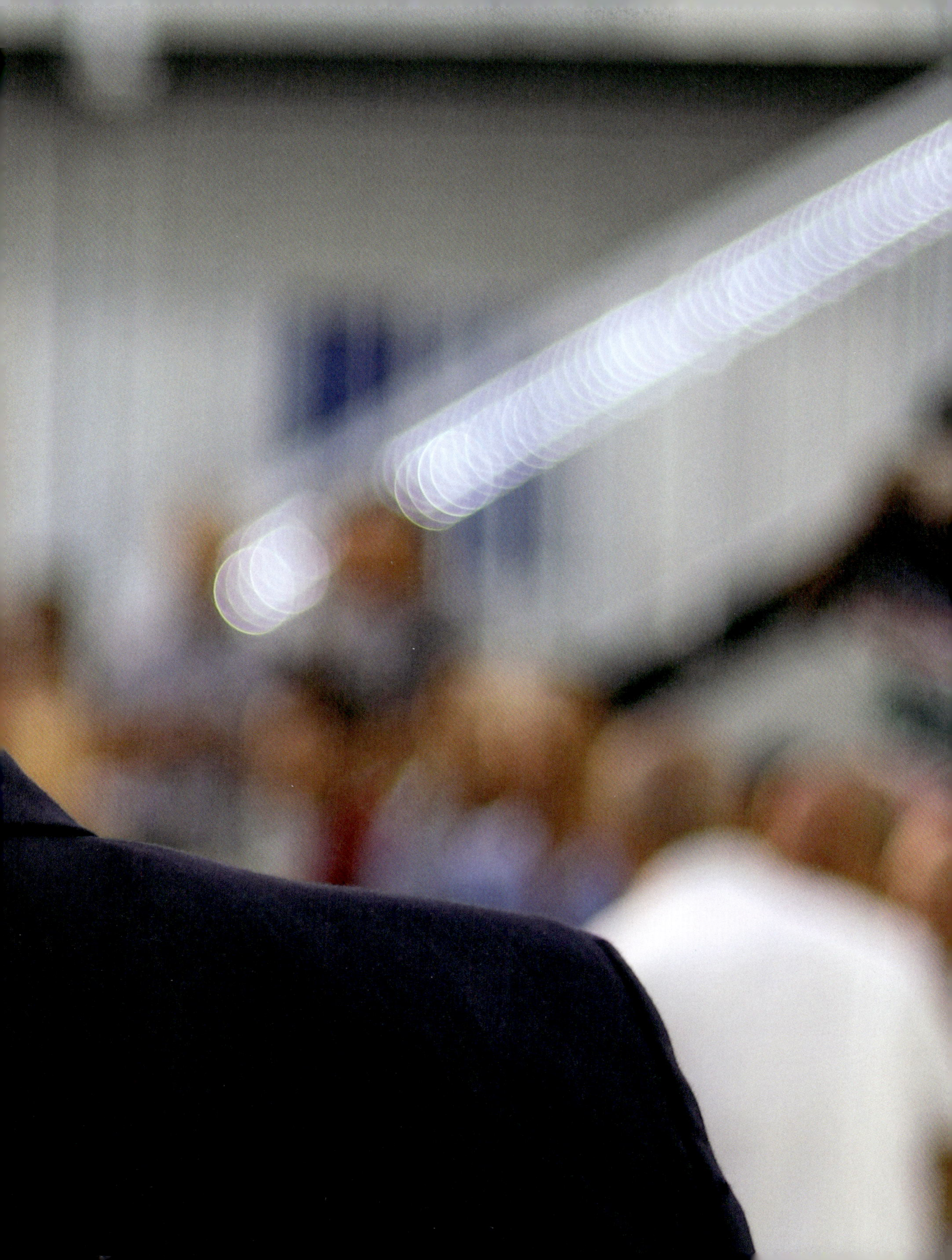

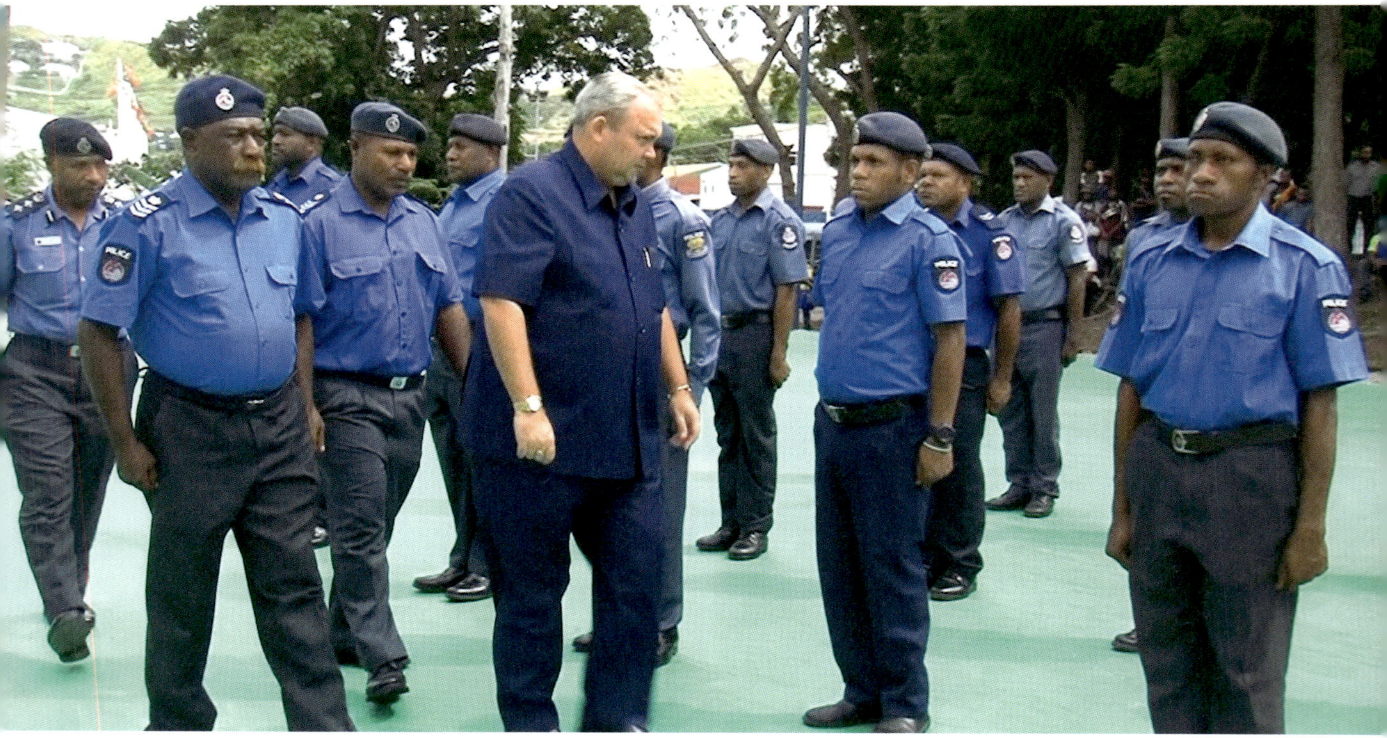

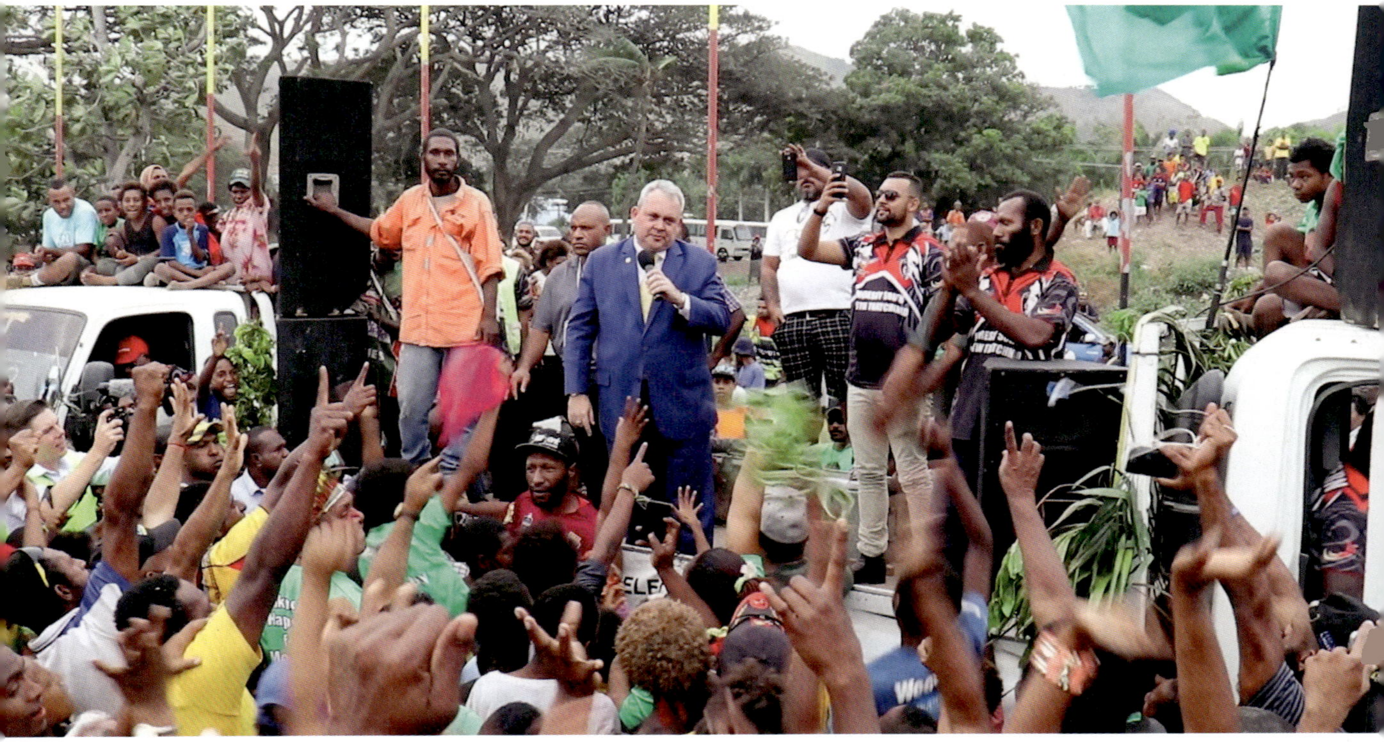

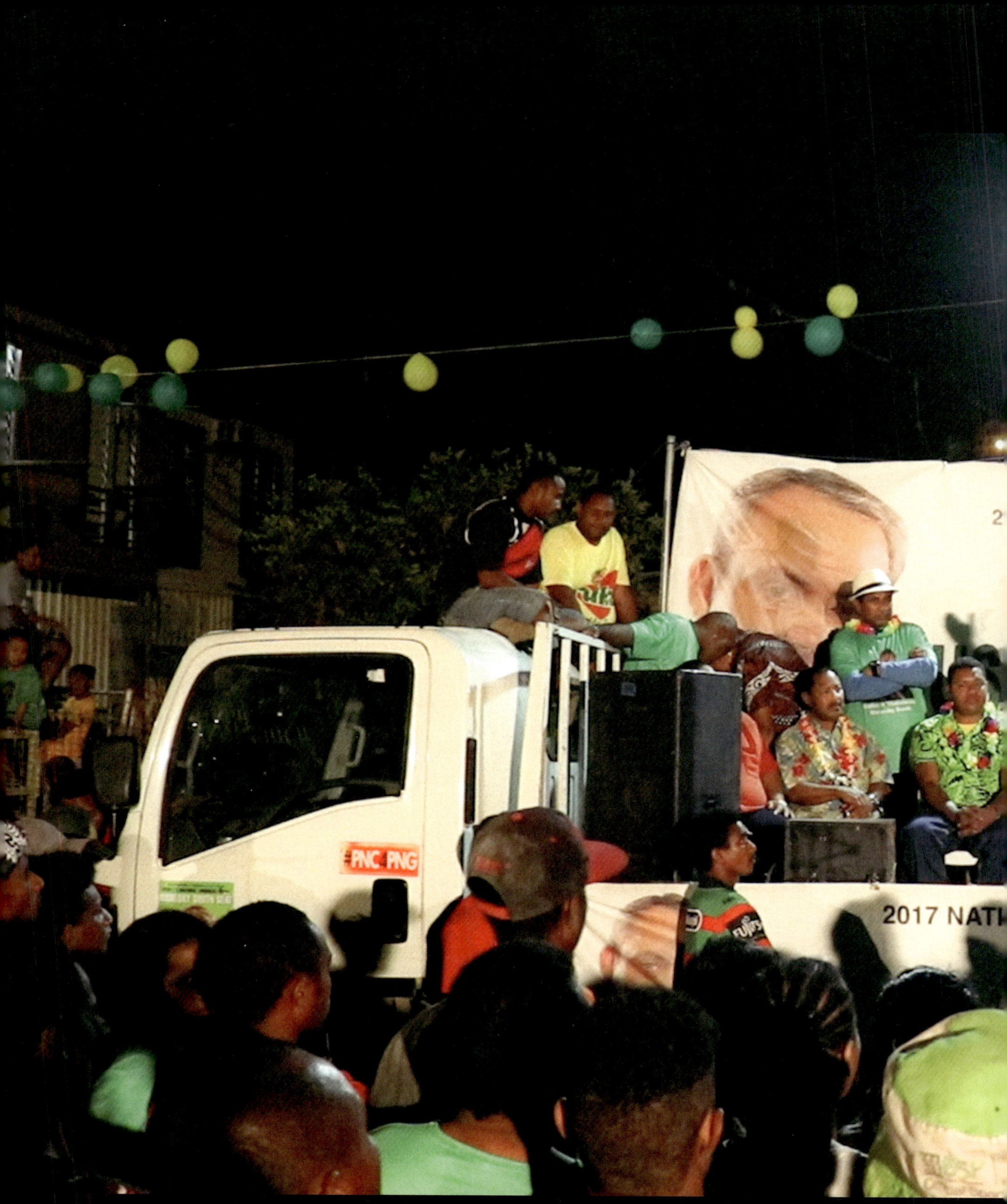

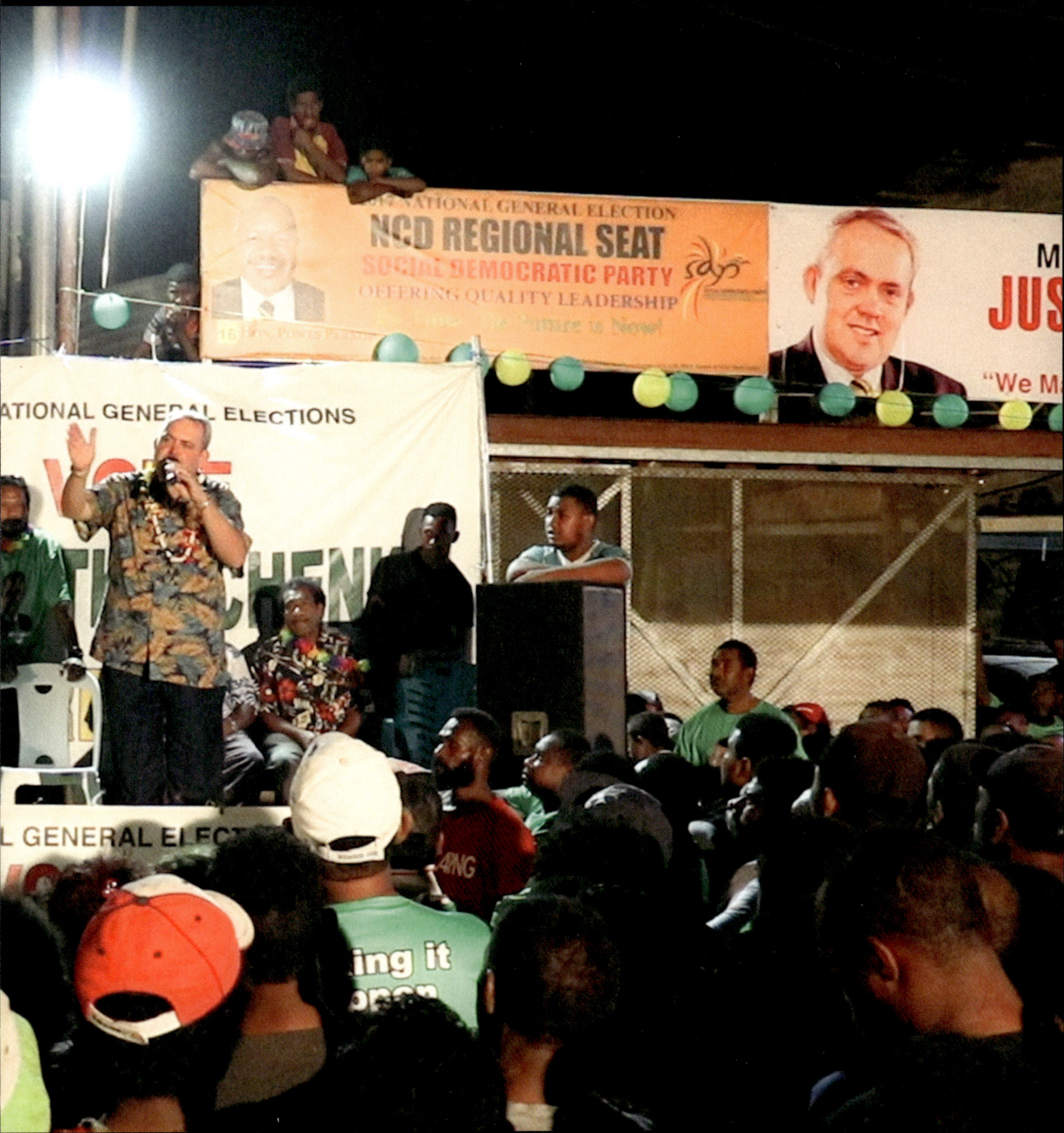
NATIONAL GENERAL ELECTION
NCD REGIONAL SEAT
SOCIAL DEMOCRATIC PARTY
OFFERING QUALITY LEADERSHIP
GENERAL ELECTIONS
VOTE

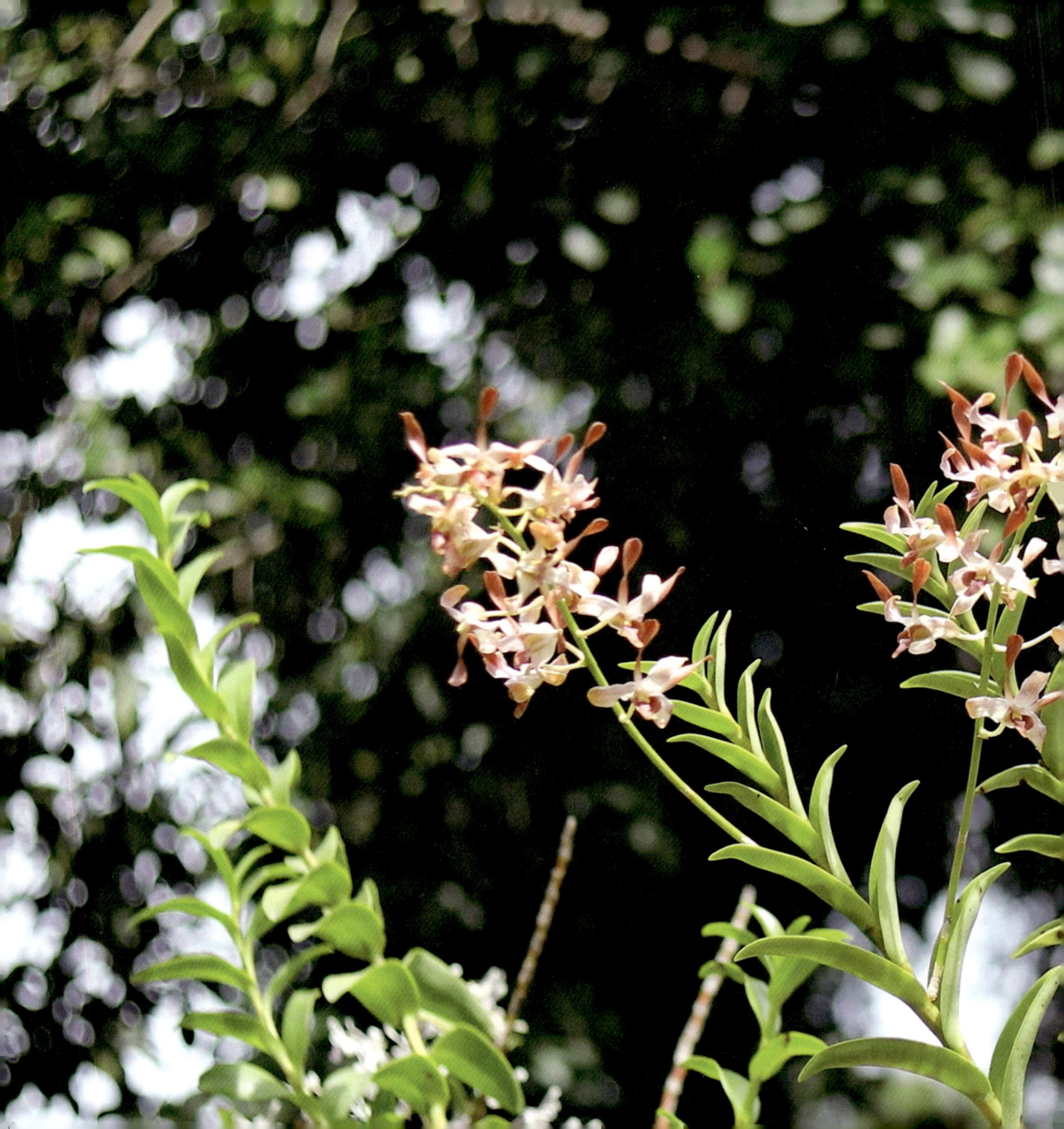

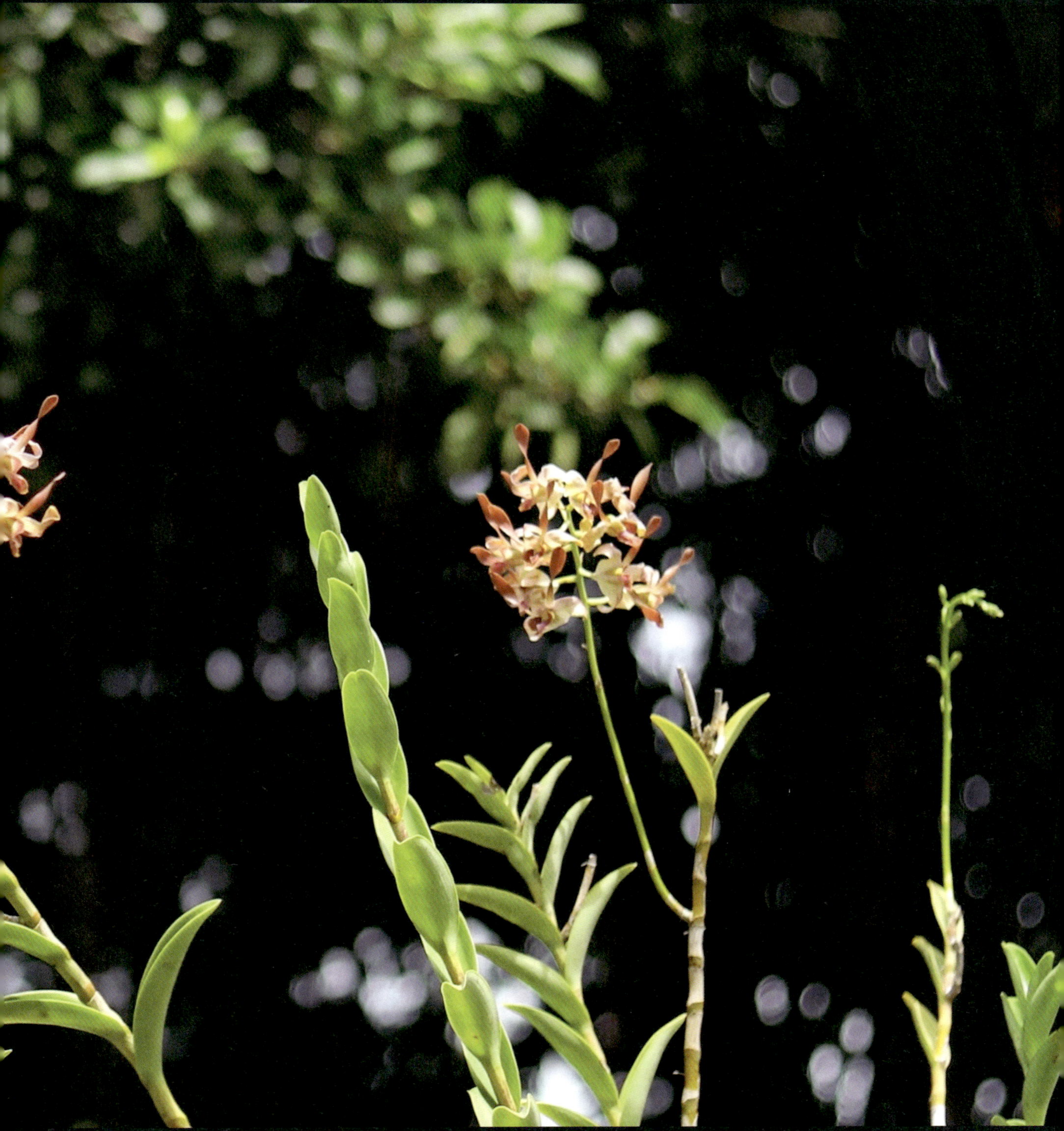

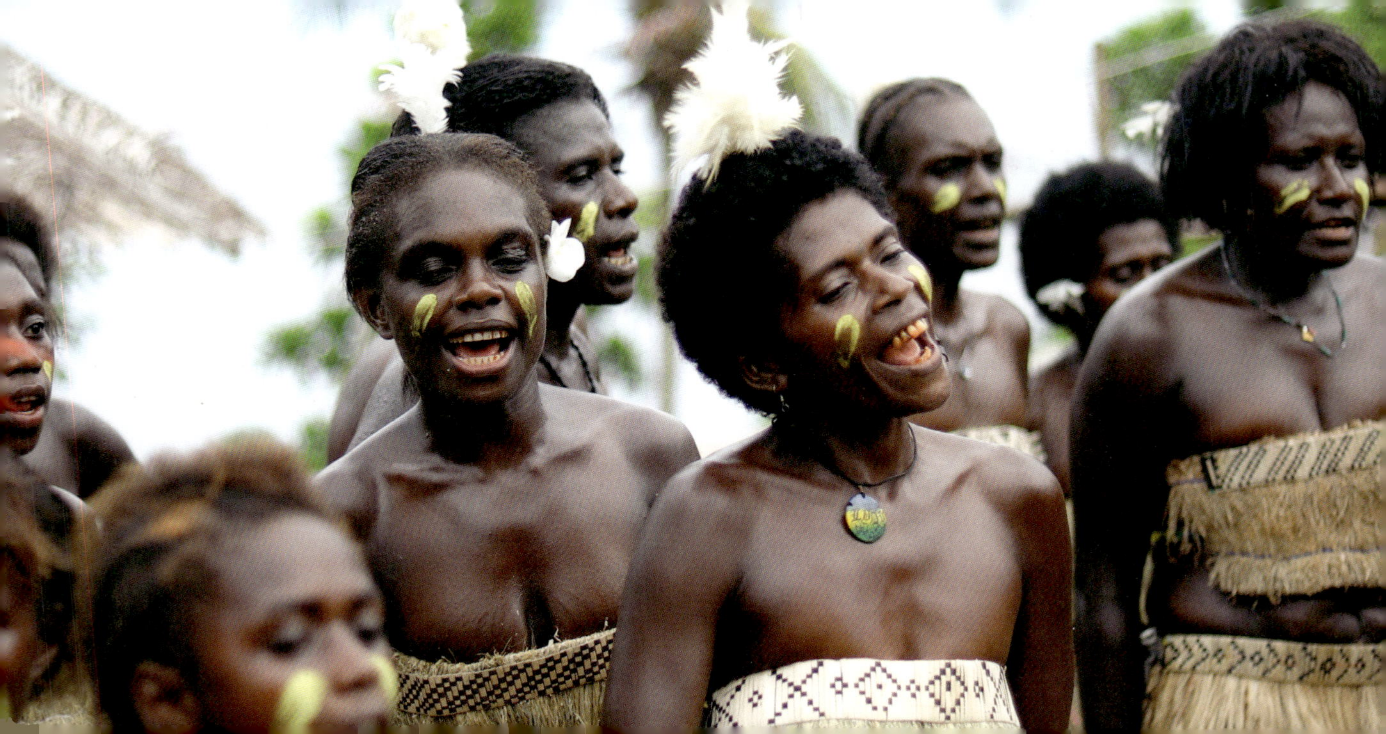

Seite / Pages 64–69

The Magical of Pipes, 2019
Zwei-Kanal-Videoinstallation, Farbe, Ton / Two-channel video installation, colour, sound, 30'

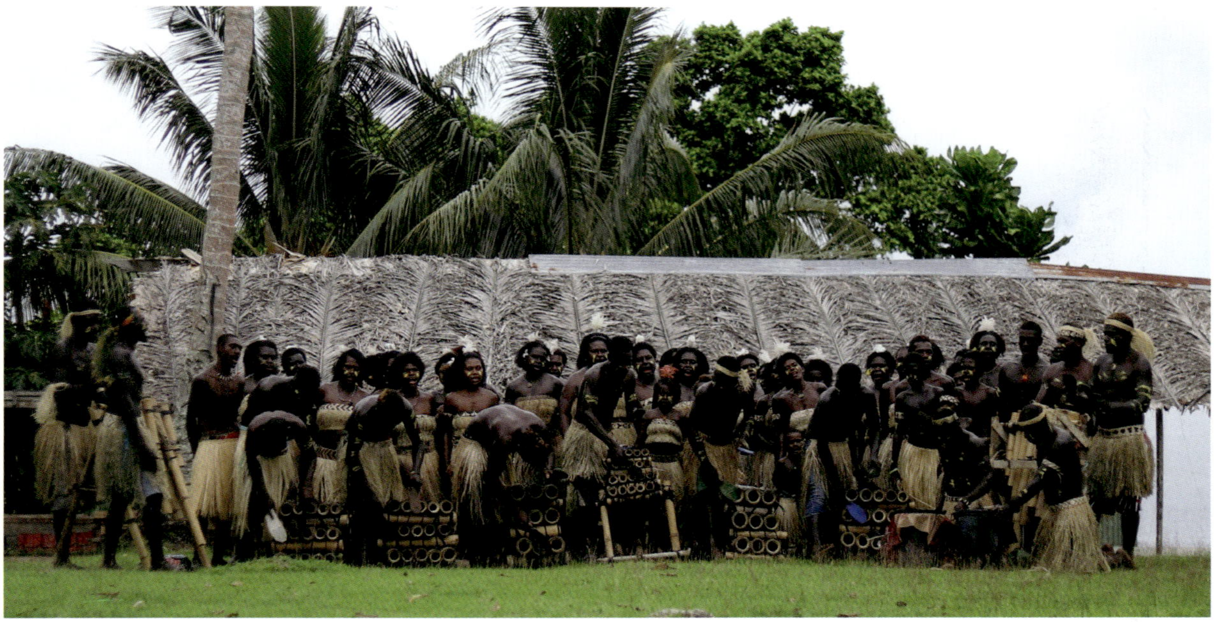

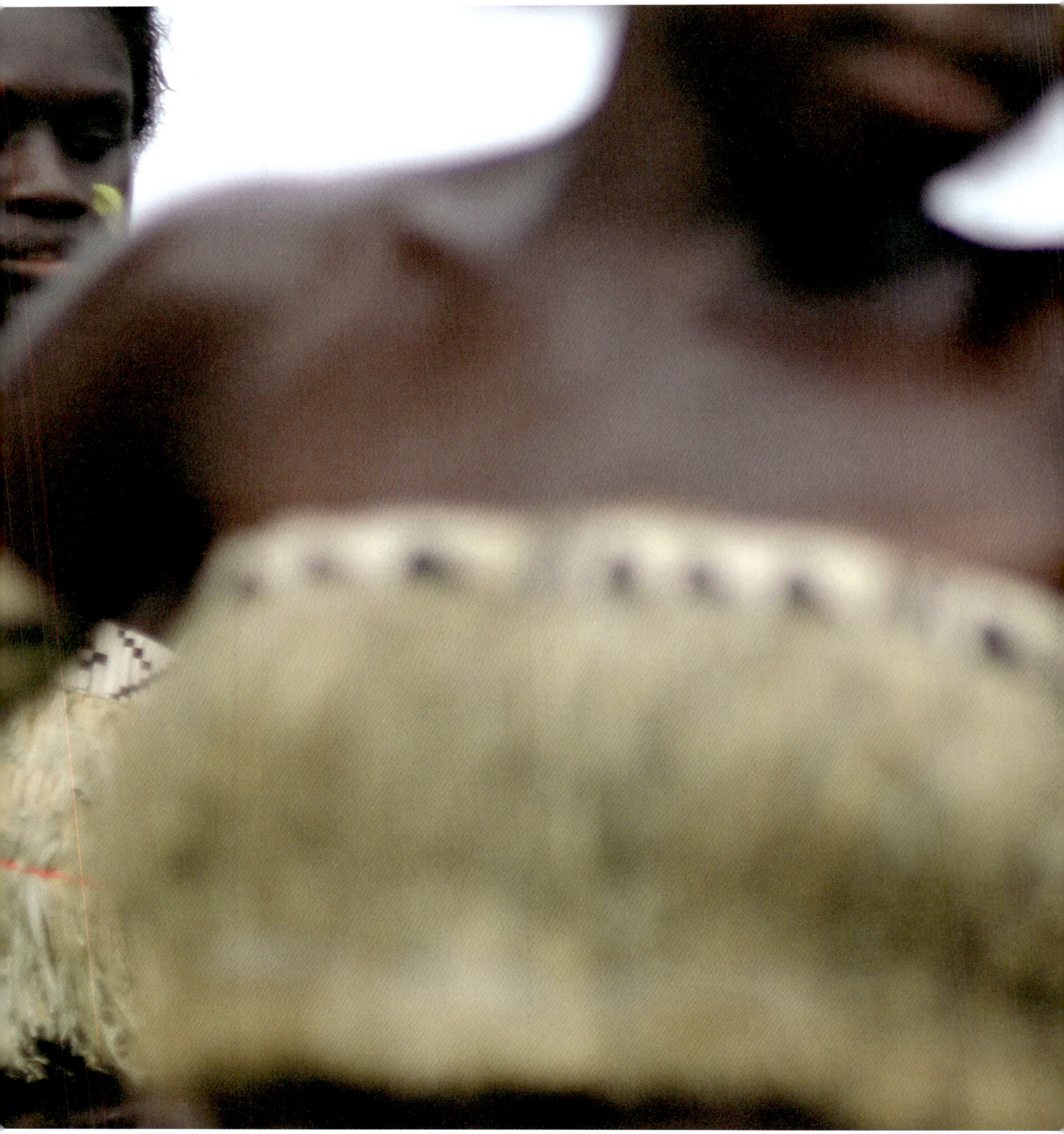

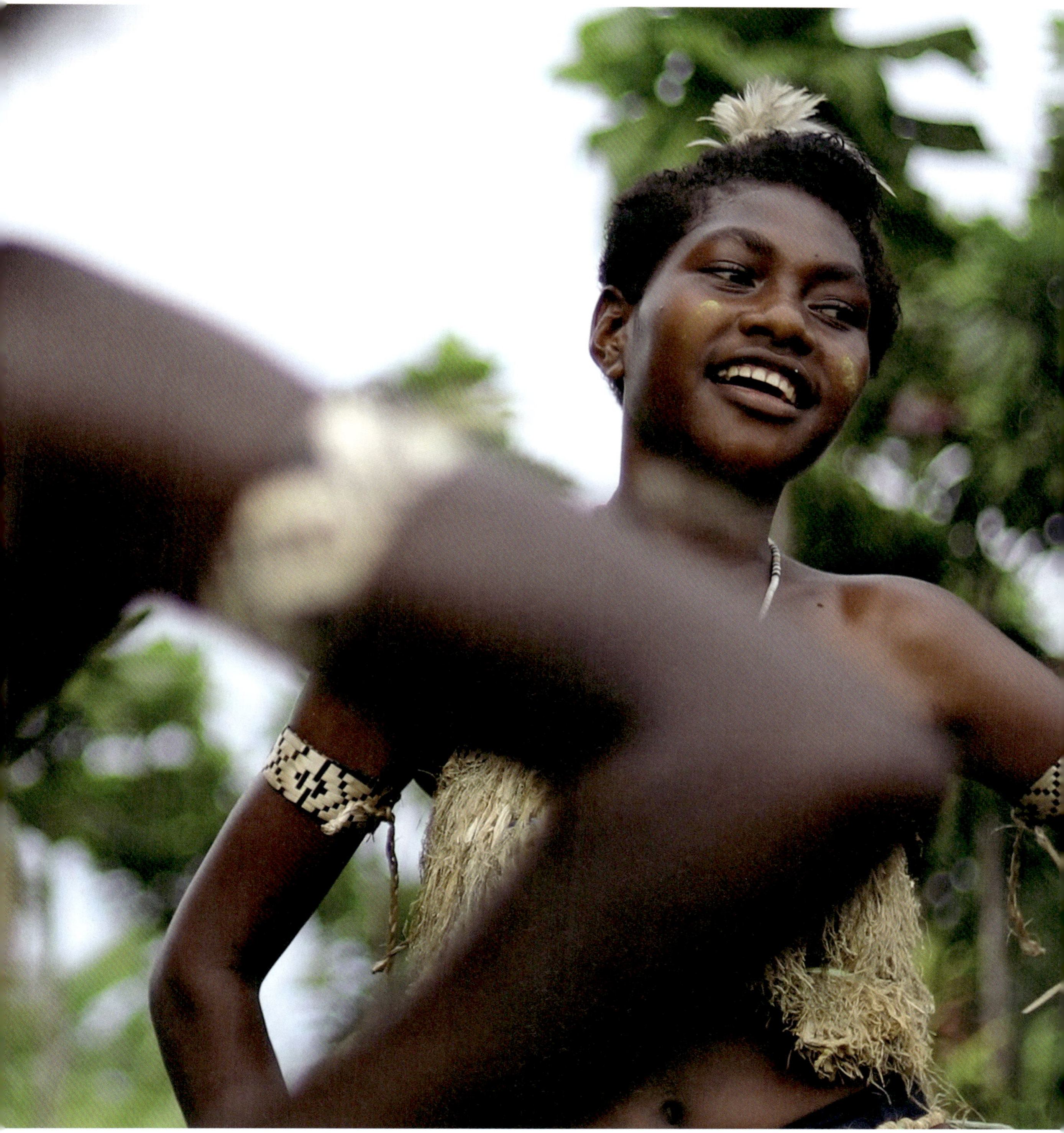

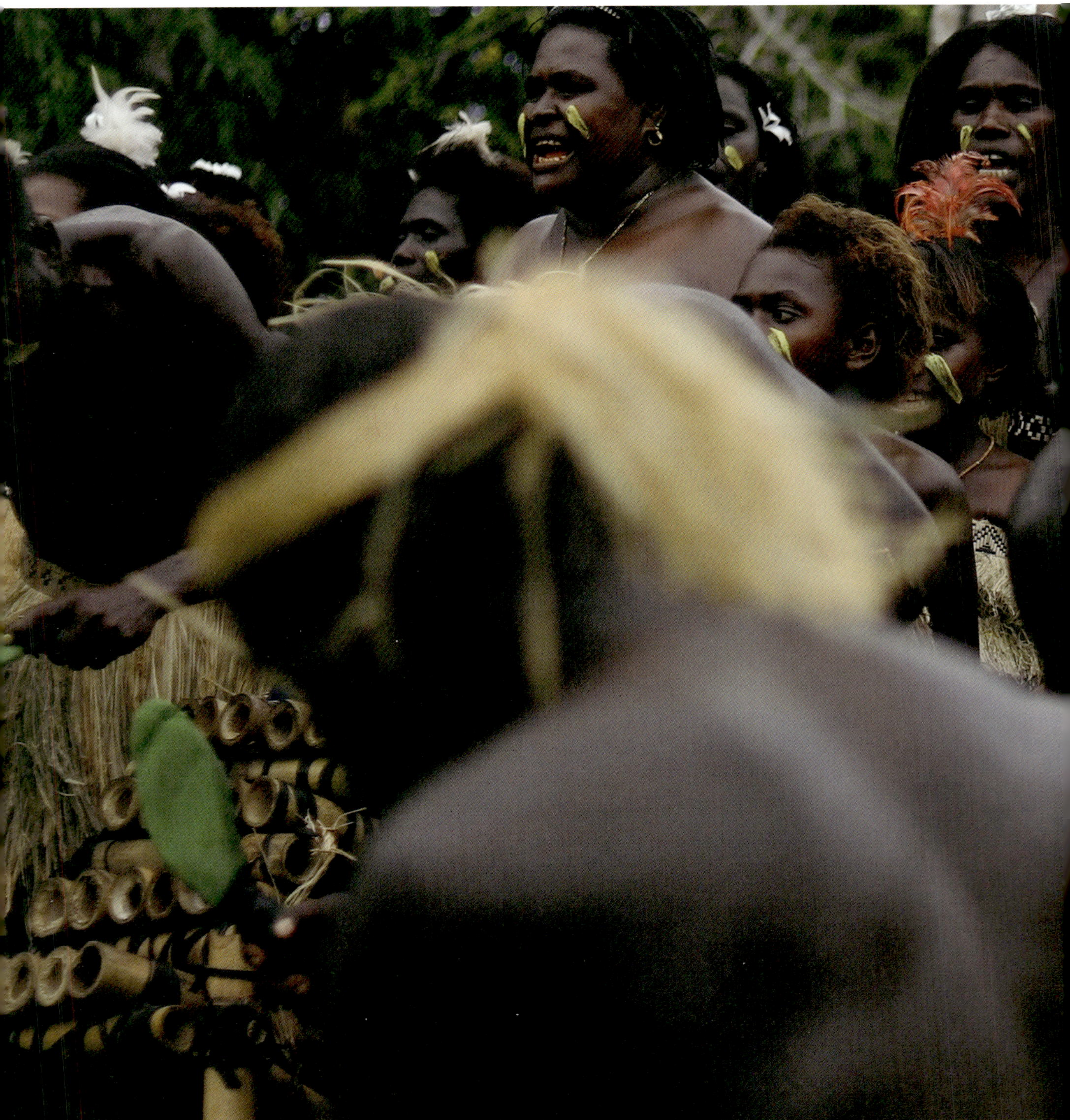

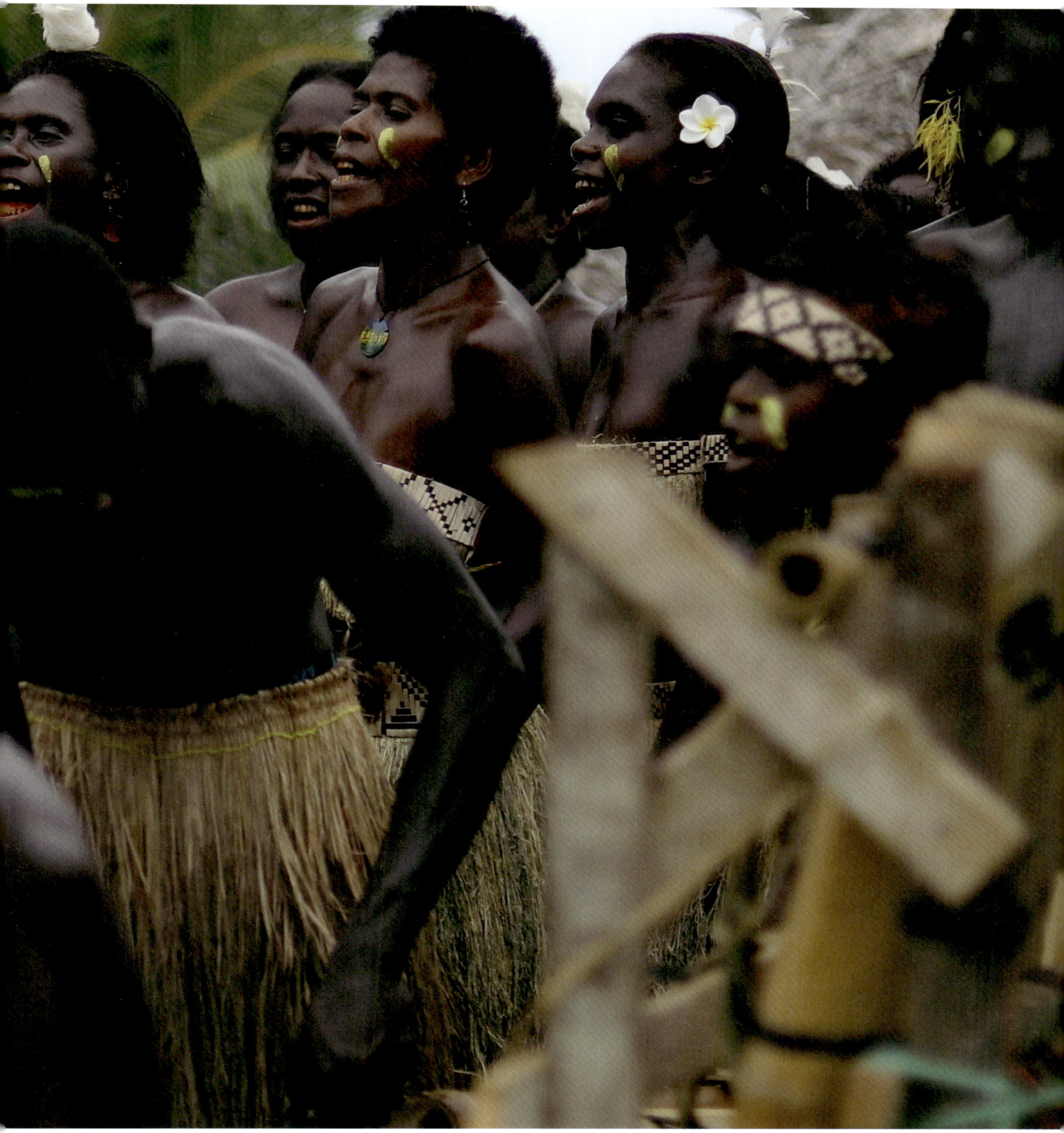

Lu Yang interweaves virtual and physical architectures in her installations and lures viewers into syncretistic hells of an augmented reality. In her works, the artist, who was born in Shanghai in 1984, reflects on our relationship to synthetic experience and on the narcissism, loss of identity, fantasy, and fetishism associated with it. With soundtracks bubbling with energy and knowledgeable references to traditional Buddhism, techno-religions, cyberfeminism, and Japanese subcultures, Lu's works evoke spiritual stimulants, a belief in science, cultures of exorcism, curious deities, death, and post-human forms of life.

In her Wagnerian total works of art, Lu interrogates gender role clichés as well as notions of cultural identity and art considered 'Chinese'. Though she lives in China, she does not regard herself as a 'Chinese artist': she grew up with and on the Internet, and her references and the environments that significantly influence her are found online.[1] And, at the latest in 2013, when Lu's anime-like character *Uterus Man* appeared in international art exhibitions, it became clear that visual art in China is undergoing a generational shift: *Uterus Man*, from the eponymous video work and computer game, is part superhero, part feminist icon, possibly a man, but his most important weapons are oestrogen and an electrical umbilical cord, while his vehicle is a pelvis-shaped chariot.

Uterus Man is only one of the central characters that shape Lu's works. Besides him, there are also diverse deities, a *Material World Knight*, or Lu Yang as an avatar and as a *Brain Control Messenger*. These characters interlink Lu's works to form a world with its own team of superheroes—similar to the comic worlds created by Marvel or DC.

For *Micro Era*, Lu Yang's world of superheroes develops in a labyrinthine arrangement of

1 See Barbara Pollock, *Brand New Art from China* (London and New York: I. B. Tauris, 2018), p. 7.

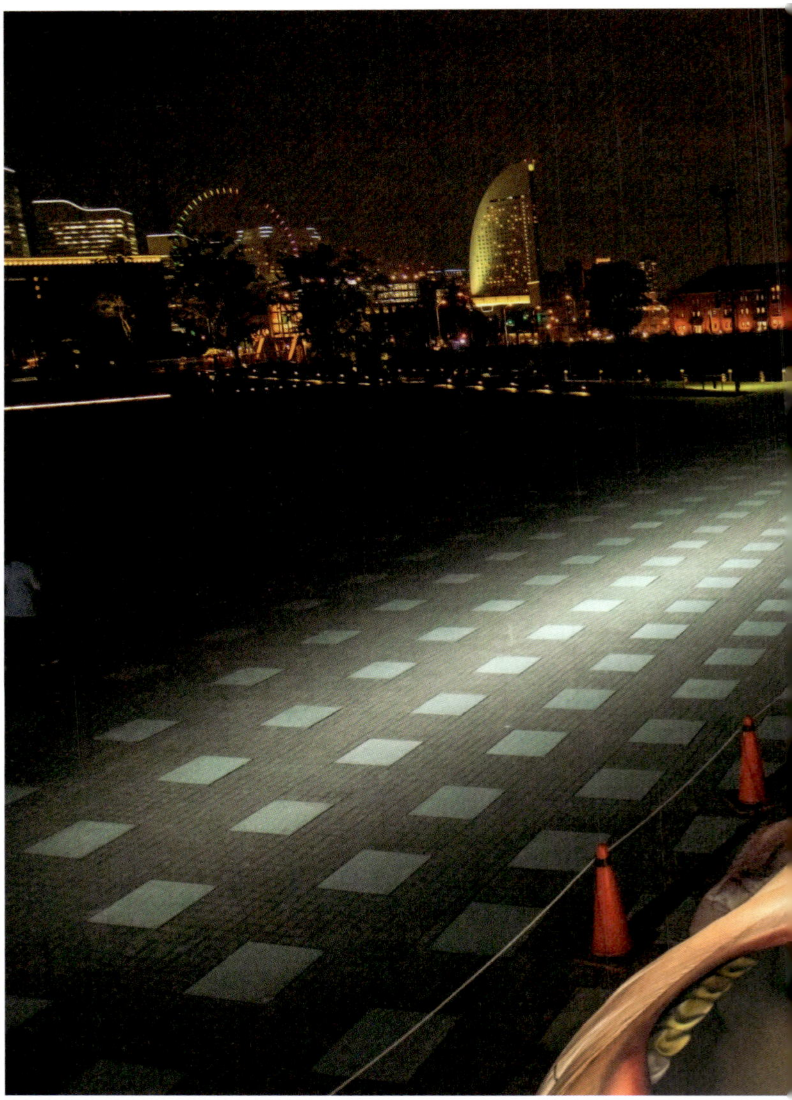

Lu Yang 陆扬

LuYang Comic Con

Lu Yang 陆扬

Power of Will – Final Shooting, 2016
Ballonkopf/aufblasbare Skulptur / Balloon head/inflatable sculpture
Installationsansicht / Installation view, Smart Illumination Yokohama, Japan, 2016

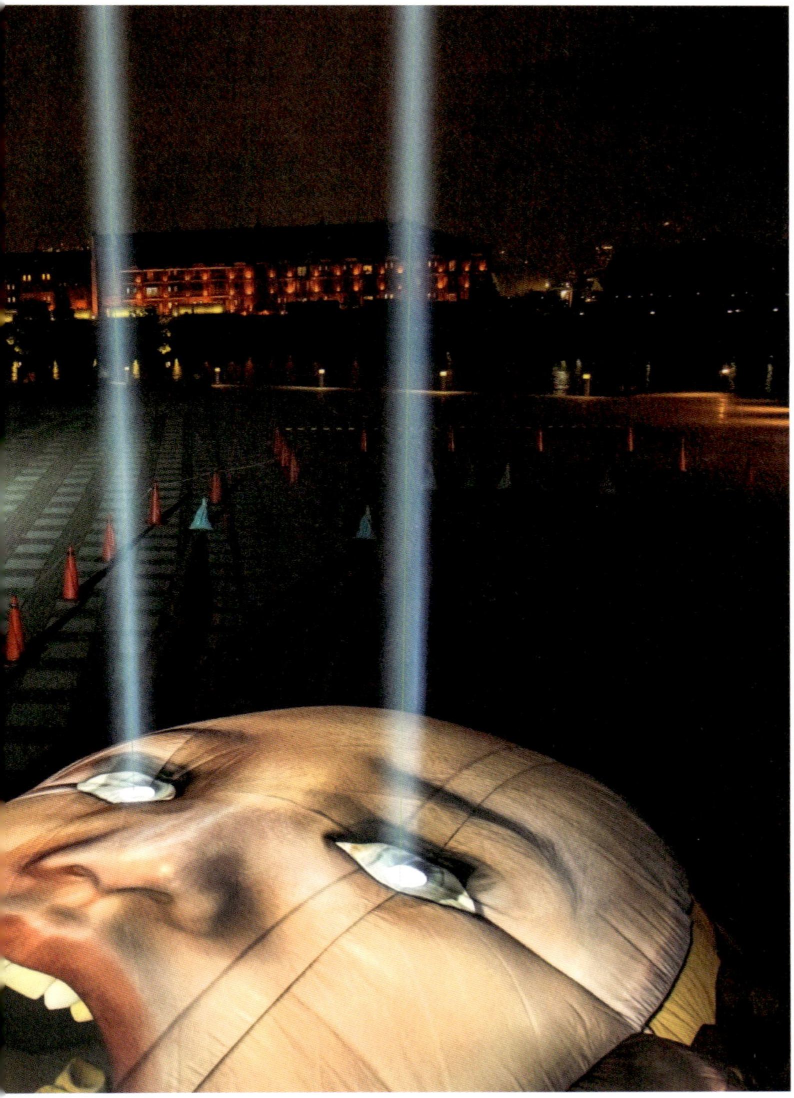

Lu Yang verwebt in ihren Installationen virtuelle mit physischen Architekturen und lockt die Betrachter*innen in synkretistische Höllen einer erweiterten Realität. In ihren Werken reflektiert die 1984 in Schanghai geborene Künstlerin unser Verhältnis zur synthetischen Erfahrung und damit einhergehend Narzissmus, Identitätsverlust, Fantasie und Fetischismus. Mit hochenergetisch sprudelnden Soundtracks und kenntnisreichen Bezügen zu traditionellem Buddhismus, Technoreligionen, Cyberfeminismus und japanischen Subkulturen beschwören Lus Werke spirituelle Stimulanzien, Wissenschaftsglaube, exorzistische Kulturen, kuriose Gottheiten, den Tod und posthumane Lebensformen.

Lu hinterfragt in ihren wagnerianischen Gesamtkunstwerken Genderrollenklischees ebenso wie Vorstellungen von kultureller Identität und als „chinesisch" geltende Kunst. In China lebend betrachtet sie sich nicht als „chinesische Künstlerin": Die Künstlerin ist mit und im Internet aufgewachsen, ihre Referenzen und ihre sie entscheidend beeinflussende Umwelt finden online statt.[1] Und spätestens als 2013 Lus Anime-artige Figur *Uterus Man* in internationalen Kunstausstellungen auftauchte, wurde klar, dass die bildende Kunst in China einen weiteren Generationenwechsel erlebt: *Uterus Man* aus der Videoarbeit und dem Computerspiel gleichen Namens ist teils Superheld, teils feministische Ikone, womöglich ein Mann, aber seine wichtigsten Waffen sind Östrogen und eine elektrische Nabelschnur, während sein Vehikel ein beckenförmiger Streitwagen ist.

Uterus Man ist nur eine der zentralen Figuren, die die Arbeiten von Lu prägen. Neben ihm gibt es diverse Gottheiten, einen *Material World Knight* oder Lu Yang als Avatar und als *Brain Control Messenger*. Diese Charaktere verbinden Lus Arbeiten zu einer Welt mit einem eigenen

1 Vgl. Barbara Pollock, *Brand New Art from China*, London/New York 2018, S. 7.

successive spaces as if at a Comic Con.[2] There, in addition to the central video or game, one finds associated materials and spheres that the artist frames with complex, iridescent laser wallpapers. But here, despite the departments and worlds following one another like exhibition booths, they are linked by a dramatic composition. Wandering from one world to the next, what unfolds for viewers is a coherent universe—Lu Yang's world system.

The first partial world is that of *Uterus Man* (2013): via this work, the viewers enter Lu Yang's man-made world, a post-Anthropocene beyond gender-essentialism.[3]

Uterus Man is followed by *LuYang Delusional Mandala* (2015) and the entry into the hell-like world of madness. With this 3D animation, Lu Yang provides the foundation for the following works, which are conceived based on this piece and connected with one another. For the transition to this sphere, the artist scans and reproduces herself using a 3D printer, to then torment the mind of her genderless clone and thus arrive at the source of her maddest dreams. Also born in this work is Lu Yang's 'LikuLiku' dance—an interpretation of Miku Hatsune's 'MikuMiku' dance.[4]

As in Dante's *Divine Comedy*, one circle of hell is merely the stage before the next inferno: what develops with *LuYang Delusional Crime and Punishment* (2016) is another delusional hell from the spirit of Lu Yang. Here, viewers encounter the Asian spirit house genre and its characters.

And above all of this hovers *Power of Will – Final Shooting* (2016), a monumental head with Lu's face as a hot-air balloon. LED lamps shine from her huge eyes like rose-coloured searchlights and capture the figures from hell in Lu Yang's world.

TMS Exorcism (2017) presents the TMS coil,[5] which can also be seen in *LuYang Delusional Mandala* and *LuYang Delusional Crime and Punishment* and serves the deities in the following work, *Electromagnetic Brainology*, as a TMS weapon for brain surveillance. Here, Lu deals with the link between sciences, neurological processes, and Asian exorcism-like methods for controlling the

2 Comic Cons are part fair, part conference, and enable visitors to transform themselves into superheroes, villains, elves, or other characters. The public frequently already shows up in suitable outfits. Otherwise, fans have the opportunity to dress up as their favourite characters or to meet these characters live on site. There are cosplay contests, photo points, and games. It is possible to buy costumes, posters, and books. Displays, sounds, and lighting transform each stand into a narrative setting. The aim of all of this is to recreate the pictorial spaces and multiple appeals of the virtual worlds of heroes, monsters, and other creatures at the stands.

3 See Harry Burke, 'Portrait Lu Yang: The Universe Is on Fire', *Spike*, 58 (Winter 2019), pp. 94–107, esp. p. 98.

4 Miku Hatsune (Jap. 初音 ミク, Hatsune Miku) was designed by the Japanese mangaka and illustrator KEI as a mascot for the Hatsune Miku software on behalf of Crypton Future Media. The artificial singing voice developed by Crypton builds on the software synthesizer Vocaloid2. In 2008, Miku Hatsune became the first synthetic pop icon and was awarded the Seiun Award in the free category. The virtual character has meanwhile become famous worldwide, has appeared in front of sold-out stadiums, and has been the opening band at various concerts, including as part of Lady Gaga's *ArtRave: The Artpop Ball* world tour in 2014.

5 Transcranial magnetic stimulation (TMS) uses strong magnetic fields to stimulate or inhibit areas of the brain. It is used

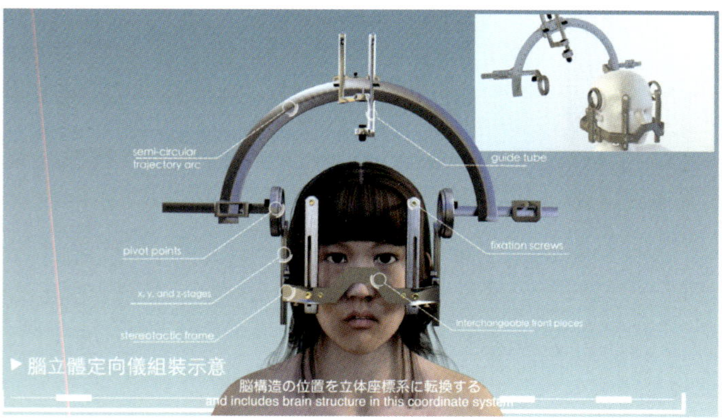

Seite / Pages 72–73

LuYang Delusional Mandala, 2015
Ein-Kanal-Video, Farbe, Ton / Single-channel video, colour, sound, 16'27"

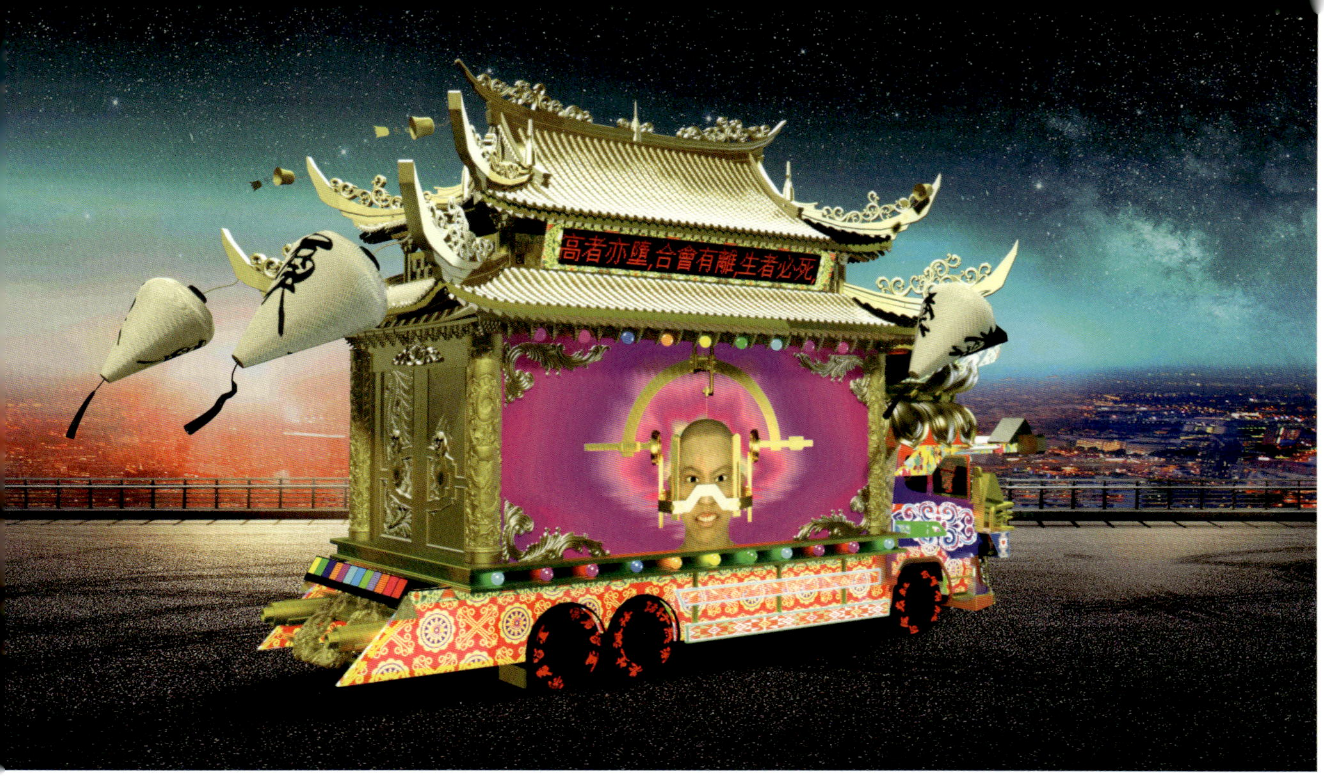

Superheld*innenteam – ähnlich der von Marvel oder DC geschaffenen Comicwelten.

Für *Micro Era* entfaltet sich Lu Yangs Superheld*innenwelt in einer labyrinthischen Anordnung von aufeinanderfolgenden Räumen wie auf einer Comic Con[2]. Dort finden sich neben dem zentralen Video oder Game dazugehörige Materialien und Sphären, die die Künstlerin durch komplexe irisierende Lasertapeten rahmt. Doch obwohl die Abteilungen und Welten messekojenartig aufeinanderfolgen, verbinden sie sich hier dramaturgisch: Von einer Welt in die nächste wandernd entfaltet sich für die Besucher*innen ein zusammenhängendes Universum – Lu Yangs Weltensystem.

Die erste Teilwelt ist die von *Uterus Man* (2013): Durch dieses Werk betritt das Publikum Lu Yangs menschenerschaffene Welt, ein Post-Anthropozän jenseits des Gender-Essenzialismus.[3]

Auf *Uterus Man* folgt *LuYang Delusional Mandala* (2015) und der Eintritt in die höllenartige Welt des Wahns. Mit der 3-D-Animation formte Lu Yang die Basis für die folgenden Werke, die von diesem Werk aus gedacht und miteinander verbunden sind. Für den Übergang in diese Sphäre scannt und reproduziert sich die Künstlerin selbst mit einem 3-D-Drucker, um anschließend das Gehirn ihres geschlechtslosen Klons zu traktieren und so die Quelle ihrer wahnsinnigsten Träume zu erreichen. Geboren wird in diesem Werk auch Lu Yangs LikuLiku-Tanz – eine Interpretation von Miku Hatsunes MikuMiku-Tanz.[4]

Wie in Dantes Göttlicher Komödie bildet ein Höllenkreis nur die Stufe vor dem nächsten Inferno: Mit *LuYang Delusional Crime and Punishment* (2016) entfaltet sich eine weitere

2 Comic Cons sind teils Messe, teils Kongress und ermöglichen den Besucher*innen, sich in Superheld*innen, Bösewichte, Elfen oder andere Charaktere zu verwandeln. Oft erscheint das Publikum bereits im entsprechenden Outfit. Ansonsten erhalten die Fans vor Ort die Chance, sich als ihre Lieblingscharaktere zu verkleiden oder diese Charaktere live zu treffen. Es gibt Cosplay-Contests, Photopoints und Games. Man kann Kostüme, Poster und Bücher kaufen. Displays, Sounds und Beleuchtung verwandeln jeden Stand in ein eigenes erzählerisches Setting. All dies dient dazu, in den Kojen die Bildräume und multiplen Reize der virtuellen Welten der Helden, Monster und sonstigen Wesen nachzuempfinden.

3 Vgl. Harry Burke, „Portrait Lu Yang. The Universe is on Fire“, in: *Spike*, Nr. 58 (Winter 2019), S. 94–107, hier S. 98.

4 Miku Hatsune (jap. 初音 ミク, Hatsune Miku) wurde vom japanischen Mangaka und Illustrator KEI im Auftrag für Crypton Future Media als Maskottchen der Software Hatsune Miku entworfen. Die von Crypton entwickelte künstliche Gesangsstimme baut auf dem Software-Synthesizer Vocaloid2 auf. 2008 wurde Miku Hatsune zur ersten synthetischen Popikone, erhielt den Seiun-Preis in der freien Kategorie. Die virtuelle Figur hat mittlerweile weltweite Bekanntheit, tritt vor ausverkauften Stadien auf und bildete u. a. bei Lady Gagas *ArtRave: The Artpop Ball*-Welttournee 2014 bei einigen Konzerten das Vorprogramm.

brain, but also as rituals of liberation and the expulsion of crippling demons.

Electromagnetic Brainology (2018) follows this like a cyber-altar—all the previous areas become a preview of this centre of Lu Yang's world: a temple dedicated to four deities, with laser and hologram wallpaper and five screens. Lu's overlaying of technology and religion is most evident here. *Electromagnetic Brainology* takes up the Hindu-Buddhist doctrine of the four elements—earth, water, fire, and air—and assigns them to the four central pain points in the neuralgic system of the brain.[6] Four deities that have become brightly coloured anime figures in the form of characters tailored to contemporary fan cultures transfer the mythological traditions to the twenty-first century and, equipped with the most modern medical technology, combat the sources of human suffering—that suffering which, according to Hindu-Buddhist teachings, leads to death. Death itself is an anxiety-causing topic in societies influenced by Chinese culture and is thus taboo. Again as if in a liberating, exorcism-like ritual, Lu addresses this taboo in the version with a fifth, centric video by having a figure that resembles her slowly slide into a coffin, before it is then loaded into a kitschy version of a traditional hearse, cluttered with ornaments. In the background of the scene, it is possible to make out a distant, microscopically small world, the post-human world that Liu Cixin describes in his short story 'The Micro-Era'.

The interweaving of Buddhist belief systems and fantasies of technology-assisted immortality shows that post-human questions arose long before the dispositifs of technoscientific thinking. This insight also includes the fact that the future is more deeply rooted in spiritual systems than is generally assumed, and that personal identity is a delusion. The deities in Lu's videos are multiplied in any case and do not stop dancing.

as therapy for neurological illnesses such as tinnitus, epilepsy, or Parkinson's disease, but also for affective disorders such as depression and schizophrenia. The fact that TMS achieves something seems to be demonstrated by changes that repeatedly occur after the magnetic coils have been used. But how the mechanism of action functions has not yet been determined. At the same time, as in the case of the TMS technique, technology is also not always connected directly with an exact science, but instead achieves its results based on the power of belief. And, conversely, religion cannot always be equated with blind superstition.

6 The four deities correspond to the four elements and the principles assigned to them: earth (stability), water (fluidity), air (gaseousness), and fire (passionate consumption). In Buddhism, the elements or the *Mahabhuta* consist of earth, water, fire, and air and serve as a basis for understanding the meaning of suffering and for liberating oneself.

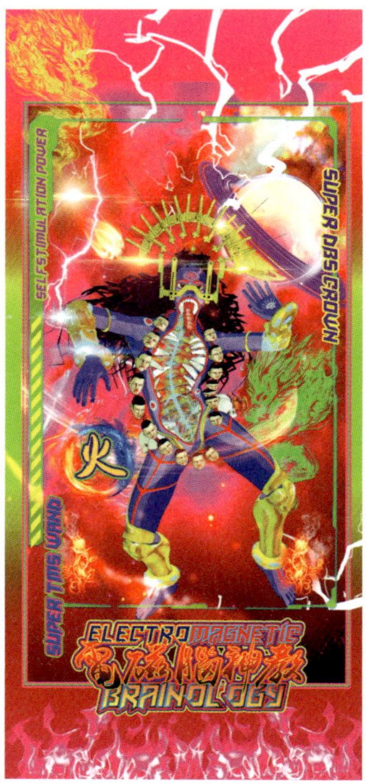

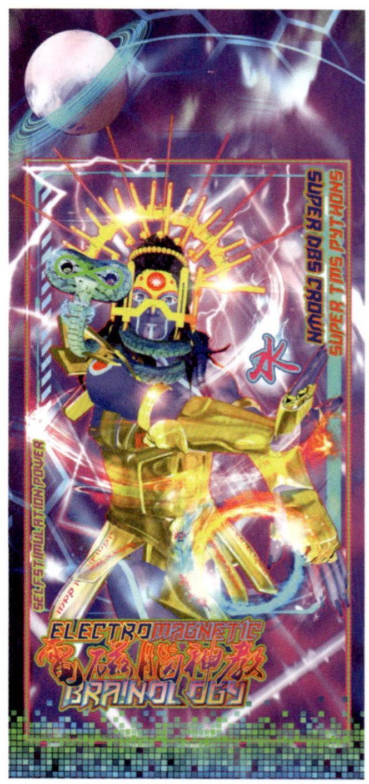

Seite / Pages 74–75

Electromagnetic Brainology, 2017
Fünf-Kanal-Videoinstallation, Farbe, Ton / Five-channel video installation, colour, sound, 13'34"

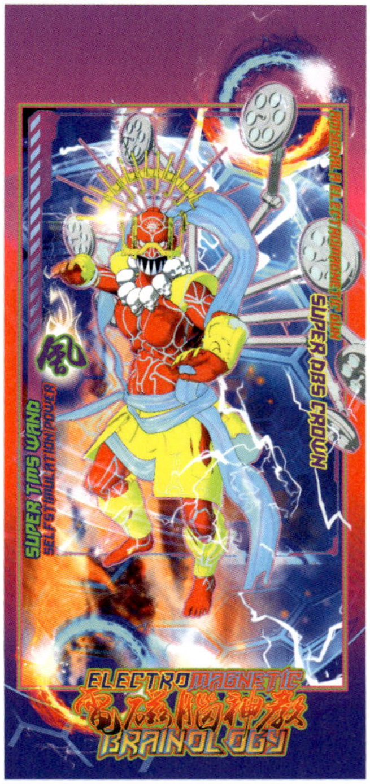

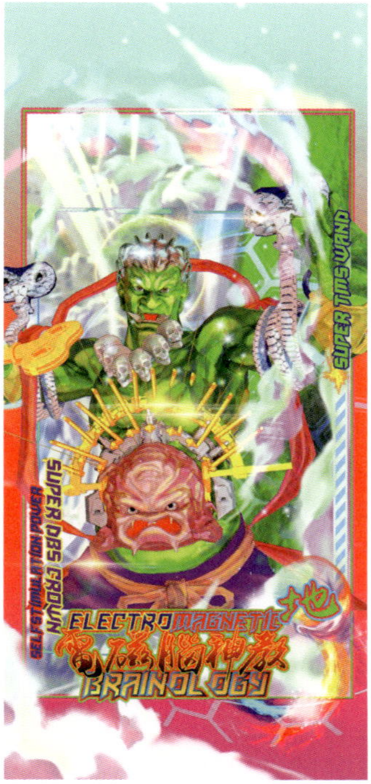

Delusional Hölle aus dem Geiste Lu Yangs. Hier treffen die Besucher*innen auf das asiatische Geisterhaus-Genre und dessen Figuren.

Und über all dem schwebt *Power of Will – Final Shooting* (2016), ein monumentaler Kopf mit Lus Gesicht als Heißluftballon. Aus ihren riesigen Augen strahlen LED-Lampen wie rosafarbene Suchscheinwerferlichter und erfassen die Höllengestalten in Lu Yangs Welt.

TMS Exorcism (2017) stellt die TMS-Spule[5] vor, die auch in *LuYang Delusional Mandala*, *LuYang Delusional Crime and Punishment* zu sehen ist und den Gottheiten des folgenden Werks *Electromagnetic Brainology* als TMS-Waffe zur Hirnüberwachung dient. Lu nimmt hier die Verbindung von Wissenschaften, neurologischen Verfahren und asiatischen Exorzismusmethoden zur Kontrolle des Gehirns, aber auch als Rituale der Befreiung und der Vertreibung von lähmenden Dämonen in den Blick.

Dem schließt sich wie ein Cyberaltar *Electromagnetic Brainology* (2017) an – alle vorhergehenden Bereiche werden zu einer Vorschau dieses Zentrums von Lu Yangs Welt: Ein vier Gottheiten gewidmeter Tempel mit Laser- und Hologramm-Wallpapers und fünf Monitoren. Hier wird Lus Überlagerung von Technik und Religion am deutlichsten. *Electromagnetic Brainology* nimmt die hinduistisch-buddhistische Lehre der vier Elemente Erde, Wasser, Feuer und Luft auf und ordnet sie den vier zentralen Schmerzpunkten im neuralgischen System des Gehirns zu.[6] Vier zu knallfarbigen Animefiguren gewordene Gottheiten in Form von auf zeitgenössische Fankulturen zugeschnittenen Charakteren übertragen die mythologischen Überlieferungen ins 21. Jahrhundert und bekämpfen mit modernster Medizintechnik ausgestattet die Quellen menschlichen Leidens. Jene Leiden, die der hinduistisch-buddhistischen Lehre zufolge zum Tode führen. Der

5 TMS, die transkranielle Magnetsimulation, nutzt starke Magnetfelder, um Gehirnbereiche zu stimulieren oder zu hemmen. Eingesetzt wird sie in der Therapie neurologischer Erkrankungen wie Tinnitus, Epilepsie oder Parkinson, aber auch affektiver Störungen wie Depressionen und Schizophrenien. Dass TMS irgendetwas bewirkt, scheinen sich immer wieder einstellende Veränderungen nach den Einsätzen der Spulen zu demonstrieren. Doch wie der Wirkungsmechanismus funktioniert, ließ sich bis heute nicht belegen. Aber wie bei der TMS-Methode geht auch Technik nicht immer unmittelbar mit exakter Wissenschaft einher, sondern erzielt ihre Ergebnisse mit der Kraft des Glaubens. Und umgekehrt ist Religion nicht immer mit blindem Aberglauben gleichzusetzen.

6 Die vier Gottheiten entsprechen den vier Elementen und den ihnen zugeordneten Prinzipien: Erde (Festigkeit), Wasser (Flüssigkeit), Luft (Gasförmigkeit) und Feuer (das glühend Verzehrende). Im Buddhismus sind die Elemente oder die *Mahabhuta* aus Erde, Wasser, Feuer und Luft und dienen als Grundlage für das Verständnis der Bedeutung des Leidens und für die Befreiung von sich selbst.

The following room presents the female character *Electromagnetic Brainology Brain Control Messenger* (2018), who resembles the artist. With the exclamation 'Henshin', the protagonist transforms herself into a heroine who possesses a new weapon developed from brain research that is based on galvanic vestibular stimulation (GVS). It is already possible to see her TMX stick for transcranial magnetic stimulation and the DBS[7] crown in the previous rooms of the exhibition. We now find ourselves on level 6 of *LuYang Comic Con*. The *Bishōjo*[8] heroine fights her way through a *Mars Attacks* and *Rampage* scenario, which resembles the Harajuku district of Tokyo, in a world designed in pink and blue, corresponding to the cuteness-*kawaii* style.

From here, visitors enter the masterpiece of the *LuYang Comic Con* world: the three-channel installation *Material World Knight* (2018) contains elements from all of the previous works. Incorporating film shot in a *tokusatsu*[9] miniature city, the wallpaper motifs engender a *tokusatsu*-like atmosphere.

The game's centre, *The Great Adventure of Material World and Hell* (2019), is part of an ongoing project that Lu is currently working on. It is the most extensive game that she has ever developed. It brings together elements from her previous works and thus completes the *LuYang Comic Con* world.

Lu Yang studied with Zhang Peili. And, like Zhang, Lu knows that every technological spectacle, however fascinating it may be, is also connected with capitalist ethics and surveillance methods. Her ambivalent worlds, populated by wrathful yet fascinating deities, thus grapple not only with floods of images, but also with augmented realities and the manipulation of emotions, which transcranial magnetic stimulation, for instance, symbolically represents. Lu Yang's vertiginous worlds bear witness to her limitless imagination and technical skills, but also to the furious search for an exit, through which we have possibly already long since eddied out in senseless ecstasy. — Anna-Catharina Gebbers

7 Deep Brain Stimulation

8 *Bishōjo* (Jap. 美少女, Eng. beautiful girl) is the Japanese term for the typical, ideal image of a beautiful young woman and in anime and manga refers to beautiful young girls, usually of school age. *Bishōjo* characters can be described with the term *kawaii*, which stands for 'endearing', 'sweet', 'childlike', or 'attractive'.

9 *Tokusatsu* (Jap. 特撮, Eng. special film shoots), portmanteau of Jap. *tokushu* + *satsuei* (Eng. special photography); also Jap. (sometimes): special filming. *Tokusatsu* entertainment generally includes genres like science fiction, fantasy, or horror, with a high concentration of special effects and live recordings of characters, which act in the game as superheroes, fantasy or horror figures, or monsters like Godzilla or Gamera. The form comes from Japanese *Kabuki* theatre and the use of puppets in special effect scenes such as the battles common there.

Tod selbst ist in von chinesischer Kultur geprägten Gesellschaften ein angstauslösendes Thema und daher mit einem Tabu belegt. Als wäre auch dies ein befreiendes exorzistisches Ritual, begegnet Lu diesem Tabu: Im zentralen, fünften Video gleitet eine ihr selbst gleichende Figur langsam in einen Sarg, bevor jener in die kitschige Version eines traditionellen, mit Ornamenten überladenen Bestattungswagens verfrachtet wird. Im Hintergrund der Szene lässt sich eine entfernte mikroskopisch kleine Welt erahnen, die posthumane Welt, die Liu Cixin in seiner Kurzgeschichte „Das Mikrozeitalter" beschreibt.

Das Verweben buddhistischer Glaubenssysteme mit Fantasien technikgestützter Unsterblichkeit zeigt, dass posthumane Fragen lange vor den Dispositiven des technowissenschaftlichen Denkens entstanden. Zu dieser Erkenntnis gehört auch, dass die Zukunft stärker in spirituellen Systemen wurzelt als gemeinhin angenommen wird, und dass persönliche Identität eine Wahnvorstellung ist. Die Götter in Lus Videos vervielfachen sich jedenfalls und hören nicht auf zu tanzen.

Der folgende Raum zeigt die der Künstlerin gleichende weibliche Figur *Electromagnetic Brainology Brain Control Messenger* (2017). Mit dem Ausruf „Henshin" transformiert sich die Protagonistin in eine Heldin, die über eine neue aus der Hirnforschung entwickelte Waffe verfügt, die auf galvanisch-vestibulärer Stimulation (GVS) basiert. Ihr TMX-Stick zur transkraniellen Magnetstimulation und die DBS[7] – Krone sind bereits in den vorherigen Ausstellungsräumen zu sehen. Wir befinden uns jetzt auf Level 6 der *LuYang Comic Con*. In einer ähnlich dem Tokioter Stadtviertel Harajuku gemäßen im Niedlichkeits-*Kawaii*-Stil gehaltenen pink-blauen Welt kämpft die *Bishōjo*[8]-Heldin sich durch ein *Mars Attacks*- und *Rampage*-Szenario.

Die Besucher*innen betreten von hier aus das Master Piece der *LuYang Comic Con*-Welt: Die Drei-Kanal-Installation *Material World Knight* (2018) beinhaltet Elemente aus allen vorhergehenden Arbeiten. Die Dreharbeiten in einer *tokusatsu*[9]-Miniaturstadt aufnehmend, erzeugen die Tapetenmotive eine *tokusatsu*-artige Atmosphäre.

Das Game-Center *The Great Adventure of Material World und Hell* (2019) gehört zu einem fortlaufenden Projekt, an dem Lu gerade arbeitet. Es ist das größte Spiel, das sie je entwickelt hat. Es verbindet Elemente ihrer früheren Arbeiten und vollendet so die *LuYang Comic Con*-Welt.

Studiert hat Lu Yang bei Zhang Peili. Und wie Zhang weiß Lu darum, dass jedes noch so faszinierende technologische Spektakel ebenso mit kapitalistischer Ethik wie mit Überwachungsmethoden verbunden ist. Ihre ambivalenten, von zornigen, aber faszinierenden Gottheiten bevölkerten Welten ringen daher nicht nur mit Bilderfluten, sondern auch mit erweiterten Realitäten und der Manipulation von Emotionen, für die symbolisch etwa die transkranielle Magnetstimulation steht. Lu Yangs wirbelnde Welten zeugen von ihrer uneingeschränkten Vorstellungskraft und technischen Geschicklichkeit, aber auch von der wütenden Suche nach einem Ausgang, durch den wir vielleicht längst schon – womöglich in sinnloser Ekstase – hinausgestrudelt worden sind. — Anna-Catharina Gebbers

7 Deep Brain Stimulation.

8 *Bishōjo* (jap. 美少女, dt. „schönes Mädchen") ist die japanische Bezeichnung für das idealtypische Bild einer schönen jungen Frau und bezeichnet in Animes und Mangas schöne junge Mädchen, üblicherweise im Schulalter. *Bishōjo*-Charaktere können mit dem Begriff Kawaii beschrieben werden, der für „liebenswert", „süß", „kindlich" oder „attraktiv" steht.

9 *Tokusatsu* (jap. 特撮, dt. „*spezielle Dreharbeiten*"), Kofferwort aus jap.: tokushu + *satsuei* (dt. etwa: „spezielle Fotografie"); auch im Japanischen manchmal: special filming. Als *Tokusatsu*-Unterhaltung werden zumeist Genres wie Science-Fiction, Fantasy oder Horror mit einer hohen Dichte von Special-Effects und Liveaufnahmen von Figuren bezeichnet, die im Spiel als Superheld*innen, als Fantasy- oder Horrorfiguren oder als Monster wie Godzilla oder Gamera agieren. Die Form entstammt dem japanischen *Kabuki*-Theater und dem dort üblichen Einsatz von Puppen in Special-Effects-Szenen wie Kämpfen.

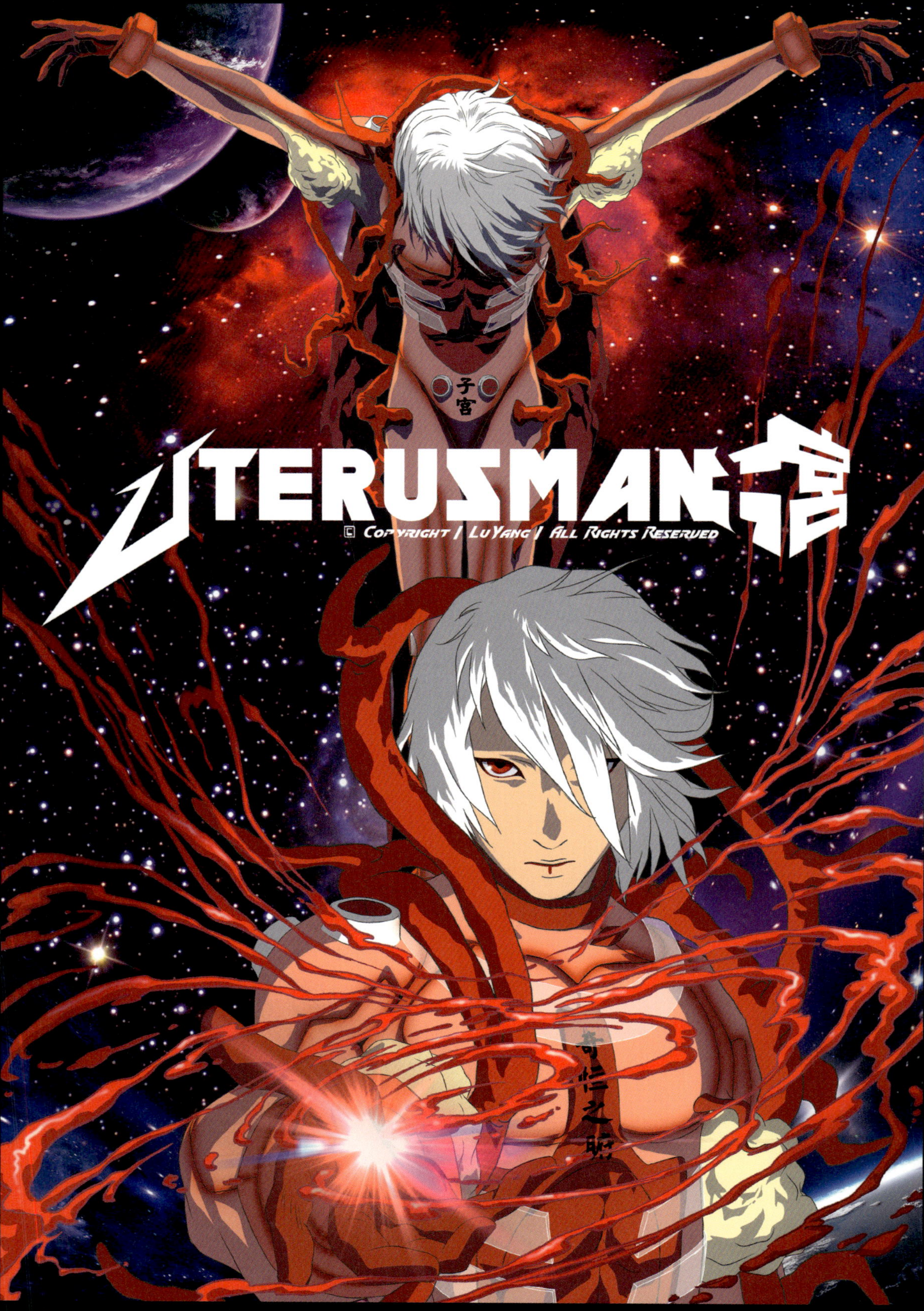
子
宫
UTERUSMAN
© Copyright | LuYang | All Rights Reserved

Uterus Man, 2013
3-D-Animation, Farbe, Ton /
3D animation, colour, sound,
11'20"

LuYang Delusional Mandala,
2015
Ein-Kanal-Video, Farbe, Ton /
Single-channel video, colour,
sound, 16'27"

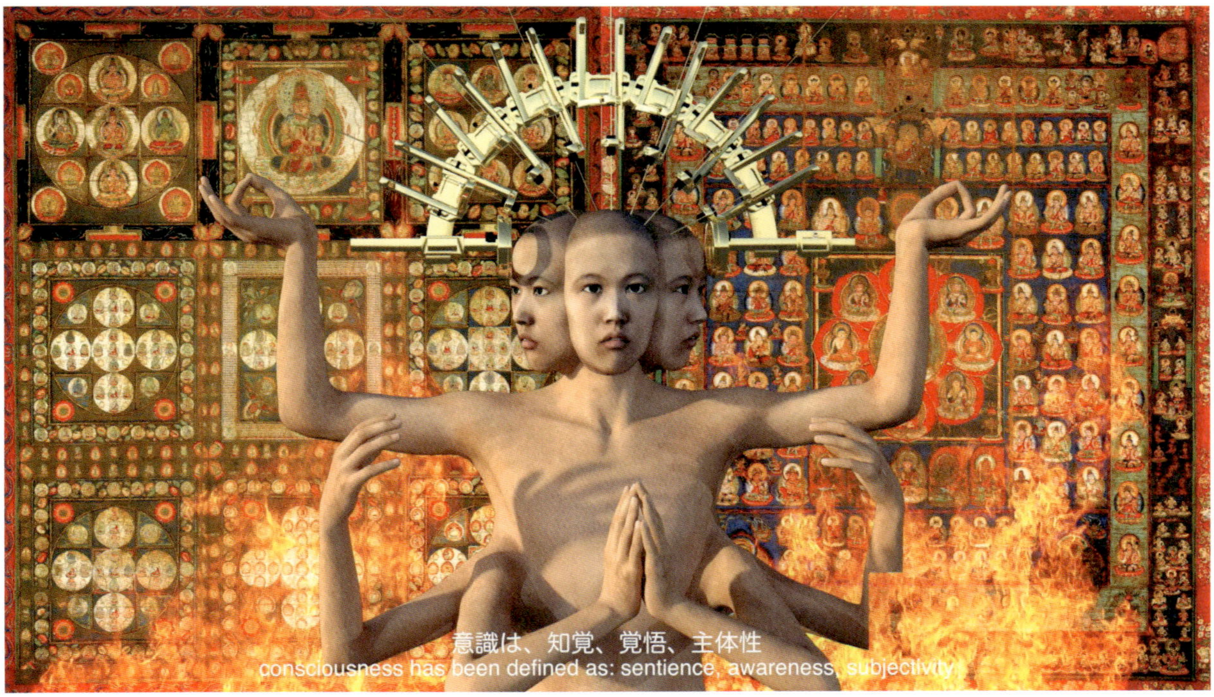

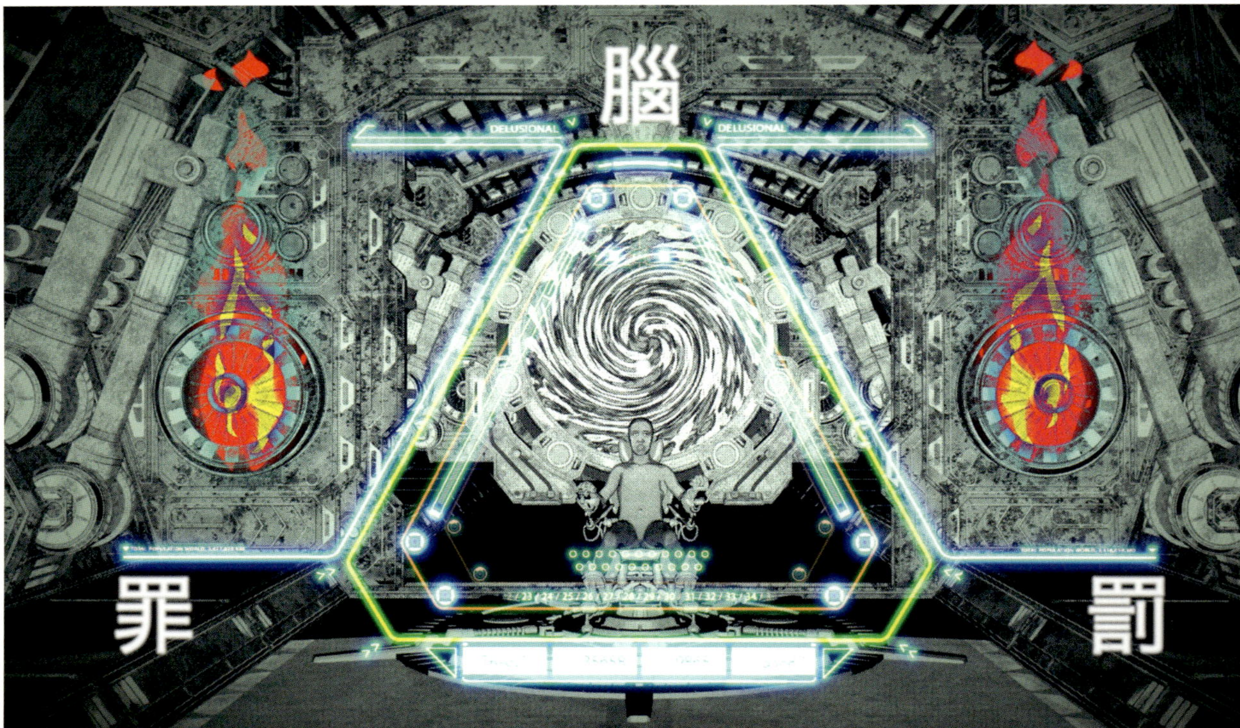

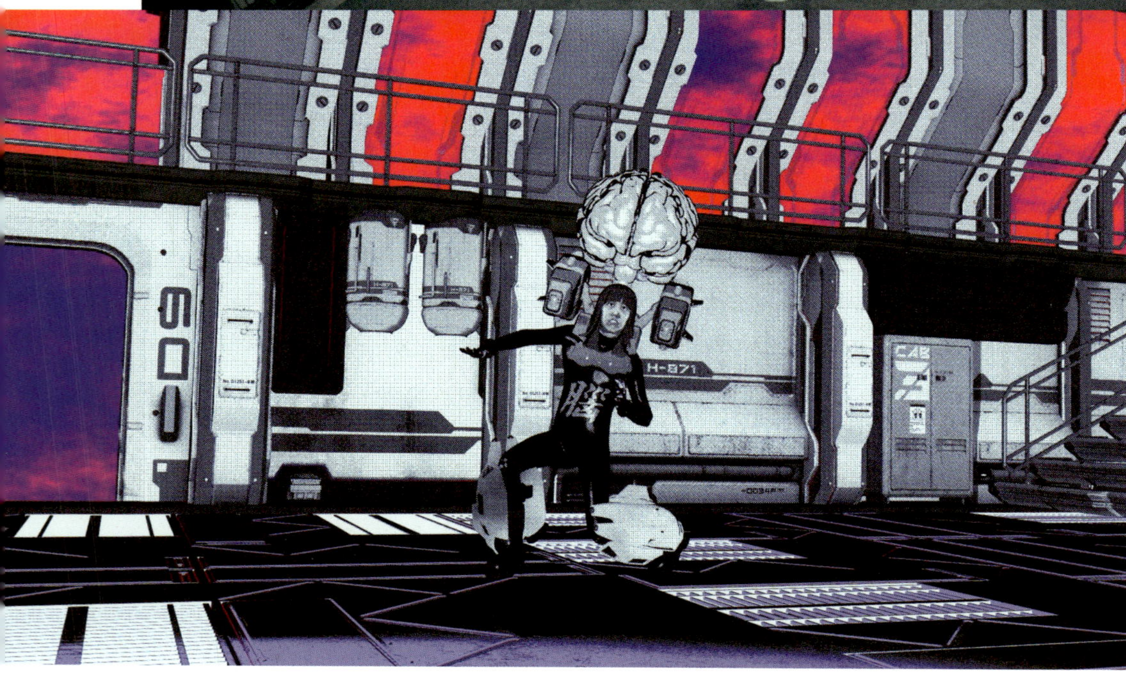

LuYang Delusional Crime and Punishment, 2016
Ein-Kanal-Video, Farbe, Ton /
Single-channel video, colour, sound, 14'37"

Seite / Pages 82–83

Installationsansicht aus der Einzelausstellung / Installation view from the solo exhibition
Lu Yang: Electromagnetic Brainology, Spiral Garden (Spiral 1F), Tokyo 2018

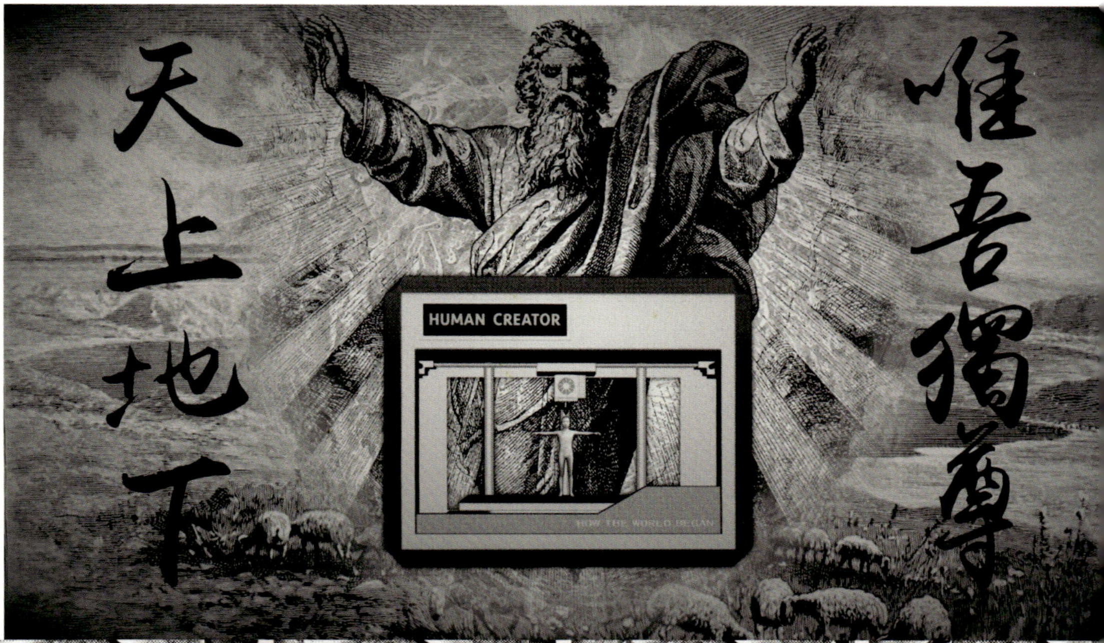
天上地下
唯吾獨尊
HUMAN CREATOR

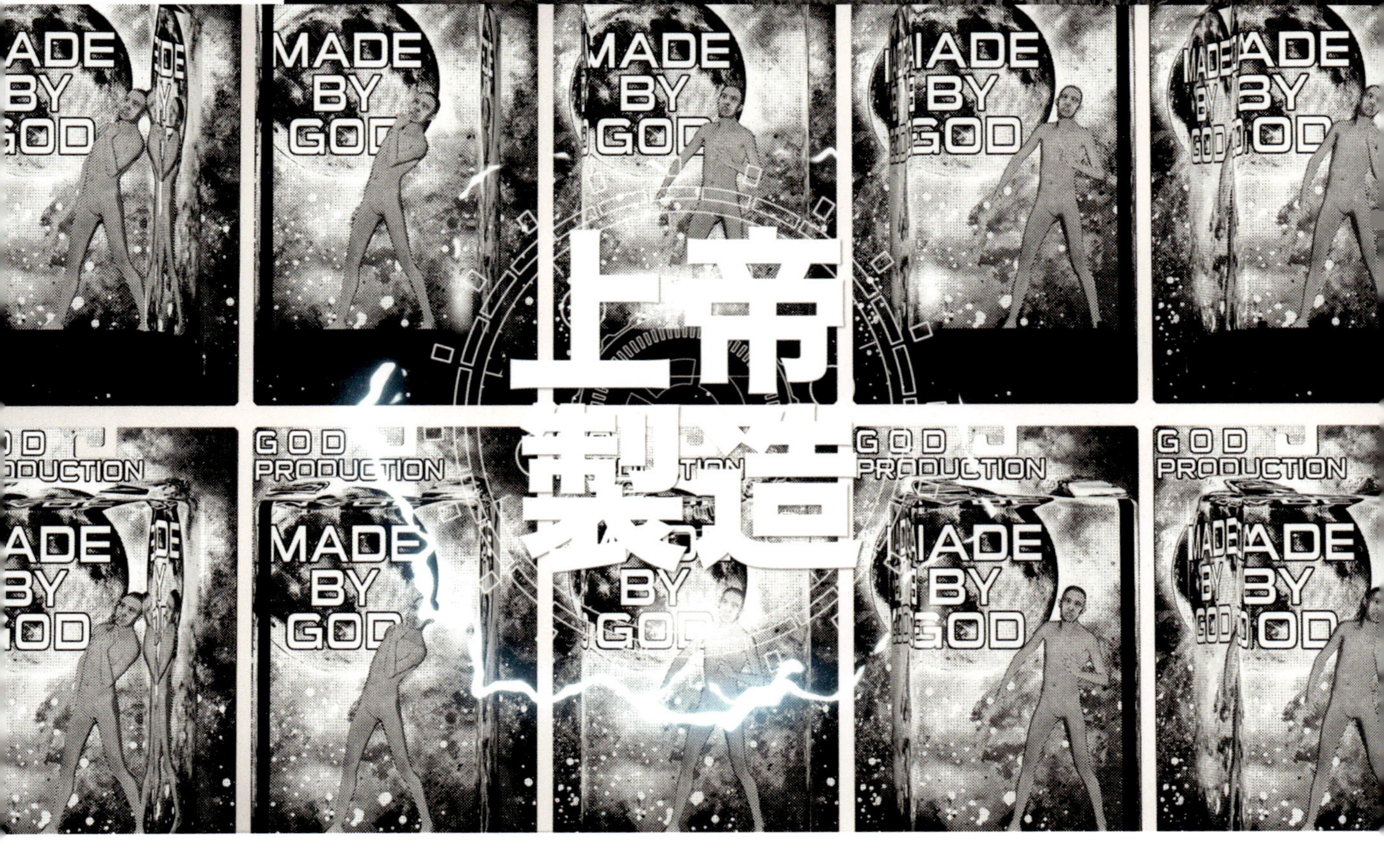
MADE BY GOD
GOD PRODUCTION
上帝製造

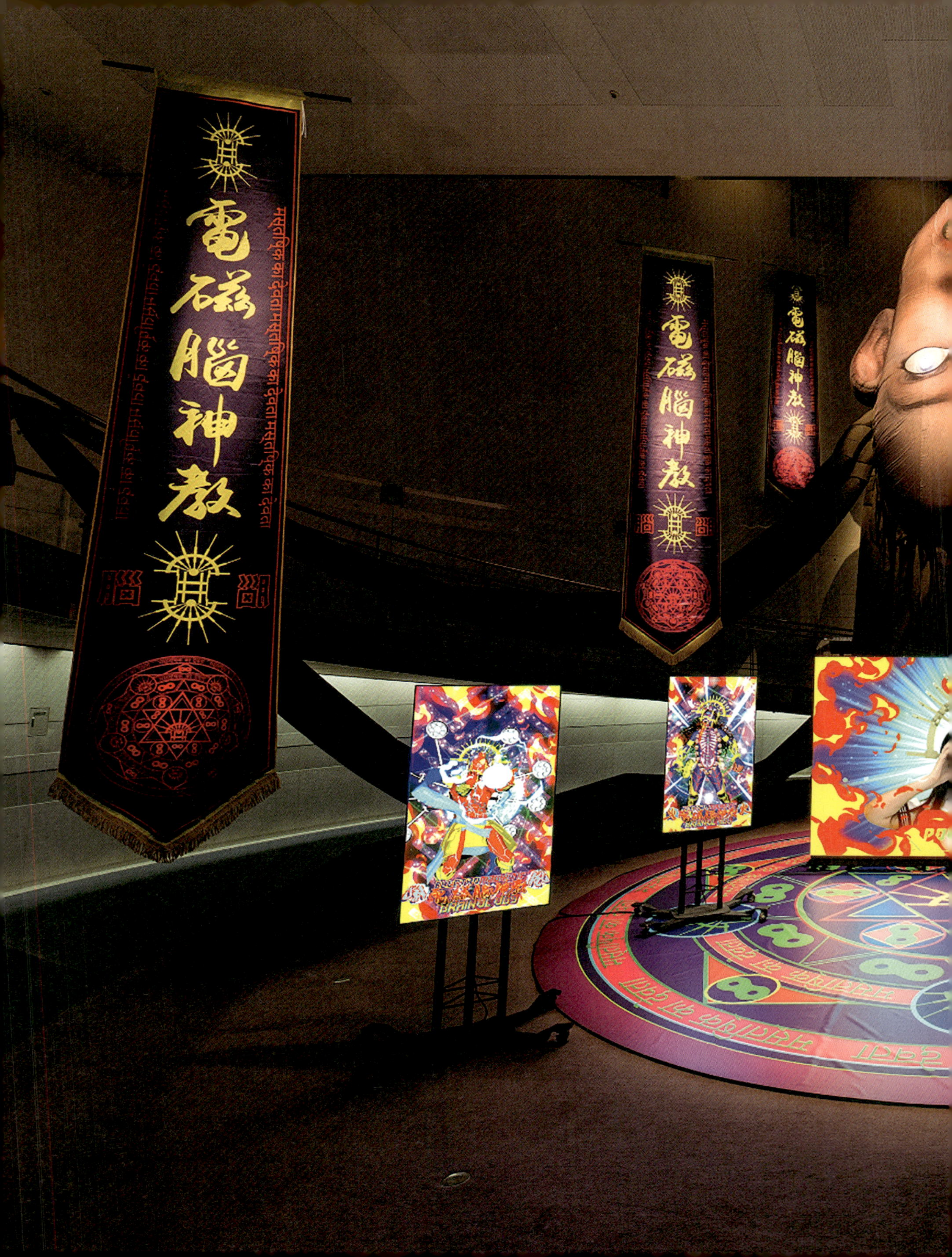
電磁脳神教
मस्तिष्क का देवता मस्तिष्क का देवता मस्तिष्क का देवता
電磁脳神教
電磁脳神教

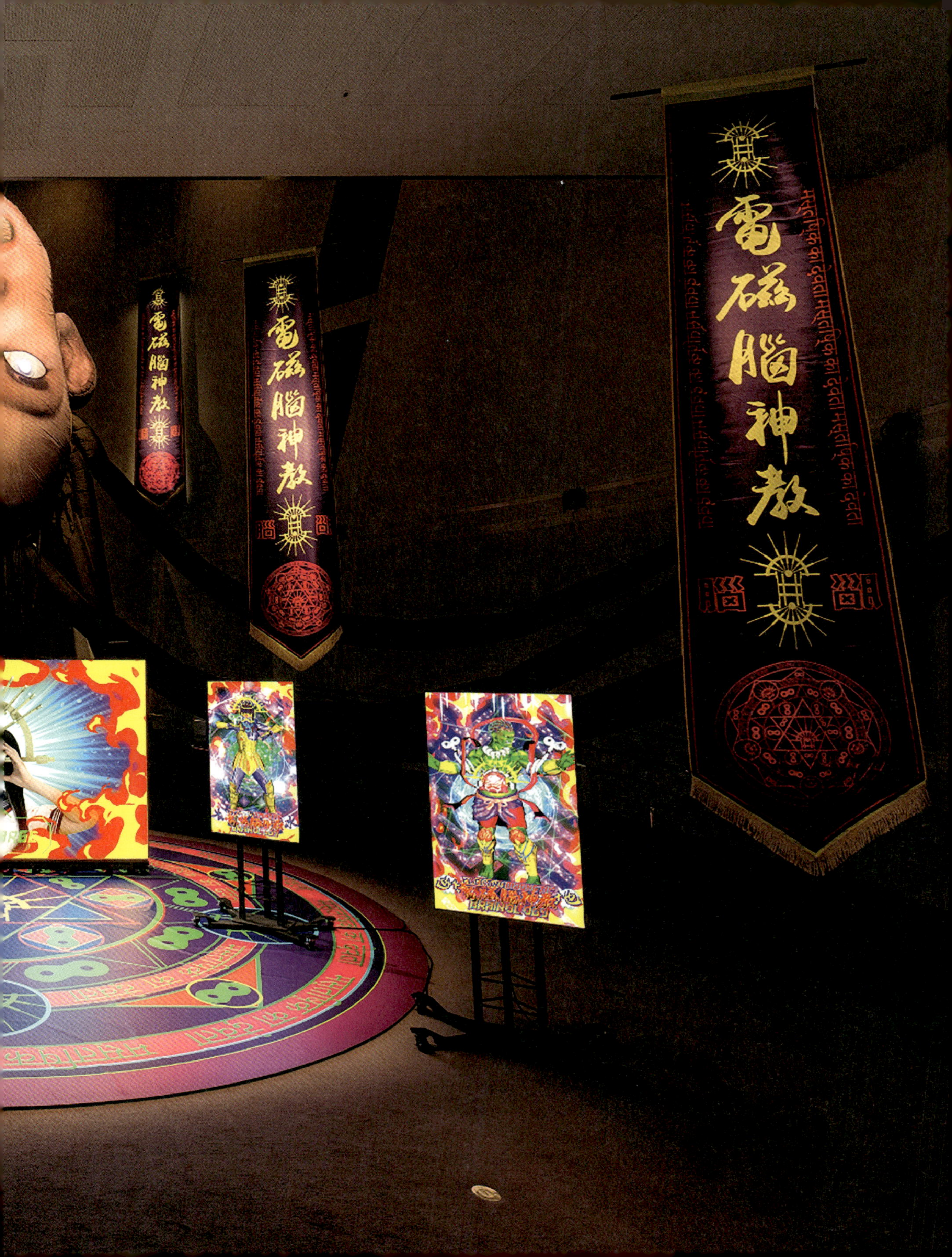
電磁脳神教

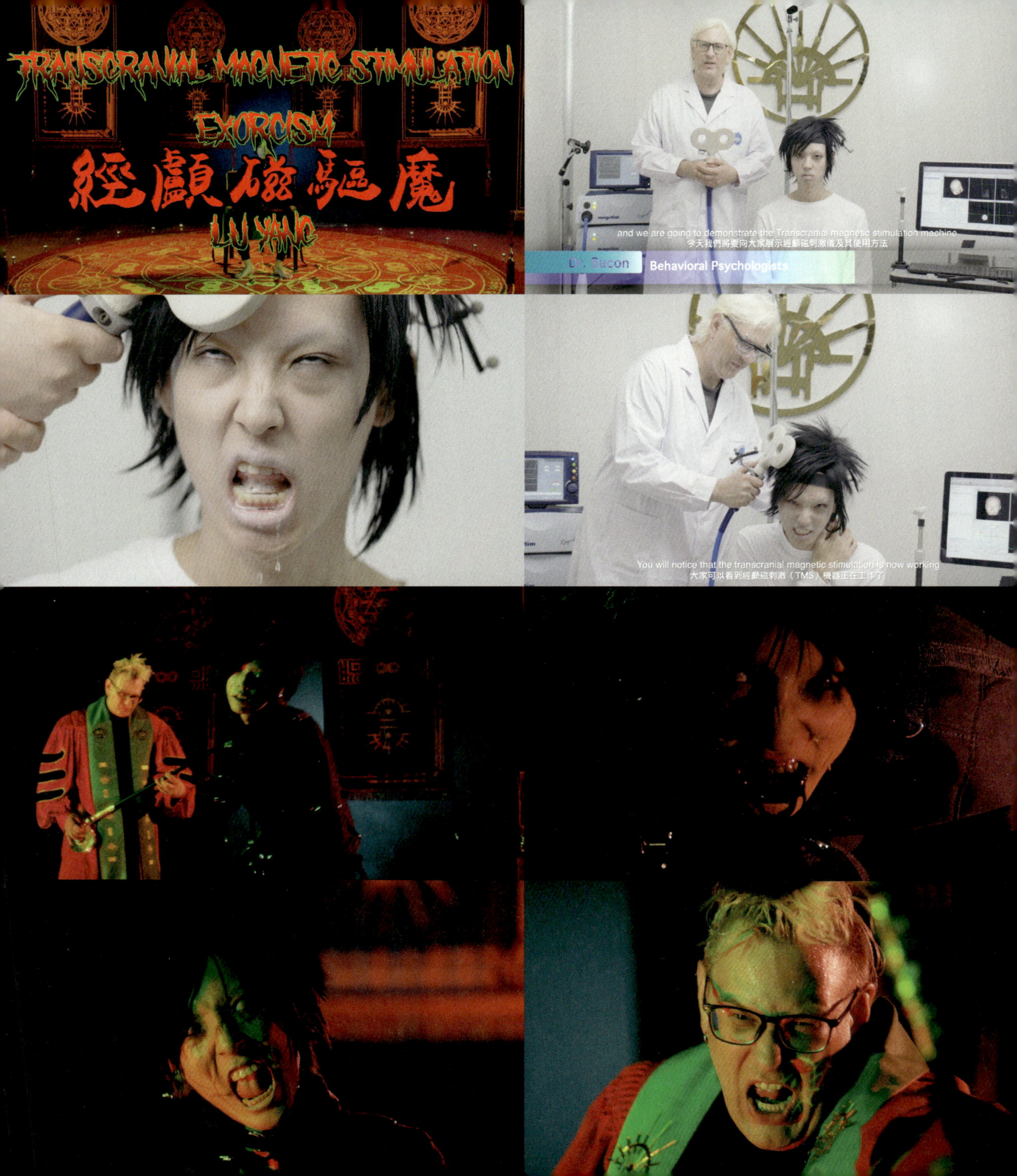
TRANSCRANIAL MAGNETIC STIMULATION
EXORCISM
經顱磁驅魔
LU YANG
and we are going to demonstrate the Transcranial magnetic stimulation machine
今天我們將要向大家展示經顱磁刺激儀及其使用方法
Behavioral Psychologists
You will notice that the transcranial magnetic stimulation is now working
大家可以看到經顱磁刺激（TMS）機器正在工作了

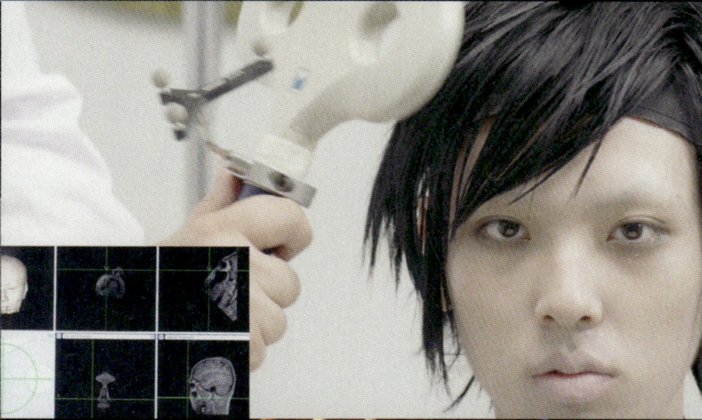

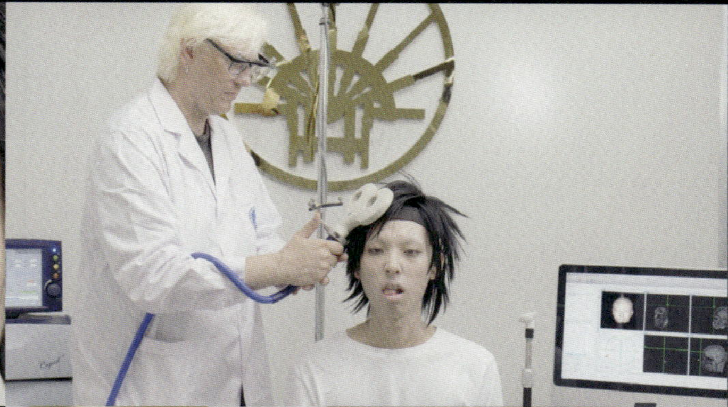

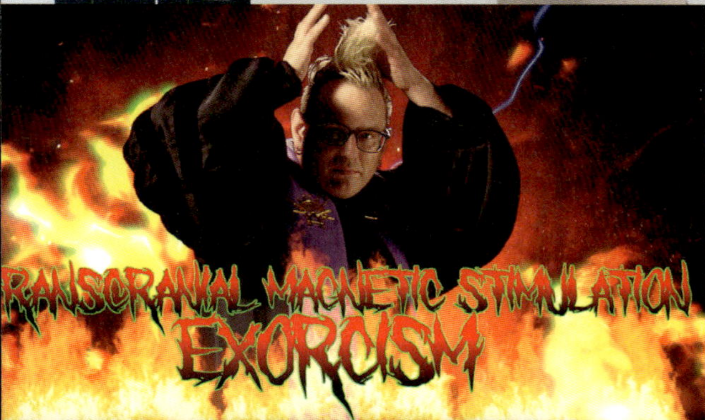

RANSCRANIAL MAGNETIC STIMULATION
EXORCISM

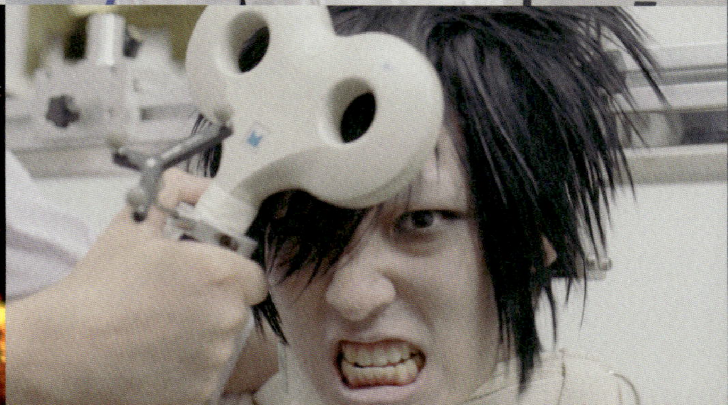

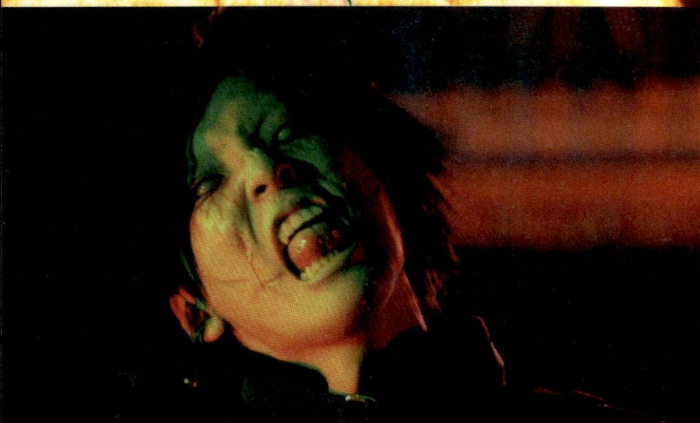

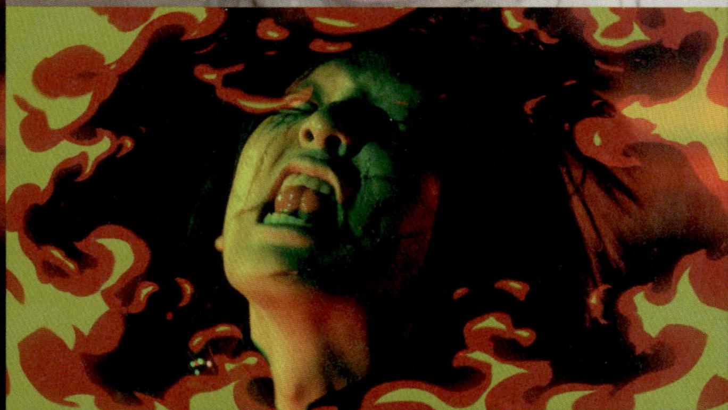

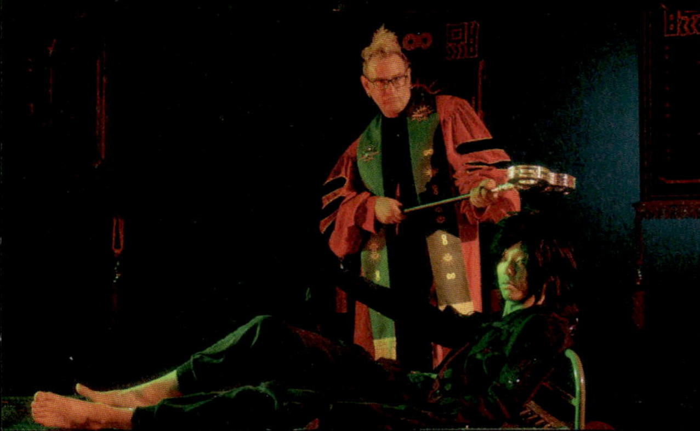

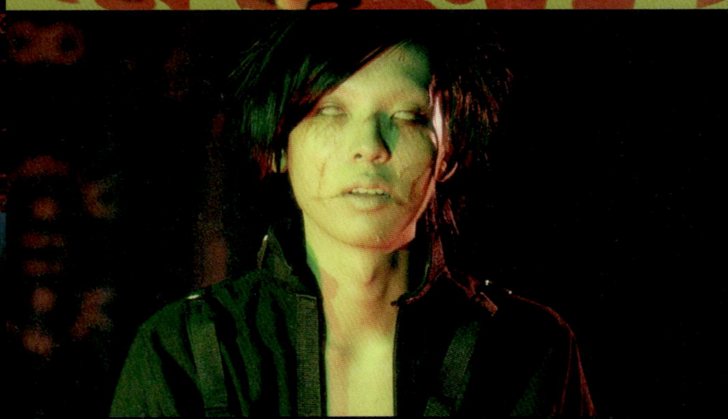

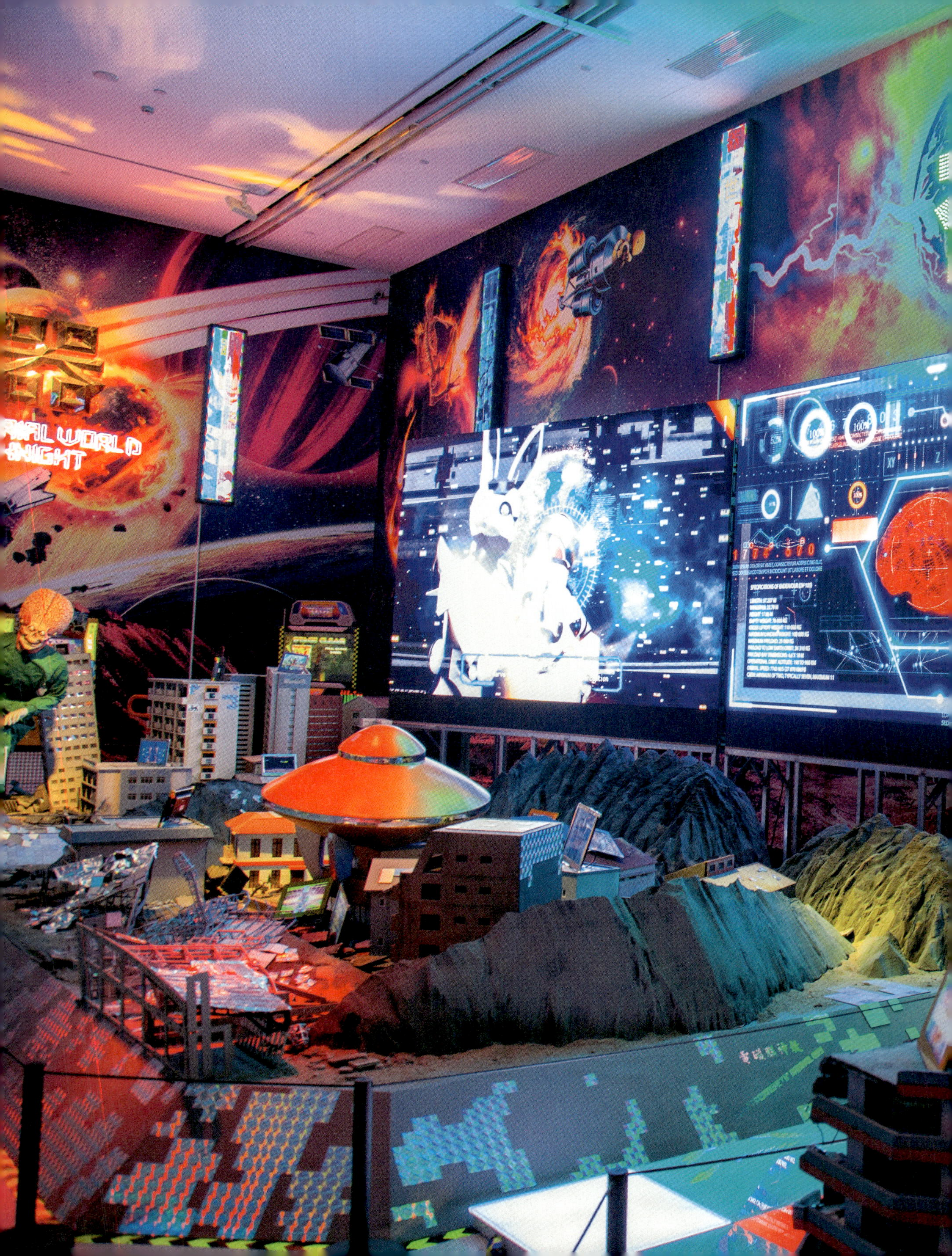

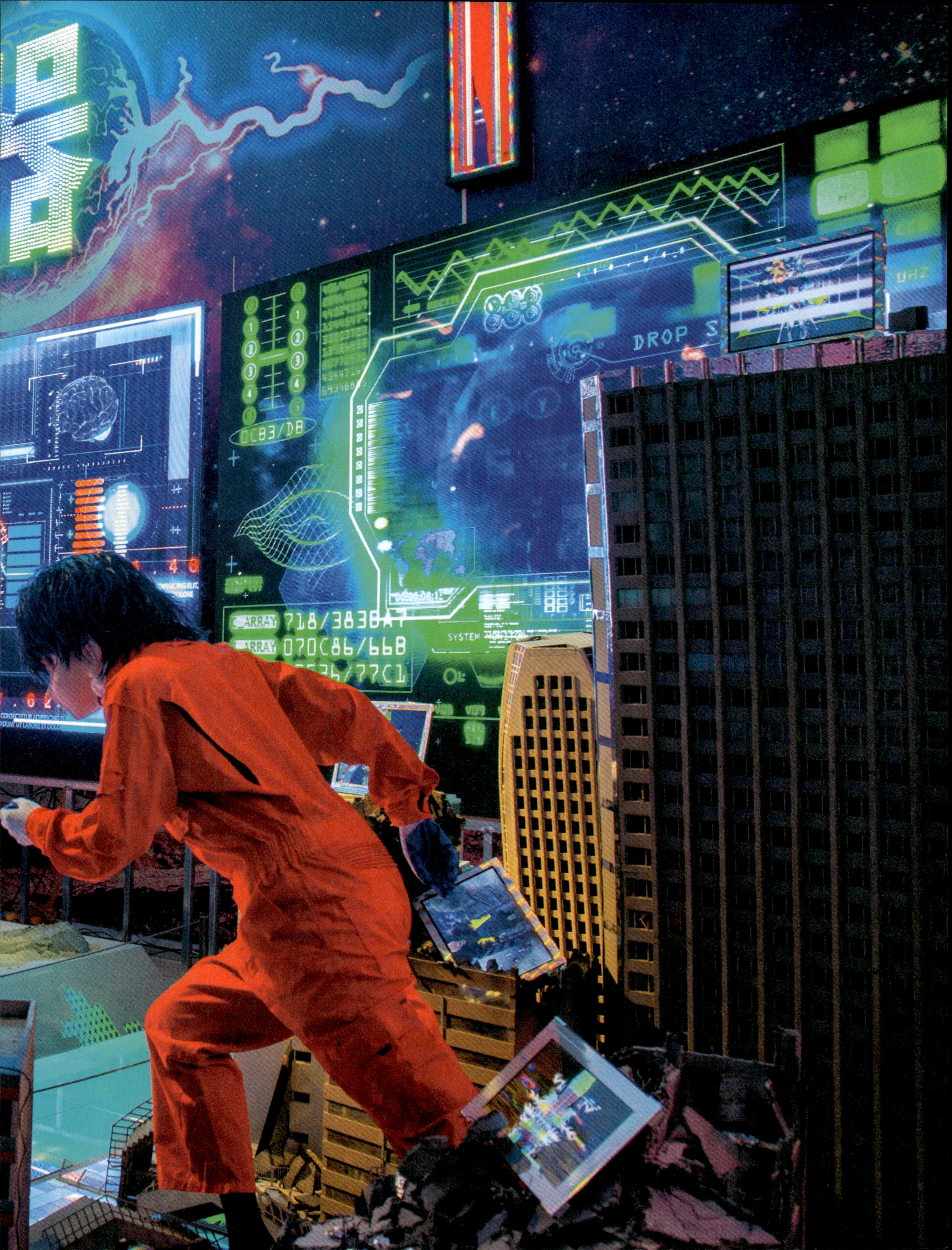
DROP S
DCB3/DB
SYSTEM
UHZ

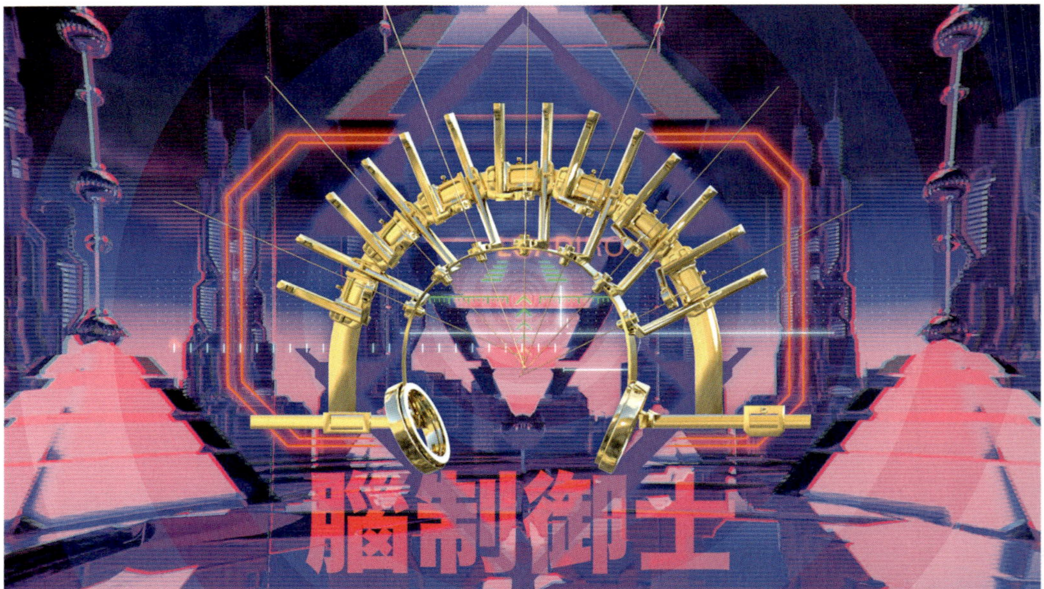

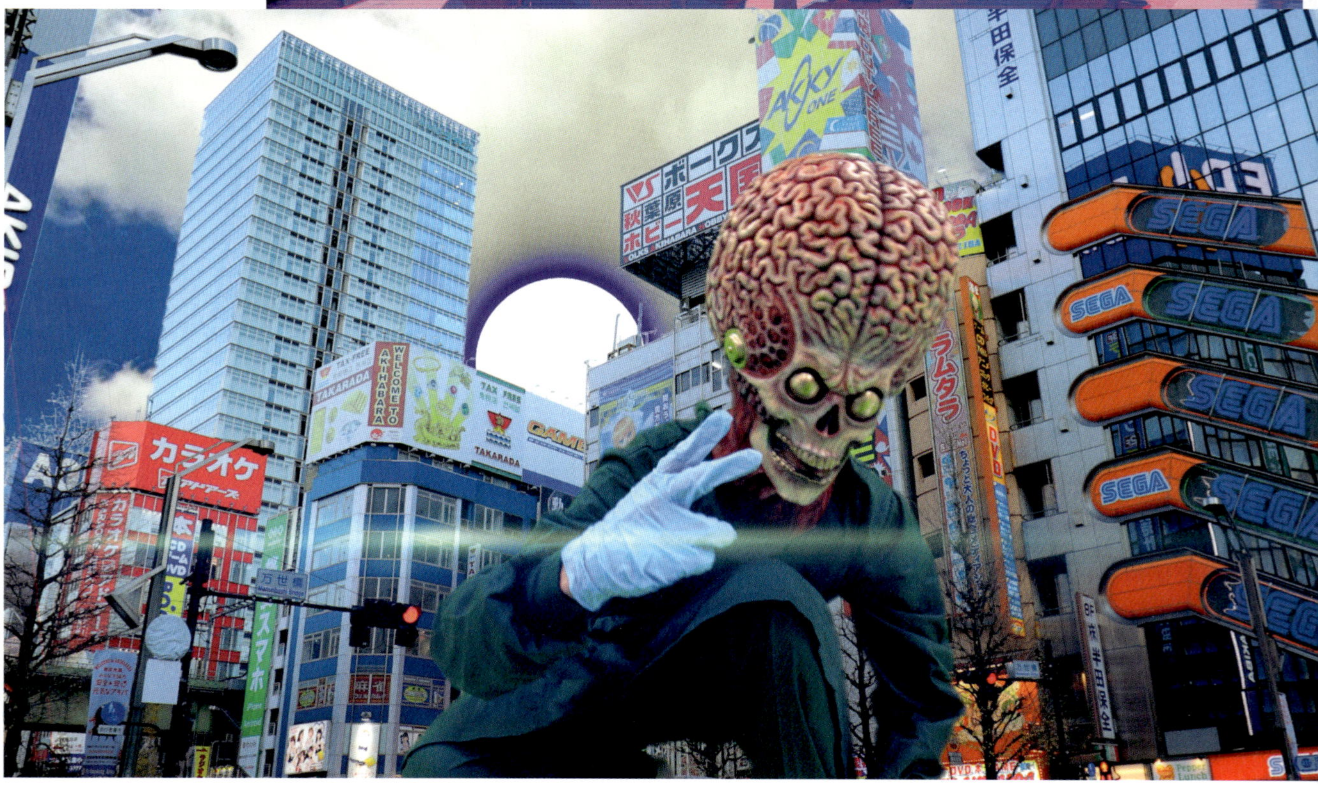

Seite / Pages 88–89

Electromagnetic Brainology
Brain Control Messenger, 2017
Zwei-Kanal-Video, Farbe, Ton /
Two-channel video, colour,
sound, 10'8''

Seite / Pages 84–85

TMS (Transcranial Magnetic Stimulation) Exorcism, 2017
Ein-Kanal-Video, Farbe, Ton /
Single-channel video, colour, sound,
15'35''

Seite / Pages 86–87

Installationsansicht / Installation view,
Shanghai Biennale 2018
Material World Knight, 2018
Drei-Kanal-Video, Multimediainstallation,
Maße variabel / Three-channel video,
multimedia installation, dimensions variable

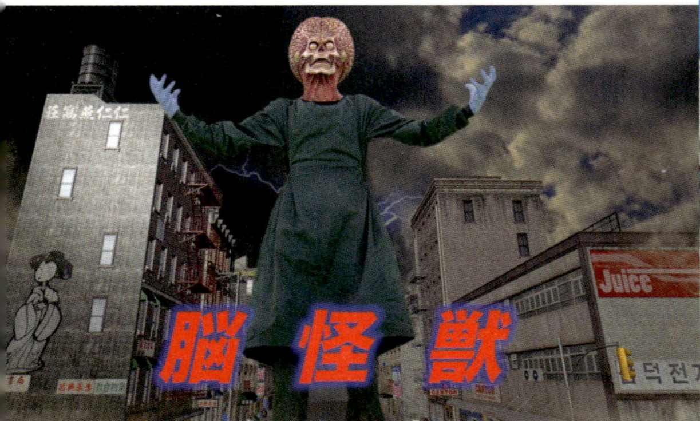

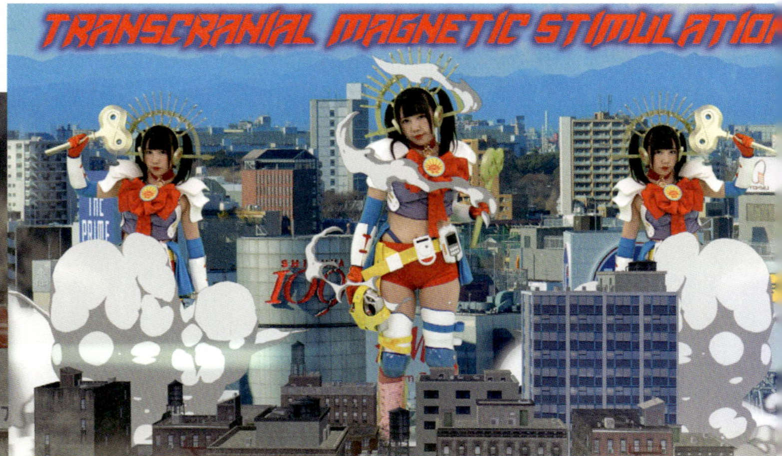

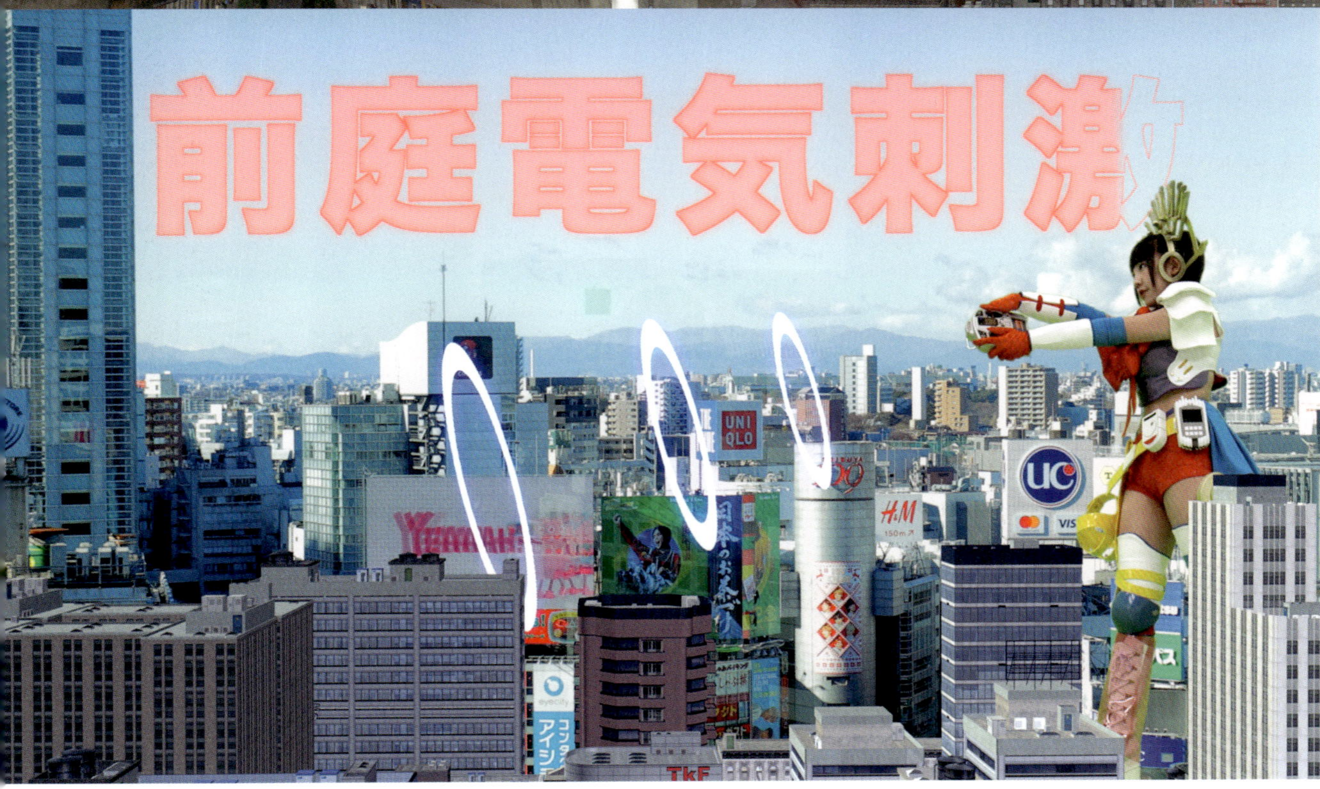

Zhang Peili 张培力 Notes on Immersion and *30×30*

How do we locate the first video artwork within the larger history of media art in China? Originally filmed using a borrowed Panasonic M7 VHS video camera, Zhang Peili's *30x30* (1988) depicts the artist meticulously and repeatedly breaking a 30 by 30 centimetre mirror into pieces, and gluing it back together using 502 glue. Zhang repeats this process for 180 minutes, or until the videotape in the camera runs out. Zhang, who was thirty-one at the time, went to the Customs Office Building in Hangzhou, where a friend of his was working, to borrow a camera and to realize the performance.

There was no predetermined space when he recorded the work, no special props or sets built, and no adjustment to the space or background made. Zhang simply had his friend, untrained in videography, press the record button. Further, there were no adjustments in either camera position or lens focus; all the 'cameraman' did was hold a fixed close-up view of Zhang performing his mirror-breaking performance. In fact, even in post-production, nothing was edited or enhanced. The main focus of the work remained the sober live event.

When speaking about the relation of the term *Jìnrù* (浸入), or 'immersion' in English, to the artists' collective Pool Society's name *Chishe* (池社), Zhang emphasized that what is important is the process of the work—for example, the act of breaking the mirror, not its final outcome.

This is unlike the early Korean precedents in the field, such as the first video work made by artist Kim Ku-lim, *The Meaning of 1/24 Second* (1969), an edited video piece that comprises twenty-four images shown at twenty-four frames a second. Or, by contrast to early American precedents like Bruce Nauman's *Walk with Contrapposto* (1968) or *Walking in an Exaggerated Manner Around the Perimeter of a Square*

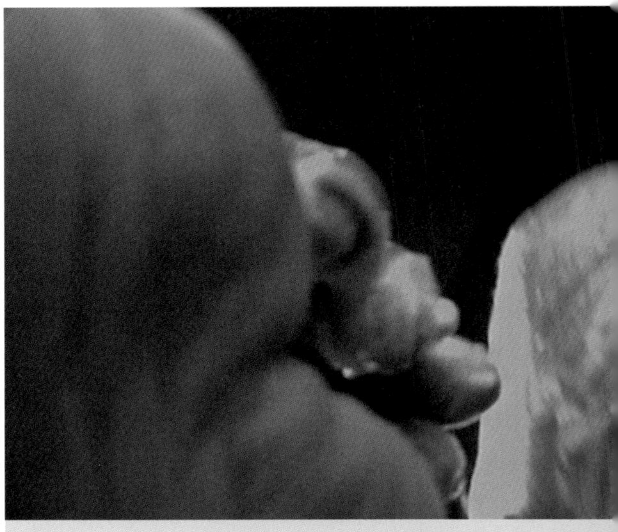

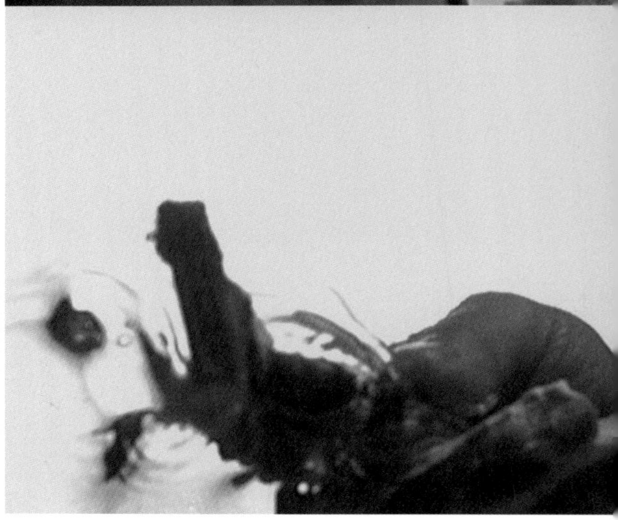

Personal Hygiene, 1998
Drei-Kanal-drei-Monitor-Videoinstallation, Farbe/schwarz-weiß, Ton / Three-channel, three-screen video installation, colour/black & white, sound, 5'49"

Installationsansicht / Installation view
Zhang Peili and Gu Wenda, Morris and Helen Belkin Art Gallery (U.B.C) Vancouver, 1998
Personal Hygiene, 1998

Bemerkungen über Immersion und *30×30*

Zhang Peili 张培力

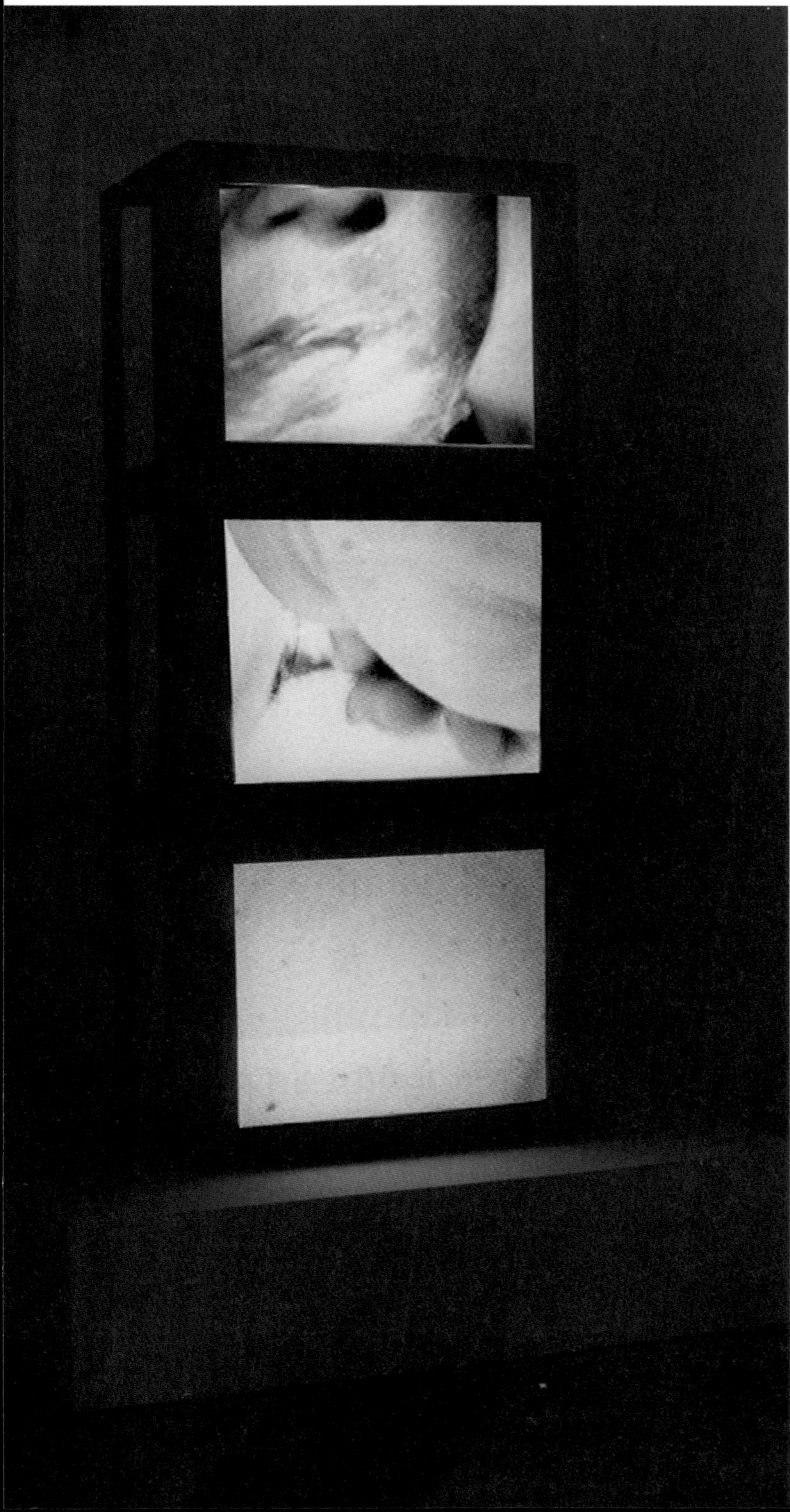

Wie verorten wir das erste Werk der Videokunst innerhalb einer breiteren Entwicklung der Medienkunst in China? Zhang Peilis Arbeit *30x30* (1988), damals mit einer geliehenen Panasonic-M7-VHS-Videokamera gefilmt, zeigt den Künstler, wie er akribisch und unablässig einen 30 mal 30 Zentimeter großen Spiegel in Stücke zerbricht und ihn dann mit Sekundenkleber der Marke 502 wieder zusammensetzt. Diesen Vorgang wiederholt Zhang 180 Minuten lang, so lange, bis das Videoband in der Kamera voll ist. Zhang war 31 Jahre alt, als er zum Zollamtsgebäude in Hangzhou ging, um sich von einem dort arbeitenden Freund eine Kamera zu leihen und die Performance durchzuführen.

Für die Aufzeichnung gab es keinen vorher festgelegten Ort, keinen Aufbau spezieller Requisiten oder Geräte, keine Abstimmung auf den Raum oder den Hintergrund. Zhang bat lediglich einen Freund, der sich mit Videoaufzeichnungen nicht auskannte, den Aufnahmeknopf zu drücken. Es gab auch keine Korrekturen der Kameraposition oder der Bildschärfe. Alles, was der „Kameramann" tat, war eine statische Nahaufnahme von Zhangs Performance festzuhalten, während dieser den Spiegel zerbrach. Auch in der Postproduktion wurde nichts nachbearbeitet oder verbessert. Der Fokus der Arbeit lag einzig auf dem nüchternen Live-Ereignis.

In einem Gespräch über die Beziehung zwischen dem Begriff *Jìnrù* (浸入) oder Immersion und dem Namen des Künstlerkollektivs Pond Society, im Chinesischen *Chishe* (池社), wies Zhang daraufhin, dass im Zentrum der Arbeit der Prozess steht, beispielsweise das Zerbrechen des Spiegels, nicht das Ergebnis.

Dies unterscheidet sich von frühen koreanischen Beispielen in diesem Genre, wie etwa der ersten Videoarbeit des Künstlers Kim Ku-lim, *The Meaning of 1/24 Second* (1969), ein zusammen-

(1968), Zhang's work was unedited and realized with a very different context and intentions.

For example, in Nauman's studio the site becomes part of a critical investigation into spaces of artistic production and the importance of the studio as a 'place' within the creative process, whereas Zhang's work is embedded in the larger sociopolitical space of the Customs Office Building in Hangzhou, during the peak of the '85 New Wave movement.

When speaking about *30x30*, Zhang says, 'I wanted to do something and say something about video, but I felt that I was also doing a performance.'[1] This merging of performance and video art that goes beyond both was the product of an initial dissemination of personal technology nationwide, and at the same time it represented the intensification of experimental artistic practices such as those of the Pool Society across China.[2] Further, all channels that might introduce Western conceptual art were blocked.[3]

Zhang's *30x30* was first informally shown at the Huangshan Conference (originally named the 1988 Chinese Contemporary Art Creative Forum) at the Jiangxinzhou Hotel in the Tunxi district of Huangshan, Anhui Province. Organized by art critic Gao Minglu, the conference invited critics and artists to discuss and select works for the forthcoming *China/Avant-Garde* exhibition (89现代艺术展), which would be held a year later. But contrary to common belief, *30x30* was never shown in the *China/Avant-Garde* exhibition; in fact, the first time the work was publicly displayed in an exhibition was four years later, in 1992, in the show titled 最近的工作 (Recent Works), an exhibition of art by Zhang Peili and Geng Jianyi held in the Diplomatic Missions Restaurant, Beijing.[4]

Dramatic changes in Chinese avant-garde art and in the development and distribution of Chinese media took place from the late 1970s to the late 1980s. The most significant of these

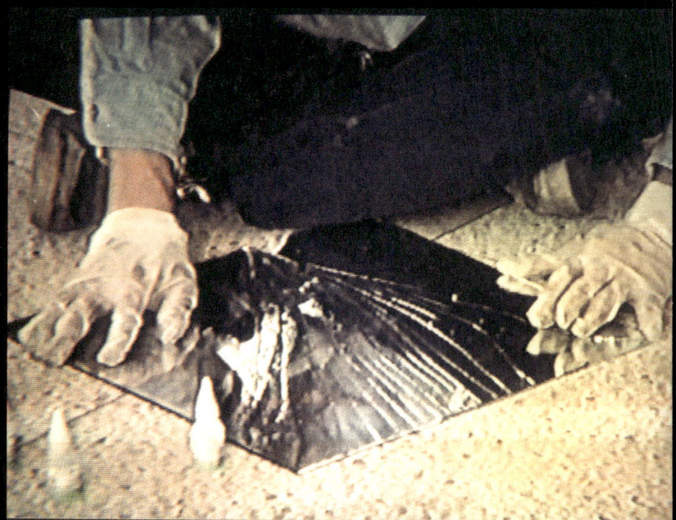

30x30, 1988
Ein-Kanal-Videoinstallation (PAL), Farbe, Ton / Single-channel video installation (PAL), colour, sound, 32'9"

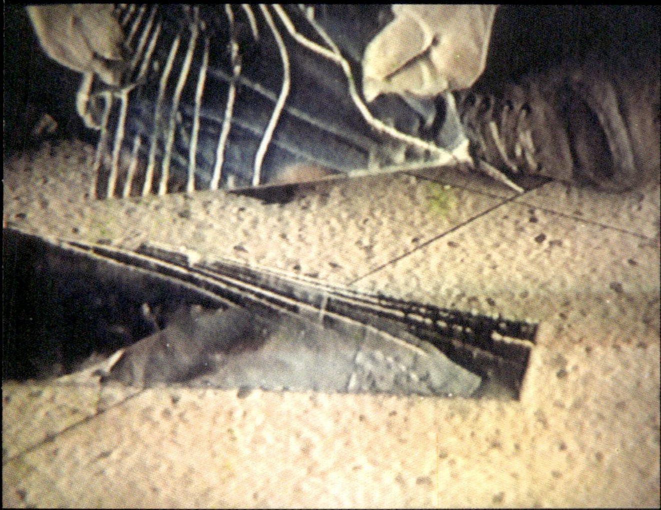

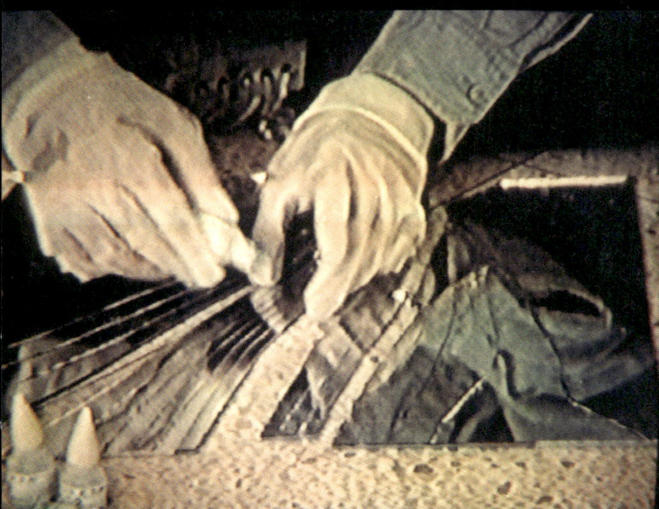

geschnittenes Video aus 24 Aufnahmen, die in 24 Bildern pro Sekunde gezeigt werden. Auch im Vergleich mit frühen amerikanischen Vorläufern wie Bruce Naumans *Walk with Contrapposto* (1968) oder *Walking in an Exaggerated Manner Around the Perimeter of a Square* (1968) wird deutlich, dass Zhang sein ungeschnittenes Werk vor dem Hintergrund sehr unterschiedlicher Kontexte und Absichten realisiert hat.

In Naumans Studio wird zum Beispiel die Umgebung Teil einer kritischen Untersuchung über Räume künstlerischer Produktion und die Bedeutung des Studios als „Ort" innerhalb des kreativen Prozesses, wohingegen Zhangs Arbeit in den größeren soziopolitischen Raum des Zollamtsgebäudes in Hangzhou eingebettet ist, zu einem Zeitpunkt, als sich die Kunstbewegung Neue Welle '85 auf ihrem Höhepunkt befand.

„Ich wollte etwas über Video machen und sagen, aber ich merkte, dass ich auch eine Performance mache", äußerte sich Zhang über *30x30*.[1] Diese Verschmelzung von Performance und Videokunst, die zugleich über beides hinausführte, war einerseits erst durch eine zunehmende landesweite Verbreitung von Verbrauchertechnologie möglich und repräsentierte andererseits zugleich die Intensivierung experimenteller Kunstpraxis in China, wie die der Pond Society[2], während alle Kanäle, die westliche Konzeptkunst hätten einführen können, blockiert waren.[3]

30x30 wurde zum ersten Mal informell auf der Huangshan-Konferenz (die offizielle Bezeichnung lautete „1988 Chinese Contemporary Art Creative Forum") im Hotel Jiangxinzhou im Stadtbezirk Tunxi in Huangshan, Provinz Anhui, gezeigt. Die von dem Kunstkritiker Gao Minglu organisierte Konferenz hatte Kritiker*innen und Künstler*innen eingeladen, Arbeiten für die bevorstehende Ausstellung *China/Avant-Garde* (89现代艺术展), die ein Jahr später stattfinden sollte, zu diskutieren und auszuwählen. Aber

changes was the establishment of regional television stations and the privatization of television sets, which allowed individual families to own televisions.[5] At that time, personal video cameras were limited and difficult to come by, and mainly belonged to government institutions, factories, schools, and neighbourhoods.

More than just a video piece, *30x30* is widely considered to be the first work of video art made in China, which with its inception heralded the emergence of a type of *jìnrù shì xingwei yingxiang* 浸入式行为影像 (immersive video performance) and the diversification of artists in China performing for the video camera—and presenting their videos and films as art. In order for *xingwei yishu* 行为艺术 (performance art) to enter the art-historical canon in China, its early relationship with *yingxiang yishu* 影像艺术 (video art) also needs to be established. In order to approach *30x30* from above and behind, we must also take a closer look at the complex historical position that *jìnrù* as immersion provides in terms of an art-historical critique of the formal evolution of video art when it comes to both concept and technology in China—from the development of single-monitor works like *30x30* and *Document on Hygiene No. 3* (1991) to multiscreen and multichannel works such as *Assignment No. 1* (1992), *Uncertain Pleasure I* (1996), and *Personal Hygiene* (1998), which, along with the video installation *Opposite Space* (1996), are all shown in the group exhibition *Micro Era*.

Established in Hangzhou, Zhejiang Province, by recent graduates of the Zhejian Academy of Fine Arts in 1986—Chishe put forward the notion of '浸入', the Chinese word for immersion, which according to Zhang emerged from the Chinese character '池' (pool) found in the collective's name. This concept of immersion, which refers to an artistic engagement with process rather than outcome,[6] can provide a framework for understanding the emergence of artistic practices that move 'between mediums' and the gradual expansion of new media in China, such as *yingxiang yishu* 影像艺术 (video art), *zhuangzhi yishu* 装置艺术 (installation art), and *xingwei yishu* 行为艺术 (performance art), through which a weaving together of different mediums and artistic practices constructs broader dialogue and links within the region and to the concept of *jìnrù shì* 浸入式 (immersive), often confirming unique origins and approaches to the medium of media art, and offering new ways of connecting these histories and practices with the wider world. — Victor Wang 王宗孚

1 Barbara Pollack, 'Breaking and Entering: In His Videos, Zhang Peili Destroys and Restores to "Capture and Emphasize Time",' *ARTnews* (5 May 2017), http://www.artnews.com/2017/05/05/breaking-and-entering-in-his-videos-zhang-pelli-destroys-and-restores-to-capture-and-emphasize-time/.

2 Wu Hung, 'Television in Contemporary Chinese Art', *OCTOBER*, 125 (Summer 2008), pp. 65–90, esp. p. 65.

3 Pi Li, 'Chinese Contemporary Video Art', *Third Text*, 23/3 (2009), pp. 303–07, esp. p. 303.

4 Zhang Peili in conversation with the author, 5 June 2019.

5 Wu Hung, 'Television in Contemporary Chinese Art', p. 66.

6 Lu Wei, 'Memories of Pool Society: Interview with Zhang Peili', *Art Ifeng* (22 March 2007), http://wap.art.ifeng.com/?action=content&app=system&contentid=2461000&controller=artmobile.

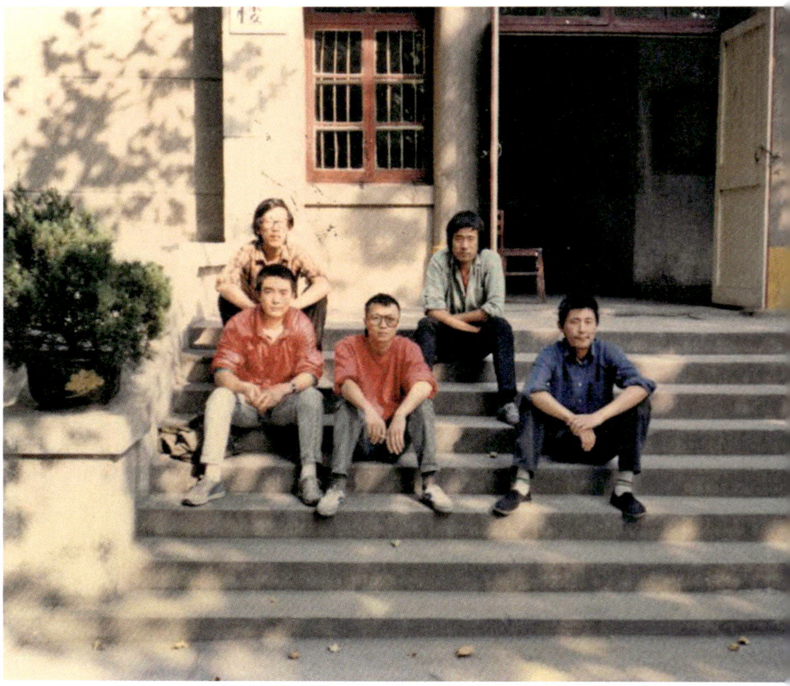

Mitglieder der Pond Society /
Members of the Pond Society, 1986

anders als allgemein angenommen wurde *30x30* nicht auf der *China/Avant-Garde* ausgestellt. Die erste öffentliche Ausstellung fand vielmehr 1992, vier Jahre später, in der von Zhang Peili und Geng Jianyi veranstalteten Schau namens 最近的工作 (Neue Arbeiten) im Pekinger Restaurant der Diplomatischen Mission statt.[4]

Bis dahin fanden zwischen den späten 1970er- und 1980er-Jahren in Chinas Avantgardekunst und der Entwicklung und Verbreitung chinesischer Medien allerdings dramatische Veränderungen statt. Zu den einschneidenden Ereignissen gehörte die Gründung regionaler Fernsehstationen und die Privatisierung von Fernsehgeräten, die es Familien erlaubte, einen Fernseher zu besitzen.[5] In dieser Zeit war der private Gebrauch von Videokameras beschränkt und es war schwierig, an sie heranzukommen, meist befanden sie sich in der Hand von Regierungsinstitutionen, Fabriken, Schulen und Stadtteilverwaltungen.

30x30 ist nicht nur eine Videoarbeit, sondern gilt darüber hinaus auch als das erste Werk der Videokunst Chinas überhaupt, das mit seiner Entstehung zum Vorboten eines eigenen Typus immersiver Videoperformance (*jìnrù shì xingwei yingxiang* 浸入式行为影像) wurde und die Diversifikation chinesischer Künstler*innen vorangetrieben hat, die mit der Videokamera arbeiten und ihre Videos und Filme als Kunst präsentieren.

Und so muss auch, um die Einführung von Performance als Kunst (*xingwei yishu* 行为艺术) in den kunsthistorischen Kanon Chinas einordnen zu können, ihre frühe Beziehung zur Videokunst (*yingxiang yishu* 影像艺术) berücksichtigt werden. Eine gründliche Auseinandersetzung mit *30x30* erfordert zudem einen genaueren Blick auf die komplexe historische Stellung, die Immersion (*jìnrù*) als Begriff einer kunsthistorischen Kritik für die formale Entwicklung von Videokunst sowohl als Konzept als auch als Technologie in China einnimmt. Diese reicht von der Entwicklung von einkanaligen Videoarbeiten, wie *30x30* und *Document on Hygiene No. 3* (1991), bis zu Multiscreen- und Multichannel-Arbeiten, wie *Assignment No. 1* (1992), *Uncertain Pleasure I* (1996) und *Personal Hygiene* (1998), die neben der Videoinstallation *Opposite Space* (1996) alle in der Gruppenausstellung *Micro Era* gezeigt werden.

Das Kollektiv Pond Society (*Chishe*, in chinesischer Schreibweise 浸入) wurde 1986 von Absolventen der Kunsthochschule in Hangzhou in der Provinz Zhejiang gegründet und brachte durch seine Namensgebung den Begriff der Immersion in Umlauf, der sich Zhang zufolge aus dem chinesischen Buchstaben 池 für Pond (oder *pool*) herleitet. Das hier formulierte Konzept der Immersion betont die künstlerisch-prozesshafte Beteiligung stärker als das Ergebnis.[6] Es bietet einen Rahmen für das Verständnis einer intermedialen Kunstpraxis „zwischen Medien" und der graduellen Verbreitung neuer Medien in China, wie der Videokunst (*yingxiang yishu* 影像艺术), der Installationskunst (*zhuangzhi yishu* 装置艺术) und der Performance (*xingwei yishu* 行为艺术). Durch diese Verknüpfung zwischen verschiedenen Medien und Kunstpraxen wird ein breiterer Dialog kreiert und eine Verbindung innerhalb dieses Bereichs mit dem Konzept des Immersiven (*jìnrù shì* 浸入式). So werden andere Ansätze und Annäherungen an das Medium der Medienkunst möglich und eigene Entwicklungen aufgezeigt, die die Spezifik dieser Entstehungsgeschichten und Praxen ausmachen. — Victor Wang 王宗孚

1 Barbara Pollack, „Breaking and Entering: In His Videos, Zhang Peili Destroys and Restores to ‚Capture and Emphasize Time', *ARTnews*, 5.5.2017, http://www.artnews.com/2017/05/05/breaking-and-entering-in-his-videos-zhang-peili-destroys-and-restores-to-capture-and-emphasize-time/ (abgerufen am 15.7.2019).

2 Wu Hung, „Television in Contemporary Chinese Art", *OCTOBER*, Nr. 125, Sommer 2008, S. 65–90, hier S. 65.

3 Pi Li, „Chinese Contemporary Video Art", in: *Third Text*, 23/3, 2009, S. 303–307, hier S. 303.

4 Zhang Peili im Gespräch mit dem Autor, 5. Juni 2019.

5 Wu 2008 (wie Anm. 2), S. 66.

6 Lu Wei, „Memories of Pool Society: Interview with Zhang Peili", Art Ifeng, 22.5.2007, http://wap.art.ifeng.com/?action=content&app=system&contentid=2461000&controller=artmobile (abgerufen am 15.7.2019).

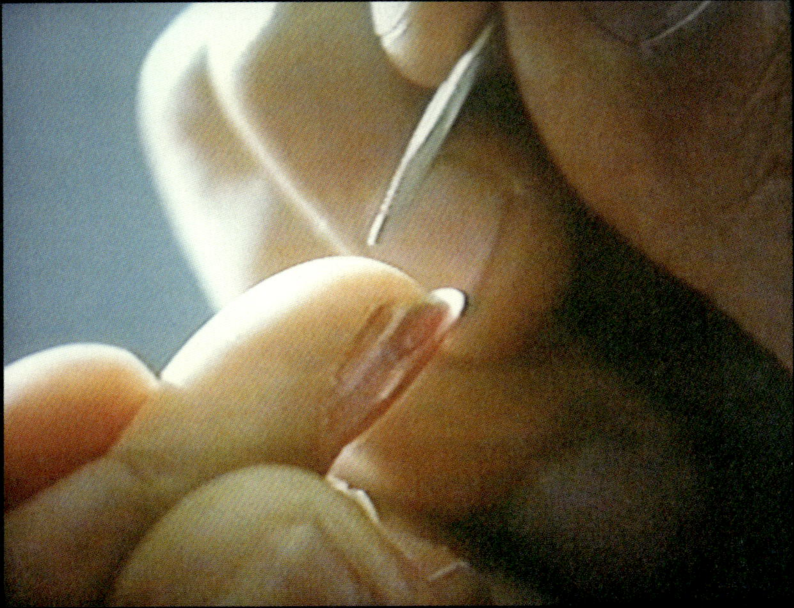

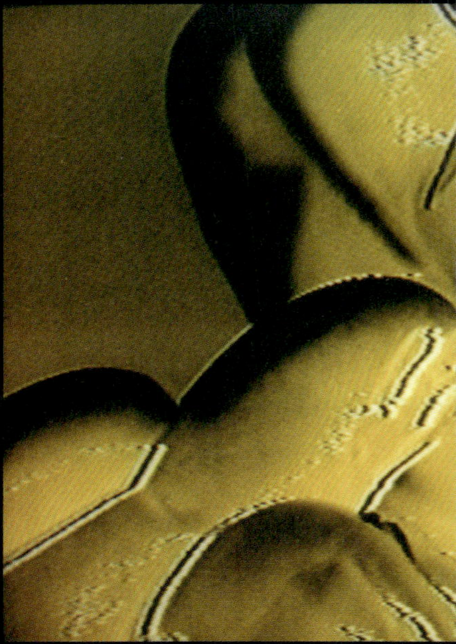

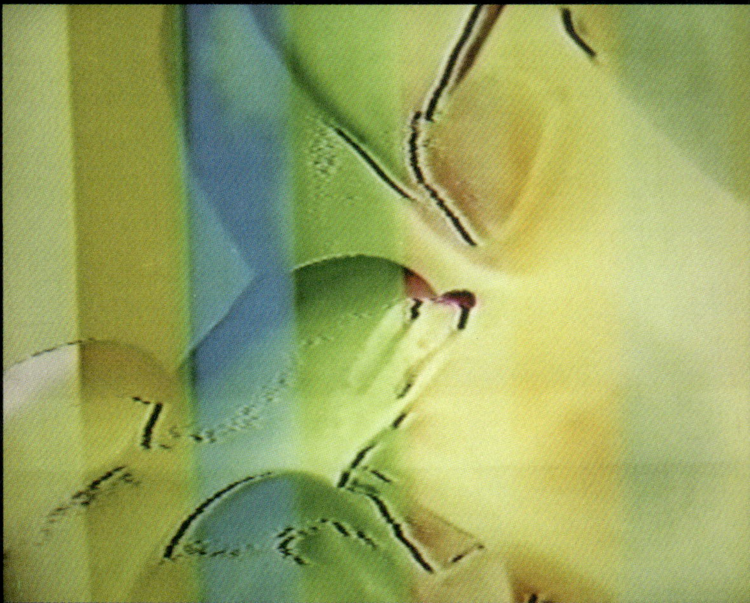

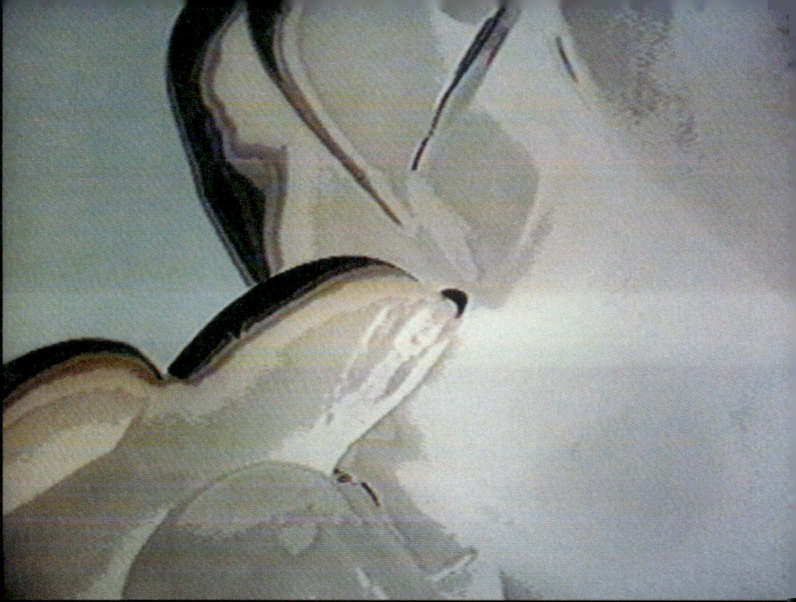
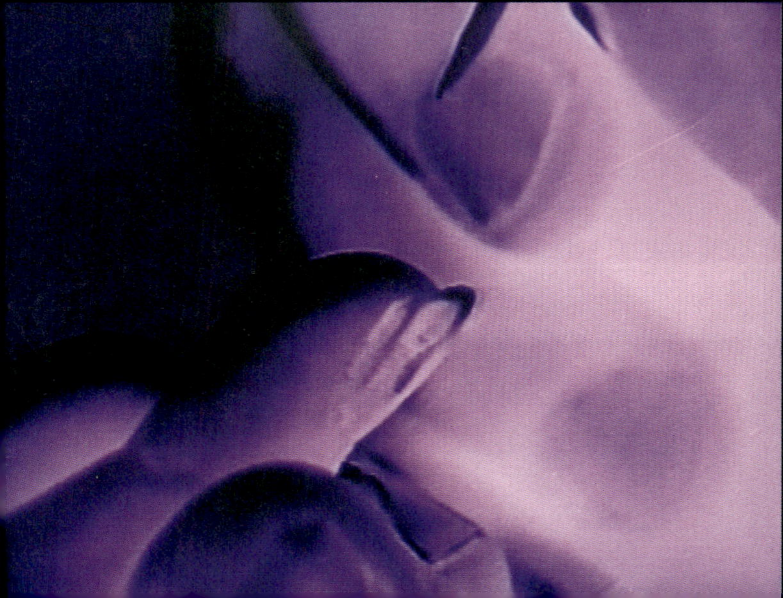

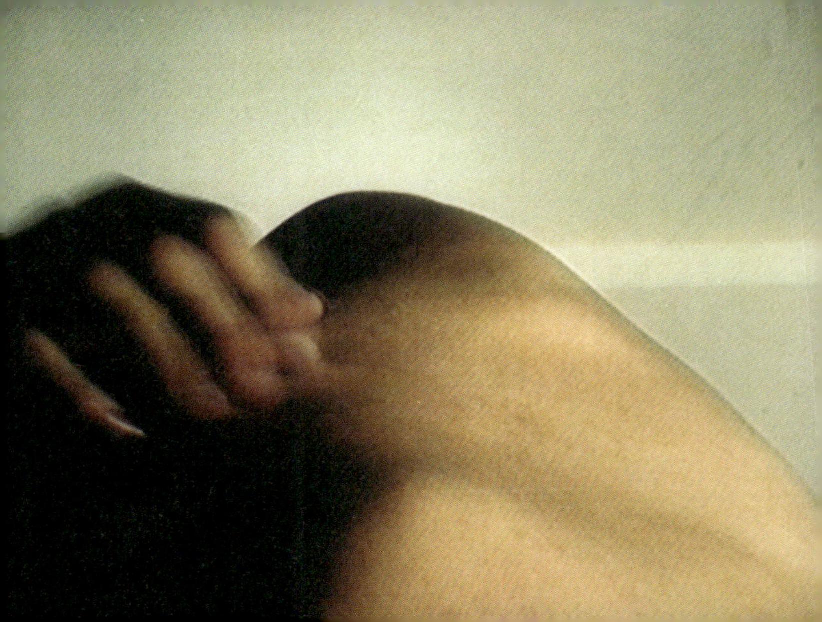

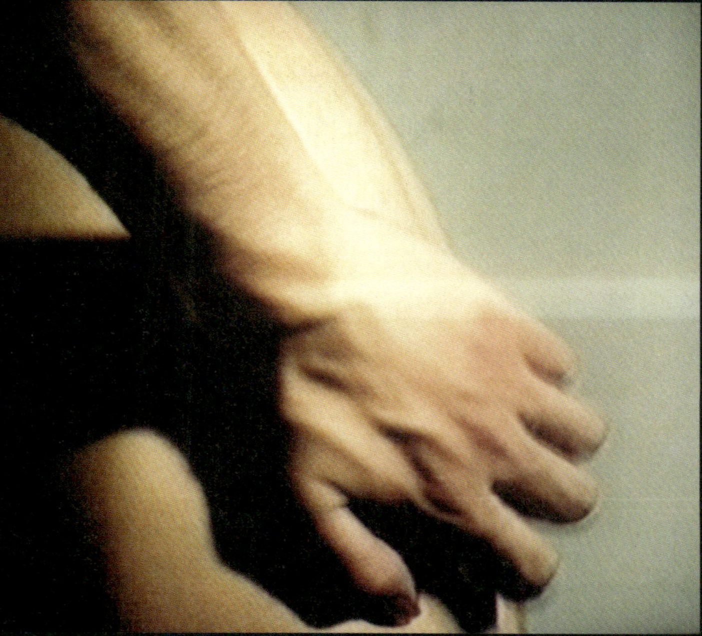

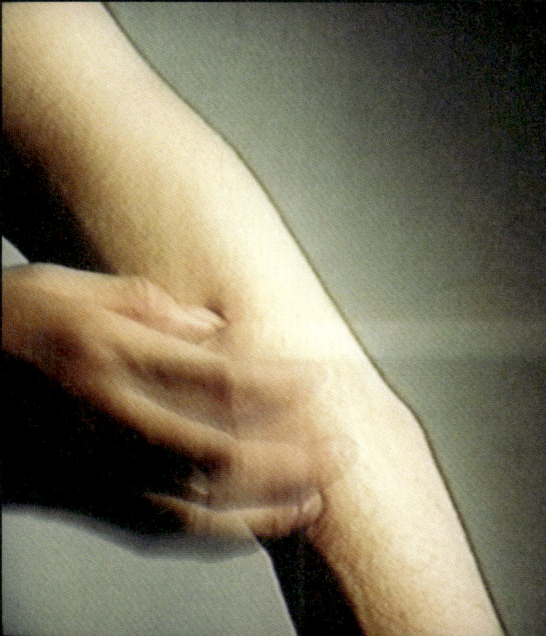

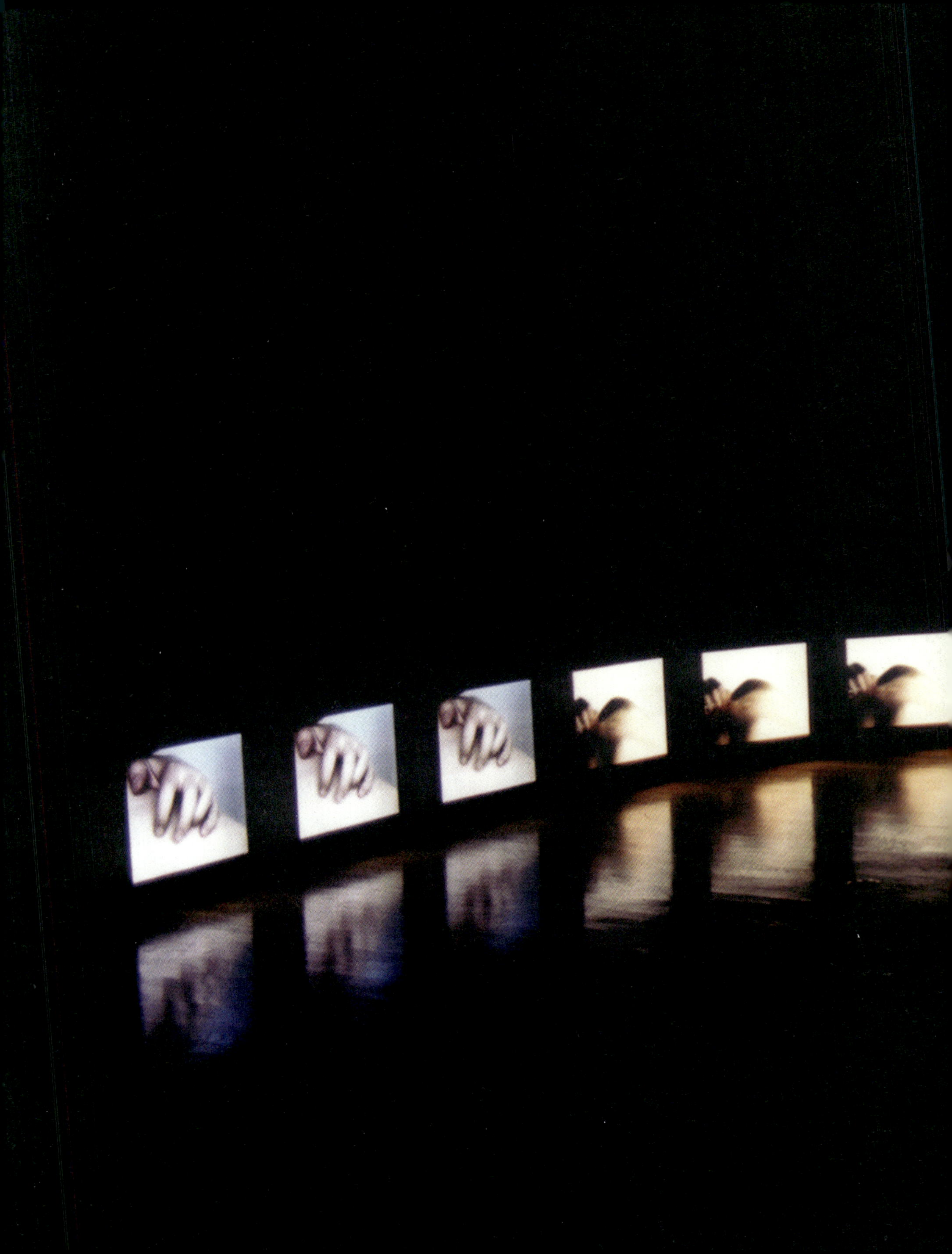

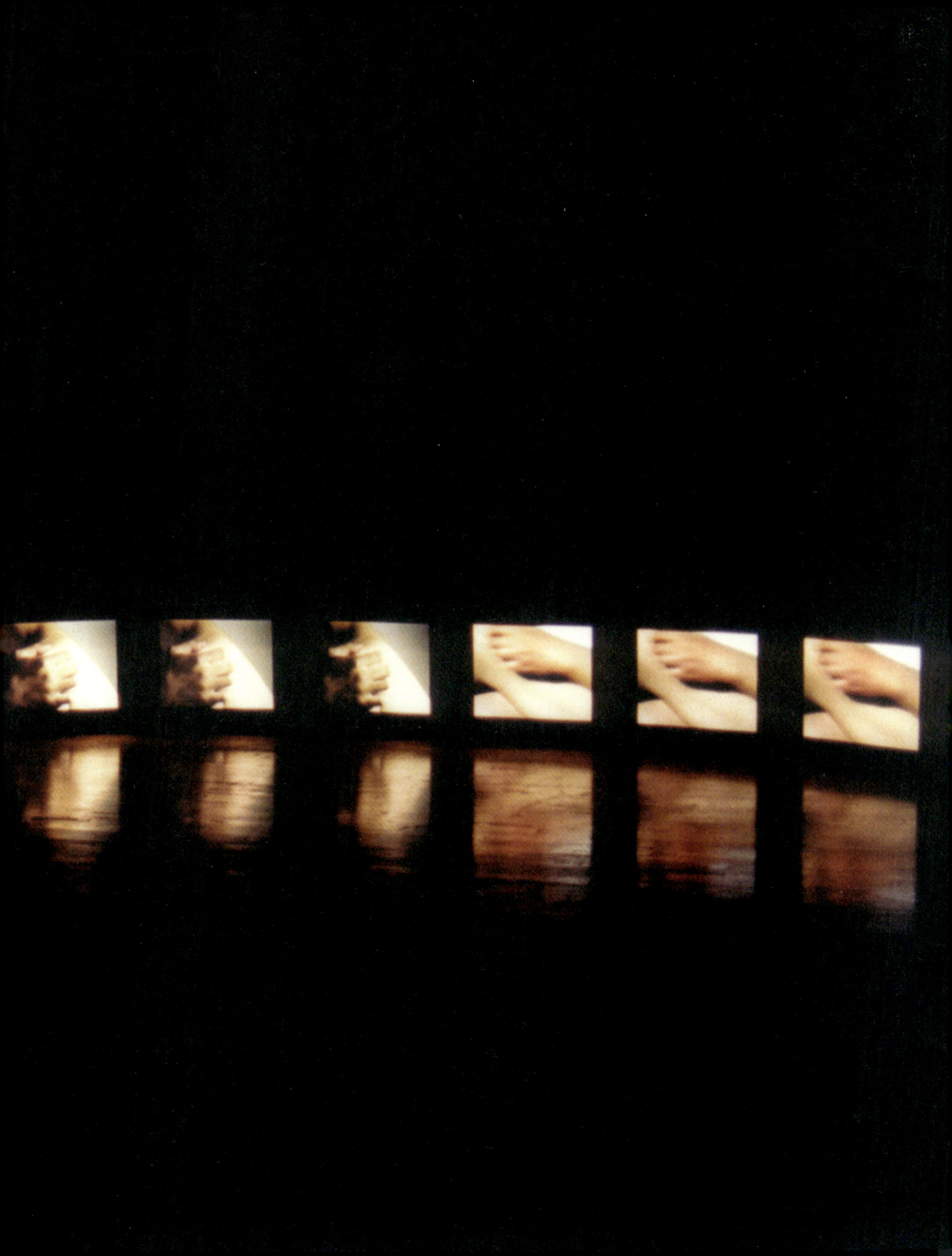

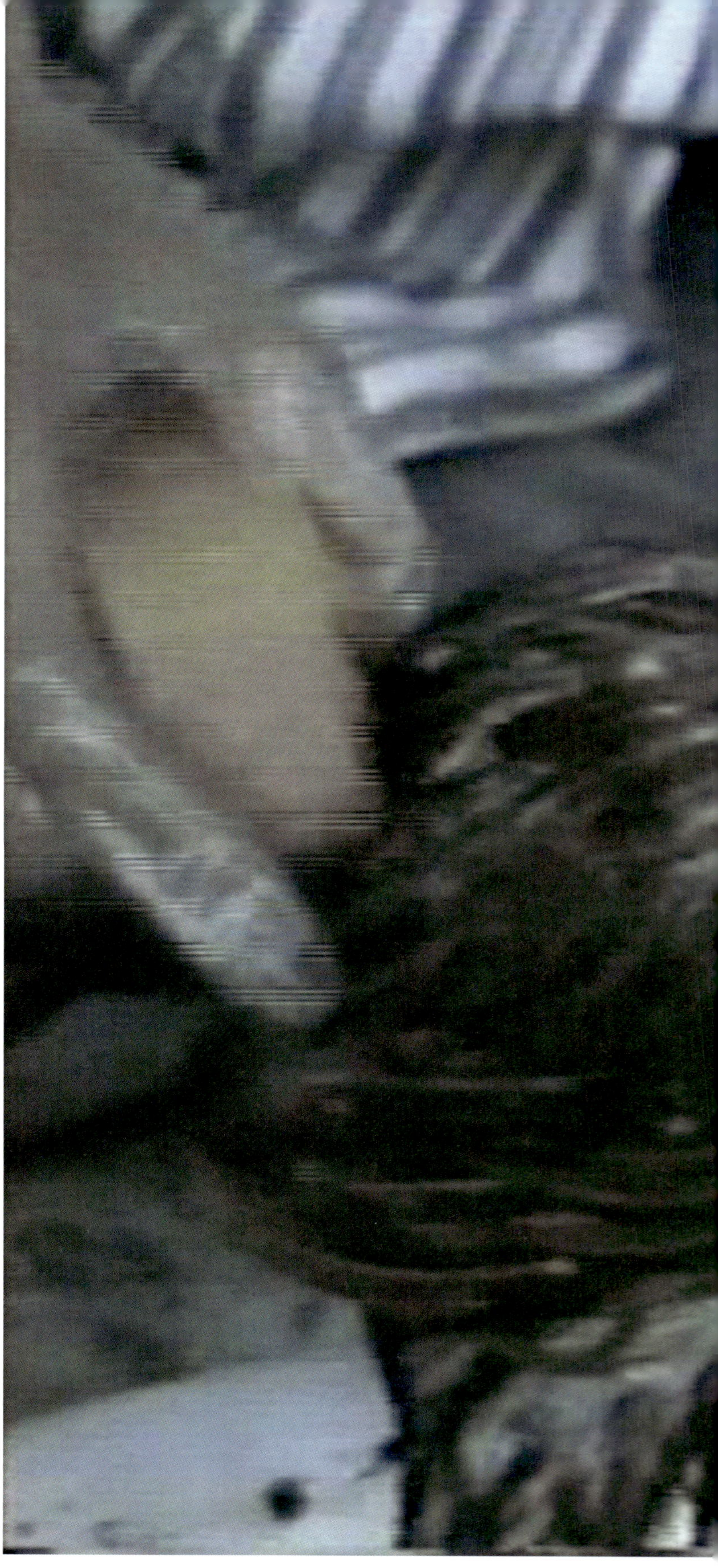

Seite / Pages 96–97

Assignment No. 1, 1992
Sechs-Kanal-zwölf-Monitor-Videoinstallation (PAL) Farbe, ohne Ton / Six-channel, twelve-screen video installation (PAL), colour, silent, 13'–14'

Seite / Pages 98–99

Uncertain Pleasure I, 1996
Vier-Kanal-zwölf-Monitor-Videoinstallation (PAL), Farbe, ohne Ton / Four-channel, twelve-screen video installation (PAL), colour, silent, 30'

Seite / Pages 100–101

Installationsansicht / Installation view, The 1st Fukuoka Asian Art Triennial 1999, Fukuoka Asian Art Museum, Japan
Uncertain Pleasure I, 1996

Diese Seite / This page

Document on Hygiene No. 3, 1991
Ein-Kanal-Videoinstallation (PAL) Farbe, ohne Ton / Single-channel video installation (PAL), colour, silent, 24'45"

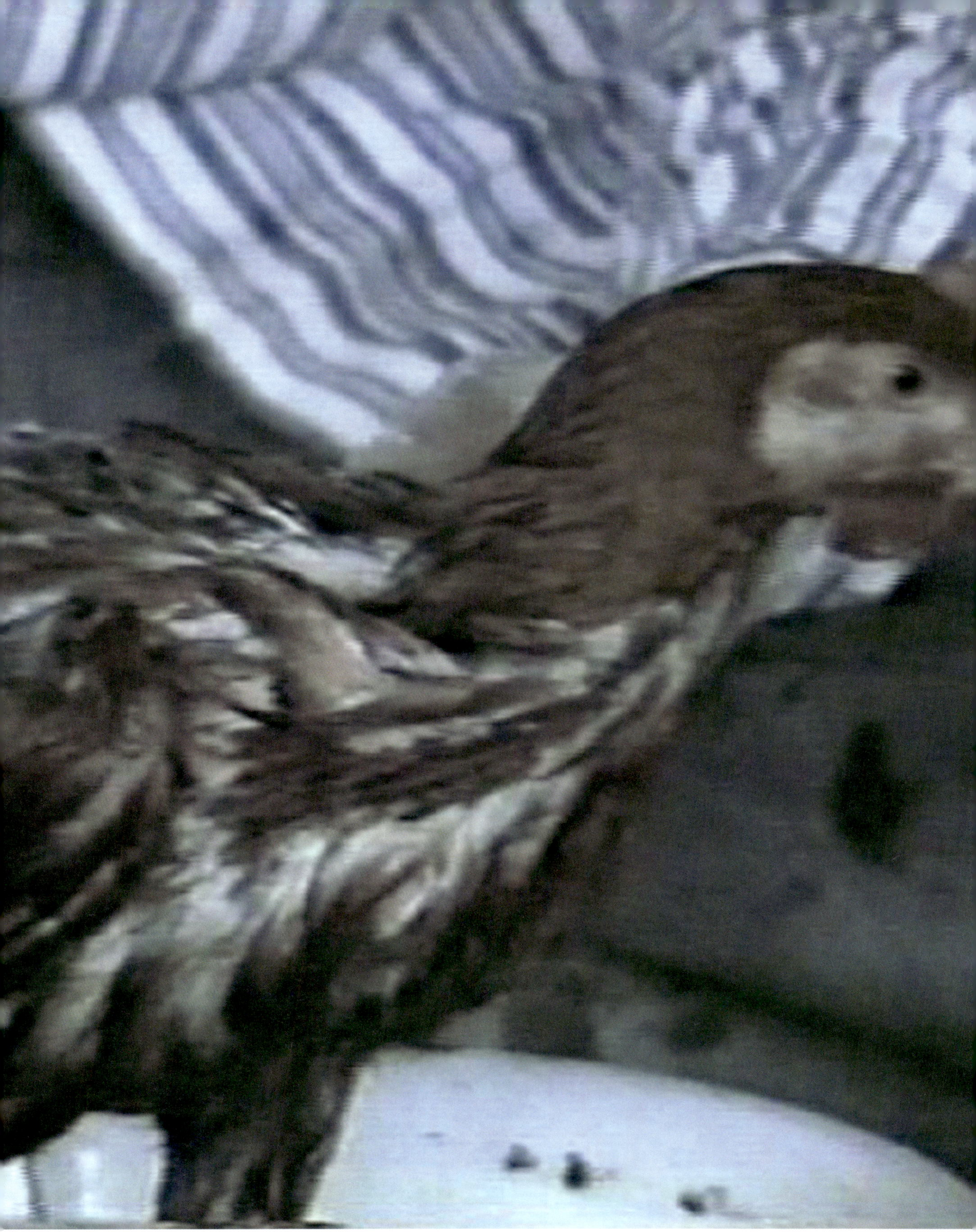

King and Queen, 1986
Performance mit Zeitungspapier /
Performance with newspapers

Das Pond-Society-Manifest / The Pond
Society Manifesto, Hangzhou, 1986

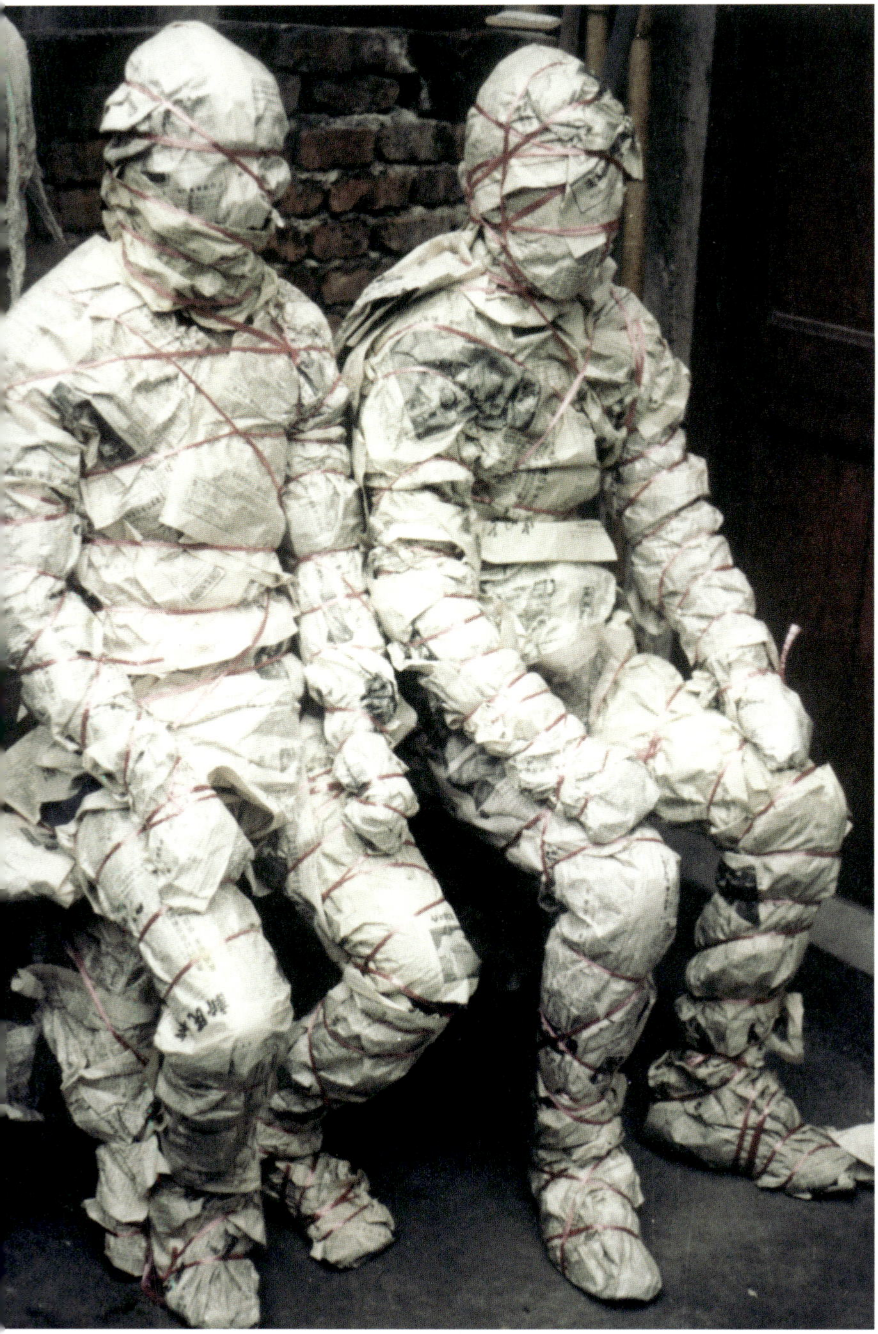

“池”社宣言

一九八六年五月

○ 艺术是一个池。

○ 我们的生存有赖于碳水化合物。

○ 不是想要这样才这样。
而是不得不这样才这样。

○ 我们的肌体覆满了灰尘。

○ 艺术是有利可图的吗?
艺术是赏心悦目的吗?

○ 我们的渴望恰当的净化。

○ 我们的思维是流动的，模糊的。

○ 我们渴望潜能的挥发。

○ 艺术的异化是学究的、机械的或被功利制约的重复生产。

○ 我们渴望疲惫而令人心醉的壮严时刻。

○ 重要的是“浸入”。

○ 有谁见过理性的冲动?

○ “浸入”的瞬间令人陶醉。
复苏的瞬间大彻大悟。

○ 对于法则，
我们通过一种“较高的服从”，
给予“严正的注意”。

○ 结果是次要的。
种子在不断发芽。

○ 真谛不可言说。

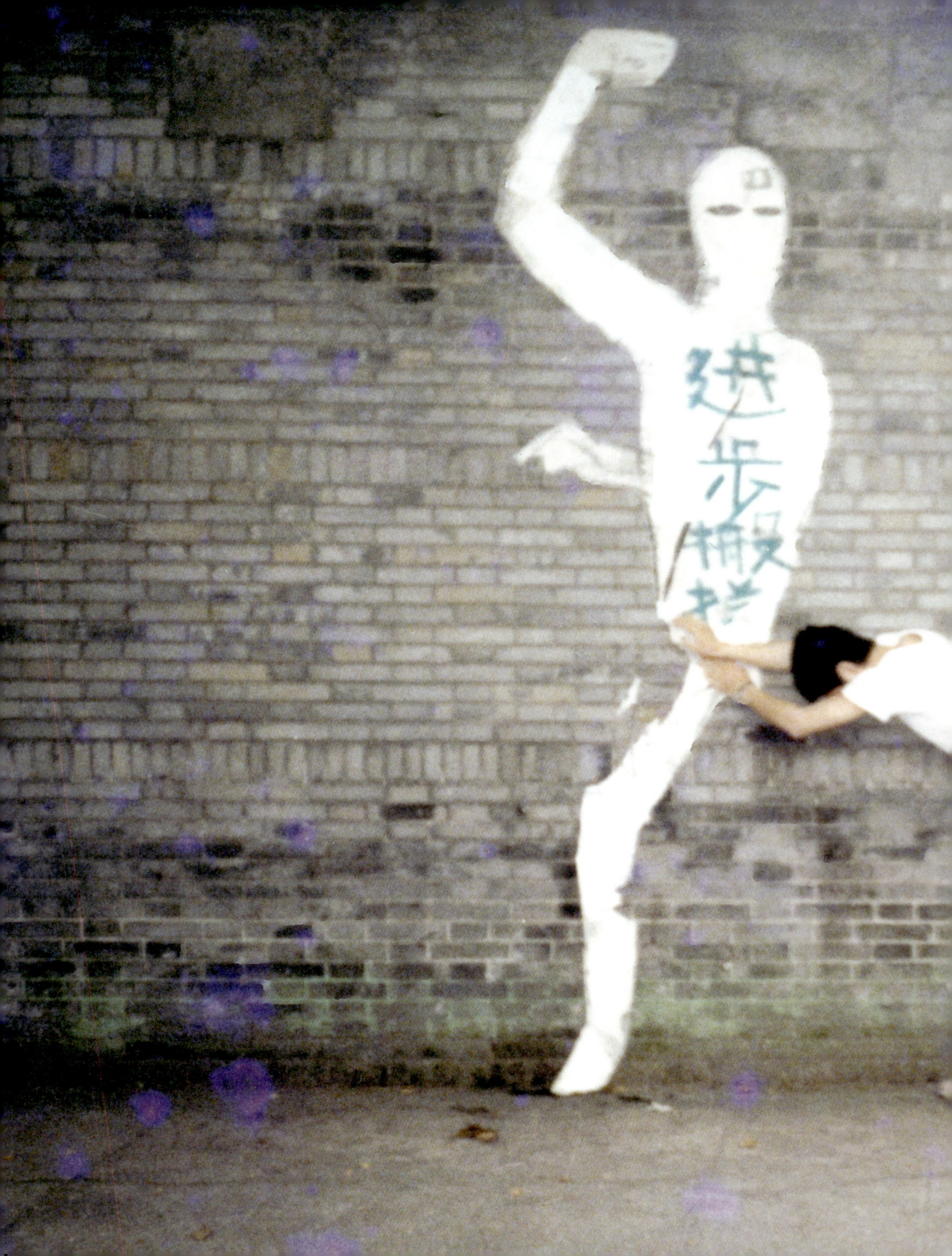

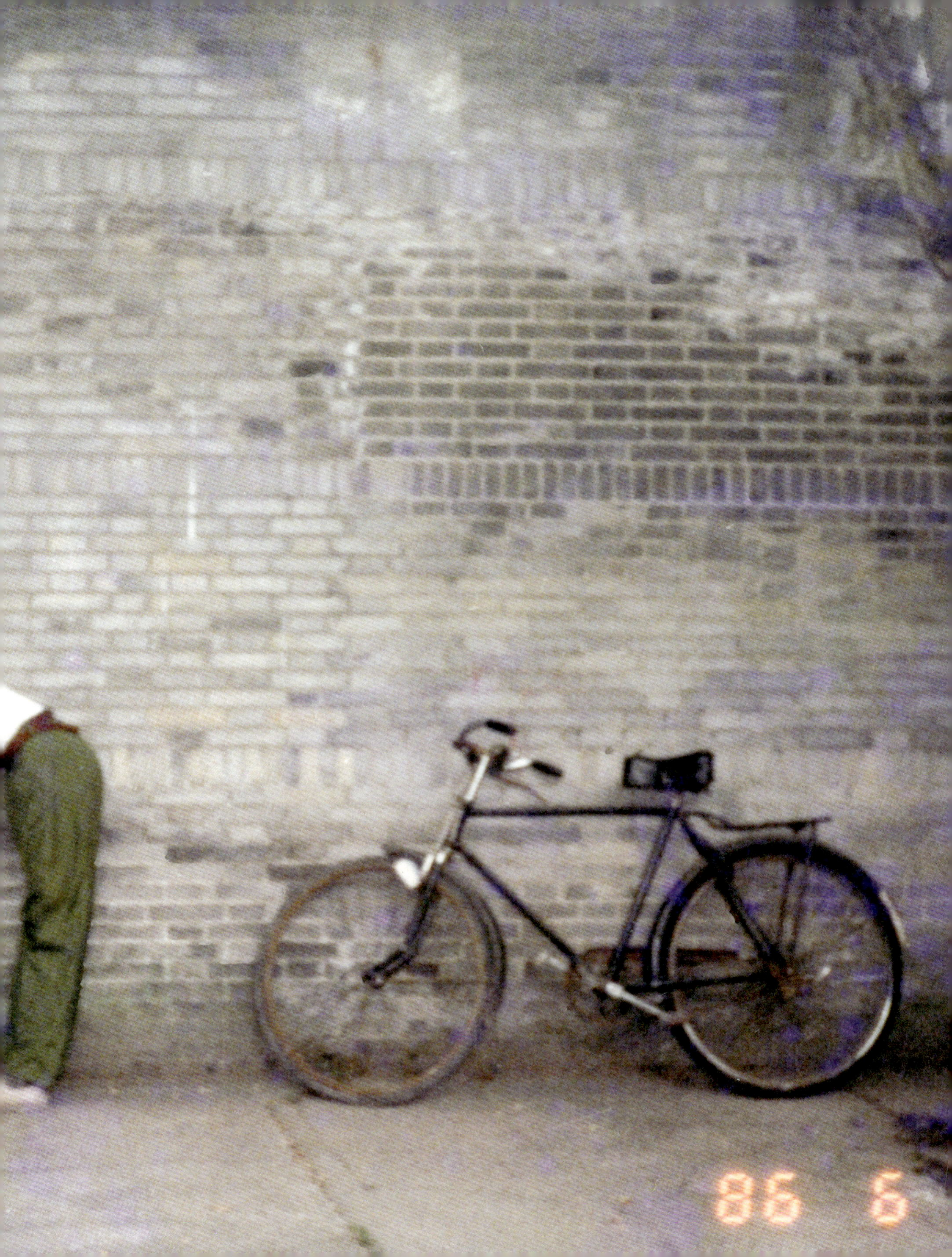
86 6

Seite / Pages 106–107

Yang-style Tai Chi Series,
Hangzhou, 1986
Altes Zeitungspapier / Old
newspapers

Installationsansicht / Installation
view, *China Artistic Avantgarde
Movements*, Centre d'Art Santa
Monica, Barcelona, Spanien /
Spain, 1995
Opposite Space, 1995
Zwei-Kanal-Videoinstallation mit
Überwachungskameras und
14-Zoll-Fernsehbildschirmen,
Farbe, Wänden / Two-channel
video installation with surveillance
cameras, 14-inch TV displays,
colour, and constructed walls,
350 x 140 x 500 cm

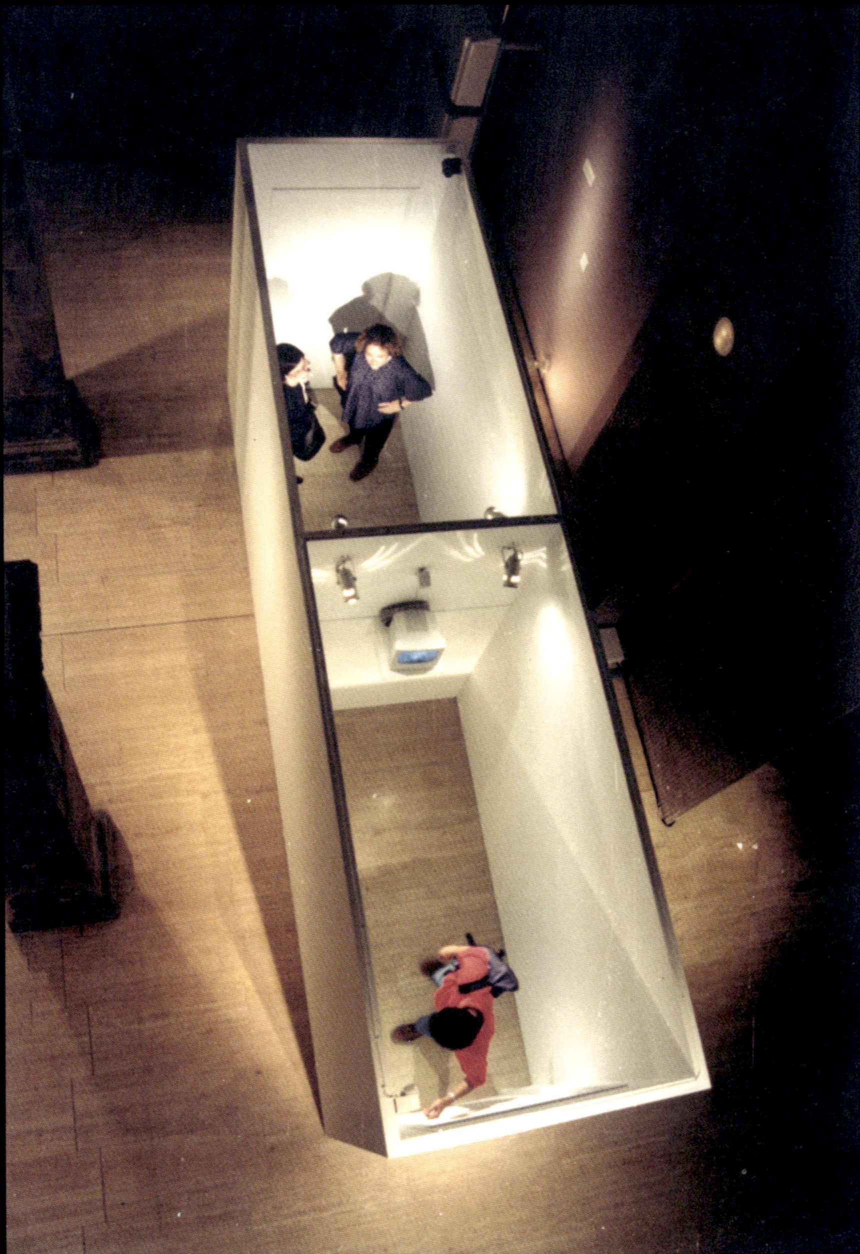

Appendix

Anhang

Künstler*innenbiografien
Werkverzeichnis
Kurator*innen
Impressum

Geboren 1978 in Guangzhou, China; Studium an der Guangzhou Academy of Fine Arts; lebt und arbeitet in Peking, China.

Born 1978 in Guangzhou, China; graduated from Guangzhou Academy of Fine Arts; livesand works in Beijing, China.

Ausgewählte Einzelausstellungen
Selected Solo Exhibitions

2019 *HX*, Centre Pompidou, Paris, FR

2018 *A hollow in a world too full*, Tai Kwun Contemporary, Hong Kong, HK

Cao Fei, K21 Kunstsammlung Nordrhein-Westfalen, Düsseldorf, DE

2016 *Cao Fei*, MoMA PS1, New York, US

2015 *Cao Fei: Shadow Plays,* The Mistake Room, Los Angeles, US

Cao Fei: La Town, Bonnefantenmuseum, Maastricht, NL

2013 *Haze and Fog*, Tate Modern, Starr Auditorium, London, GB

2011 *RMB City Opera*, The Nelson-Atkins Museum of Art, Kansas City, US

2010 *Cao Fei: RMB City*, CrossFade Lounge, Yerba Buena Center for the Arts, San Francisco, US

2008 *Cao Fei*, Frac Île-de-France, Le Plateau, Paris, FR

Cao Fei: RMB City, Serpentine Gallery (2008–09), London, GB

2007 *Cao Fei: Whose Utopia?*, Orange County Museum of Art, Newport Beach, US

2006 *PRD Anti-Heroes*, Museum Het Domein, Sittard, NL

Ausgewählte Gruppenausstellungen
Selected Group Exhibitions

2019 *Vertiginous Data*, National Museum of Modern and Contemporary Art, Seoul, KR

Is This Tomorrow?, Whitechapel Gallery, London, GB

Cao Fei 曹斐

2018 *9th Asia Pacific Triennial of Contemporary Art*, Queensland Art Gallery, Gallery of Modern Art (QAGOMA), South Brisbane, AU

One Hand Clapping, Solomon R. Guggenheim Museum, New York, US

BMW Art Car #18, Art Basel, Hong Kong, HK

2015 *All the World's Future*, Arsenale, 56th International Art Exhibition, La Biennale di Venezia, Venice, IT

2014 *Whose Utopia, Poetry and Dream*, Tate Modern, London, GB

15 Years CCAA (China Contemporary Art Award) exhibition, Shanghai Power Station of Art, Shanghai, CN

2011 *Future Generation Art Prize, ILLUMInations*, 54th International Art Exhibition, La Biennale di Venezia, Venice, IT

2010 *17th Biennale of Sydney*, Sydney, AU

Contemplating the Void, Guggenheim Museum, New York, US

2009 *The Generational: Younger Than Jesus*, The New Museum, New York, US

2008 *Yokohama Triennale*, Yokohama, JP

2007 *10th International Istanbul Biennial*, Istanbul, TR

Everyday Miracles, 52nd International Art Exhibition, La Biennale di Venezia, Chinese Pavilion, Venice, IT

2006 *China Power Station: Part 1*, Battersea Power Station, Serpentine Gallery, London, GB

Taipei Biennial, Taipei Fine Arts Museum, Taipei, TW

15th Biennale of Sydney, Sydney, AU

2005 *Dialectics of Hope, 1st Moscow Biennale*, Moscow, RU

2004 *5th Shanghai Biennale,* Shanghai Museum of Art, Shanghai, CN

2003 *Z.O.U. (Zone of Urgency)*, 50th International Art Exhibition, La Biennale di Venezia, Venice, IT

2002 *Reinterpretation: A Decade of Experimental Chinese Art – The 1st Guangzhou Triennial,* Guangdong Museum of Art, Guangzhou, CN

China on Screen, Tate Modern, London, GB

2001 *living in time – 29 contemporary artists from China*, Hamburger Bahnhof – Museum für Gegenwart – Berlin, Berlin, DE

1999 *4th Cross-Strait*, Hong Kong and Macau Student Film & Video Festival, Hong Kong, HK

Geboren 1987 in Yangjiang, Provinz Guangdong, China; Studium der bildenden Künste an der Guangzhou Academy of Fine Arts und an der Mount Royal School of Art; lebt und arbeitet in Shenzhen, China, und Port Moresby, Papua-Neuguinea.

Born 1987 in Yangjiang, Guangdong Province, China; graduated from the Department of Fine Art at Guangzhou Academy of Fine Arts and at Mount Royal School of Art; lives and works in Shenzhen, China, and Port Moresby, Papua New Guinea.

Ausgewählte Einzelausstellungen Selected Solo Exhibitions

2019 *Jiū Society: Lost in Shenzhen*, Centre for Chinese Contemporary Art, Manchester, GB

2017 *GAS STATION IX: DÀ QǏDÀ LUÒ*, Fang Di and Jiū Society (Fang Di, Ji Hao, Jin Haofan), Vanguard Gallery, Shanghai, CN

2016 *Lost in Shenzhen, Presented by Jiū Society*, 33 Artspace, Shenzhen, CN

2013 *Hit Me!*, Delaware Center for the Contemporary Arts, Wilmington, US

2009 *433*, Sabaki Space, Guangzhou, CN

Ausgewählte Gruppenausstellungen Selected Group Exhibitions

2019 *Extreme Mix 2019 Airport Biennale*, Guangzhou Airport Resort, Fenghe Village, Guangzhou, CN

Hic sunt leones, 798 Art Center, Beijing, CN

Hic sunt leones, Surplus Space, Wuhan, CN

Not for the faint of heart, White Rabbit Gallery, Sydney, AU

2018 *12th Shanghai Biennale – Progress: Art in an Age of Historical Ambivalence*, Power Station of Art, Shanghai, CN

Fang Di 方迪

New Metallurgists,
Julia Stoschek Collection,
Düsseldorf, DE

OMG, It's a Party!, Vtape's,
Toronto, CA

The Precariousness, Hyundai
Motorstudio, Beijing, CN

2017 *Chinafrika: blackout*, curated by
Jochen Becker/metroZones with
Huang Xiaopeng, *Bi-City Biennale of Urbanism Architecture*,
Nantou Village, Shenzhen, CN

Art, Making Cities Buy Me,
by Jiū Society, *Bi-City Biennale of Urbanism/Architecture*,
Nantou Village, Shenzhen, CN

The Ecstasy of Time – Reframing the Medium of Knowing,
He Xiangning Art Museum,
Shenzhen, CN

Millennial Millionaires and the Survivor's Club, LITHIUM gallery,
Chicago, US

Southern Climate, N3 Gallery,
Beijing, CN

2016 *Shenzhen New Media Art Festival*,
Jiū Society, Huigang Art Center,
Shenzhen, CN

Wet Dreams, Salt Project No.4
Langjia Hutong, Beijing, CN

The Suggestive Wheel: An Era of Metaphors, Boxes Art Space of OCT
Harbour, Shenzhen, CN

2015 *Institution Production: Ecology Investigation of Contemporary Art of Young Guangzhou Artists*, Guangdong
Museum of Art, Guangzhou, CN

Magic International Art Exhibition 2015, New Media Industrial Park,
Shenzhen, CN

IVY ART 2015 · Chinese Young Artists Annual Exhibition Today,
Art Museum, Beijing, CN

2014 *IV Moscow International Biennale for Young Art*, The Museum of Moscow,
Moscow, RU

2013 *COLUMBUS RESORT*,
Storefront for Art and Architecture,
New York, US

Youngblood 2013, Maryland Art Place,
Baltimore, US

Academy 2013, CONNERSMITH
Gallery, Washington, D.C., US

BRAZEN, Project Gallery,
Toronto, CA

Geboren 1984 in Schanghai, China; Studium der Medienkunst an der China Academy of Art, Hangzhou; lebt und arbeitet in Schanghai, China.

Born 1984 in Shanghai, China; graduated from the Department of New Art Media at the China Academy of Art, Hangzhou; lives and works in Shanghai, China.

Ausgewählte Einzelausstellungen Selected Solo Exhibitions

2019 *The Game World of Material World Knight*, CC Foundation & Art Center Shanghai, CN

Cyber Altar, Art Basel Hong Kong under the auspices of Société, Hong Kong, HK

2018 *Electromagnetic Brainology*, Spiral, Tokyo, JP

2017 *Lu Yang Asia Character Setting Show*, Special Special, New York, US

Lu Yang: Encephalon Heaven, M WOODS, Beijing, CN

Welcome to LuYang Hell, Société, Berlin, DE

Delusional Mandala, MOCA Cleveland, Cleveland, US

2016 *LuYang Delusional Crime and Punishment*, NYU Shanghai Art Gallery, Shanghai, CN

Ausgewählte Gruppenausstellungen Selected Group Exhibitions

2019 *Stumbling Through the Uncanny Valley: Sculpture and Self in the Age of Computer Generated Imagery*, The Center for Contemporary Art, Tel Aviv, IL

Chinernet Ugly, Center for Chinese Contemporary Art, Manchester, GB

LOW FORM: Imaginaries and Visions in the Age of Artificial Intelligence, MAXXI (National Museum of XXI Arts), Video Gallery, Rome, IT

Lu Yang 陆扬

2018 *"Lumen Quarterly" by World Organization of Video Culture Development*, Ullens Center for Contemporary Art, Beijing, CN

Computer Grrrls, HMKV, Dortmund, DE

Computer Grrrls, La Gaité Lyrique, Paris, FR

Nowness Anniversary Exhibition, Shanghai, CN

From / To: The Frontier of Chinese Art Education, China Academy of Art at SFAI/San Francisco Art Institute, San Francisco, US

6th Athens Biennale, "ANTI", Athens, GR

12th Shanghai Biennale, Shanghai, CN

2017 *Zhongguo 2185*, Sadie Coles, London, GB

Culture City of East Asia 2017 Kyoto: Asia Corridor Contemporary Art Exhibition, Kyoto Art Center, Kyoto, JP

After Party 1: Collective Dance and Individual Gymnastics, Blindspot Gallery, Hong Kong, HK

one world expo 2.1 # like4like, K11, Hong Kong, HK

After Us, K11, Shanghai, CN

2016 *Hyperlinks 2*, Center for Contemporary Art, Tel Aviv, IL

Moscow Biennale 2016, Moscow, RU

2015 *Breaking Joints*, Institute of Contemporary Arts, London, GB

Absolute Collection Guideline, SiFang Art Museum, Nanjing, CN

Pavilion of China, 56th International Art Exhibition, La Biennale di Venezia, Venice, IT

Rendez-vous, Institute of Contemporary Arts, Singapore, CN

New Directions in Chinese Animation, Institute of Contemporary Art, Boston, US

Fridericianum-Inhuman, Museum Fridericianum, Kassel, DE

Zhang Peili 张培力

1957 geboren in Hangzhou, China; Studium der Ölmalerei an der Zhejiang Academy of Fine Arts (heute China Academy of Art), wo er jetzt Professor ist. Zhang lebt und arbeitet derzeit in Hangzhou und ist zudem Leiter von OCAT Shanghai, China.

Born 1957 in Hangzhou, China; graduated from the Department of Oil Painting at Zhejiang Academy of Fine Arts (now China Academy of Art), where he is now a professor. Zhang currently lives and works in Hangzhou. He is also the executive director of OCAT Shanghai, China.

Ausgewählte Einzelausstellungen
Selected Solo Exhibitions

2018 *Now That*, Boers-Li Gallery, Beijing, CN

Uplifting, S.M.A.K., Ghent, BE

The Flickering Uncertain – Jim Campbell & ZHANG Peili joint solo, Chronus Art Center (CAC), Shanghai, CN

2017 *Record. Repeat.*, The Art Institute of Chicago, Chicago, US

2016 *From Painting to Video*, CIW Gallery, Australian National University, Canberra, AU

2013 *Zhang Peili*, ACAF Art Space, Melbourne, AU

2012 *Zhang Peili*, MAAP (Media Art Asia Pacific), Brisbane, AU

2011 *Certain Pleasures/Zhang Peili Retrospective*, Minsheng Art Museum, Shanghai, CN

2009 *Zhang Peili*, Govett-Brewster Art Gallery, New Plymouth, NZ

2008 *Mute*, OCT Contemporary Art Terminal, Shenzhen, CN

2007 *Zhang Peili, "Best Artist" (Tilton Gallery, New York)*, 07 Shanghai Art Fair International Contemporary Art Exhibition, Shanghai Exhibition Centre, CN

2006 *Phrase*, Currents/Art & Music, Beijing, CN

2000 *Zhang Peili*, Artist Project Rooms (Art & Public, Switzerland) Arco2000, Madrid, ES

1999 *Zhang Peili*, Jack Tilton Gallery, New York, US

1998 *Eating*, The Museum of Modern Art, New York, US

1997 *Zhang Peili*, The Art Center, Centers of Academic Resources, Chulalongkorn University, Bangkok, TH

1996 *Uncertain Pleasure*, Video Forum / Art27'96, (Art & Public) Basel, CH

1993 *Zhang Peili*, Maison des Cultures du Monde, Galerie du Rond Point, Paris Galerie Crousel-Robelin, Paris, FR

Ausgewählte Gruppenausstellungen Selected Group Exhibitions

2018 *Thailand Biennale, "Edge of the Wonderland"*, Krabi, TH

Institute of Asian Performance Art: Tokyo, Tokyo Art and Space, Tokyo, JP

This is Shanghai, Cunard Building, Tate Exchange Liverpool, Museum of Liverpool, Mann Island, GB

Devided We Stand, Busan Biennale, Busan, KR

2017 *Simultaneous Eidos*, Guangzhou Image Triennial 2017, Guangdong Museum of Art, Guangzhou, CN

Art and China after 1989: Theater of the World, Solomon R. Guggenheim Museum, New York, US

2016 *Slaying Monsters – Kuandu Biennale 2016*, Taipei, TW

Hybridizing Earth – Discussing Multitude, Busan Biennale 2016, Busan, KR

Time Test: International Video Art Research Exhibition, CAFA Art Museum, Beijing, CN

Wrap Around the Time: Remembrance Exhibition for Nam Jun Paik's 10th Anniversary, Nam Jun Paik Art Center, KR

M+Sigg Collection: Four Decades of Chinese Contemporary Art, ArtisTree, Hong Kong, HK

2015 *Mobile M+ – Moving Images*, Midtown POP, Hong Kong, HK

A Hundred Years of Shame – Songs of Resistance and Scenarios for Chinese Nations, PARA SITE, Hong Kong, HK

2014 *Hans van Dijk: 5000 Names*, Ullens Center for Contemporary Art, Beijing, CN; Witte de With Center for Contemporary Art, Rotterdam, NL

2013 *Passage to History: 20 Years of La Biennale di Venezia and Chinese Contemporary Art*, Collateral Event at the 55th International Art Exhibition – La Biennale di Venezia, Venice, IT

2012 *Reactivation – 9th Shanghai Biennale*, Power Station of Art, Shanghai, CN

The 7th Shenzhen Sculpture Biennale, Shenzhen, CN

2010 *Artistic Impression of Chinese*, National Art Museum of China, Beijing, CN

Not Only Time: Zhang Peili and Zhu Jia, REDCAT, Los Angeles, US

2009 *Timelapse*, National Art Museum of China, Beijing, CN

Avant-Garde China: 20 Years of Chinese Contemporary Art, National Museum of Art, Osaka, JP; Aichi Prefectural Museum of Art, Nagoya, JP

A Gift to Marco Polo, Collateral Event at the 53rd International ArtExhibition – La Biennale di Venezia, Venice International University, Island of San Servolo, Venice, IT

2008 *Avant-Garde China: 20 Years of Chinese Contemporary Art*, National Art Center, Tokyo, JP

2007 *We are your future (Video Box)*, 2nd Moscow Biennale, Moscow, RU

Chinese Contemporary Art, Kunsthaus Graz, Graz, AT

China Onward: The Estella Collection/ Chinese Contemporary Art, 1966–2006, Louisiana Museum of Modern Art, Humlebæk, DK

85 New Wave, The Birth of Chinese Contemporary Art, Ullens Center for Contemporary Art, Beijing, CN

2006 *China Power Station Part 1*, Serpentine Gallery, London, GB

2005 *Shaun Gladwell/Tracey Moffatt/ Zhang Peili*, Institute of Modern Art, Brisbane, AU

2004 *Techniques of the Visible/Shanghai Biennale 2004*, Shanghai Art Museum, Shanghai, CN

2003 *Z.O.U. – Zone of Urgency*, 50th International Art Exhibition – La Biennale di Venezia, Venice, IT

Happiness: a survival guide for art and life, Mori Art Museum, Tokyo, JP

Alors, la Chine?, Centre Pompidou, Paris, FR

The First Guangzhou Triennial, Guangzhou Museum of Art, CN

2002 *PAUSE/Gwanju Biennale 2002*, Gwangju, KR

2001 *living in time*, Nationalgalerie im Hamburger Bahnhof – Museum für Gegenwart – Berlin, Berlin, DE

China Art Now Singapore Art Museum, National Heritage Board, Singapore, CN

2000 *Open Ends: art at the MoMA since 1980*, Museum of Modern Art, New York, US

Media-city Seoul 2000, Seoul Metropolitan Museum, Seoul, KR

Shanghai Biennale 2000, Shanghai Art Museum, Shanghai, CN

1999 *APERTO over ALL*, 48th International Art Exhibition – La Biennale di Venezia, Venice, IT

Global Conceptualism: Points of Origin 1950s–1980s, Queens Museum of Art, New York, US

Third Asia-Pacific Triennial of Contemporary Art, Queensland Art Gallery, Brisbane, AU

The 1st Fukuoka Asian Art Triennale 1999, Fukuoka Asian Art Museum, Fukuoka, JP

Cities on the Move 5, Hayward Gallery, London, GB

Inside Out: New Chinese Art, San Francisco Museum of Modern Art, San Francisco, US

1998 *Every day / 11th Biennial of Sydney*, Sydney, AU

Inside Out: New Chinese Art, PS1 Contemporary Art Center, New York, US

1997 *La 4e Biennial d'Art Contemporain de Lyon*, Lyon, FR

Cities on the Move 1, Group Exhibition of Contemporary Asian Art, Vienna Secession, Vienna, AT

1993 *Passaggio a Oriente*, 45th International Art Exhibition – La Biennale di Venezia, Venice, IT

China Avant-garde, Haus der Kulturen der Welt, Berlin, DE; Kunsthal Rotterdam, NL; Museum of Modern Art, Oxford, GB; Kunsthallen Brandts Klædefabrik, Odense, DK

Mao goes Pop, Sydney Museum of Contemporary Art, AU

1992 *Recent Works – Art Show by Zhang Peili and Geng Jianyi Since 1991*, Diplomatic Missions Restaurant, Beijing, CN

1991 *I don't want to play cards with Cezanne and other works*, Pacific Asia Museum, Pasadena, US

Garage Show, Education Congress Hall, Shanghai, CN

1989 *Documentary Exhibition on Chinese Contemporary Art*, Tokyo Gallery, JP

China Avant-garde, China National Gallery, Beijing, CN

1987 *Beyond the open door*, Pacific Asia Museum, Pasadena, US

1986 *Performances and street installations with the "Pool Society"*, Hangzhou, CN

1985 *New Space 85*, exhibition hall of the Zhejiang Academy of Fine Arts, Hangzhou, CN

Cao Fei

Multimediainstallation mit den folgenden Videoarbeiten / Multimedia installation including the following video works:

Asia One, 2018
Ein-Kanal-Videoinstallation, Farbe, Ton / Single-channel video installation, colour, sound, 63'20''
Leihgabe von / Courtesy of Cao Fei, Sprüth Magers, Vitamin Creative Space

11.11, 2018
Ein-Kanal-Videoinstallation, Farbe, Ton / Single-channel video installation, colour, sound, 60'36''
Leihgabe von / Courtesy of Cao Fei, Sprüth Magers, Vitamin Creative Space

Fang Di

Multimediainstallation mit Holztisch, Stühlen, Bühne, LED-Farblicht und den folgenden Videoarbeiten / Multimedia installation with wooden table, chairs, stage, LED colour lights and the following video works

Minister, 2019
Ein-Kanal-Videoinstallation, Farbe, Ton / Single-channel video installation, colour, sound, 60'
Leihgabe von / Courtesy of Vanguard Gallery

The Magical of Pipes, 2019
Zwei-Kanal-Videoinstallation, Farbe, Ton / Two-channel video installation, colour, sound, 30'
Leihgabe von / Courtesy of Vanguard Gallery

Sepik River Ring, 2019
Diamant, Smaragd, Rubin, Saphir, schwarzer Diamant, gelber Diamant, Achat, 18K Gold, Ringdisplay, Maße variabel / Diamond, emerald, ruby, sapphire, black diamond, yellow diamond, agate, 18K gold, cone ring display, dimensions variable
Leihgabe von / Courtesy of Vanguard Gallery

Lu Yang

Multimediainstallation mit den folgenden Medienkunstwerken / Multimedia installation with the following media art works:

Uterus Man, 2013
3-D-Animation, Farbe, Ton / 3D animation, colour, sound, 11'20''
Leihgabe von / Courtesy of Lu Yang and Société

LuYang Delusional Mandala, 2015
Ein-Kanal-Video, Farbe, Ton / Single-channel video, colour, sound, 16'27''
Leihgabe von / Courtesy of Lu Yang and Société

Hearse Delusional Mandala No. 6, 2015
Künstlicher Kristall / Artificial crystal, 19,5 × 25 × 13 cm
Leihgabe von / Courtesy of Lu Yang & Société

Hearse Delusional Mandala No. 7, 2015
Künstlicher Kristall / Artificial crystal, 35,5 × 36 × 12 cm
Leihgabe von / Courtesy of Lu Yang & Société

LuYang Delusional Crime and Punishment, 2016
Ein-Kanal-Video, Farbe, Ton / Single-channel video, colour, sound, 14'37''
Leihgabe von / Courtesy of Lu Yang and Société

Power of Will – Final Shooting, 2016
Ballonkopf / aufblasbare Skulptur, UV-Inkjet-Druck auf PU-Textil, Gebläse, Stroboskop-LED-4-Farben-Beleuchtungssystem, Maße variabel / Balloon head / inflatable sculpture, UV inkjet print on PU-Textile, fans, strobe LED 4-colour lighting system, dimensions variable
Leihgabe von / Courtesy of Lu Yang and Société

TMS (Transcranial Magnetic Stimulation) Exorcism, 2017
Ein-Kanal-Video, Farbe, Ton / Single-channel video, colour, sound, 15'35''
Leihgabe von / Courtesy of Lu Yang and Société

Electromagnetic Brainology, 2017
Fünf-Kanal-Videoinstallation, Farbe, Ton / Five-channel video installation, colour, sound, 13'34''
Leihgabe von / Courtesy of Lu Yang and Société

Electromagnetic Brainology Brain Control Messenger, 2017
Zwei-Kanal-Video, Farbe, Ton / Two-channel video, colour, sound, 10'8''
Leihgabe von / Courtesy of Lu Yang and Société

Material World Knight, 2018
Drei-Kanal-Video, Multimediainstallation, Maße variabel / Three-channel video, multimedia installation, dimensions variable
Leihgabe von / Courtesy of Lu Yang and Société

The Great Adventure of Material World, 2019
Computerspiel, Multimediainstallation, Maße variabel / PC-Game, multimedia installation, dimensions variable
Leihgabe von / Courtesy of Lu Yang and Société

Zhang Peili

30×30, 1988
Ein-Kanal-Videoinstallation (PAL), Farbe, Ton / Single-channel video installation (PAL), colour, sound, 32'9''
Leihgabe von / Courtesy of Zhang Peili and Boers-Li Gallery

Document on Hygiene No. 3, 1991
Ein-Kanal-Videoinstallation (PAL), Farbe, ohne Ton / Single-channel video installation (PAL), colour, silent, 24'45''
Leihgabe von / Courtesy of Zhang Peili and Boers-Li Gallery

Assignment No. 1, 1992
Sechs-Kanal-zwölf-Monitor-Videoinstallation (PAL), Farbe, ohne Ton / Six-channel, twelve-screen video installation (PAL), colour, silent, 13'–14'
Leihgabe von / Courtesy of Zhang Peili and Boers-Li Gallery

Opposite Space, 1995
Zwei-Kanal-Videoinstallation mit Überwachungskameras und Fernsehbildschirmen, Farbe / Two-channel video installation with surveillance cameras and TV displays, colour, 350 × 140 × 500 cm
Leihgabe von / Courtesy of Zhang Peili and Boers-Li Gallery

Uncertain Pleasure I, 1996
Vier-Kanal-zwölf-Monitor-Videoinstallation (PAL), Farbe, ohne Ton / Four-channel, twelve-screen video installation (PAL), colour, silent, 30'
Leihgabe von / Courtesy of Zhang Peili and Boers-Li Gallery

Personal Hygiene, 1998
Drei-Kanal-drei-Monitor-Videoinstallation, Ton, Farbe /schwarz-weiß / Three-channel, three-screen video installation, sound, colour/black & white, 5'49''
Leihgabe von / Courtesy of Zhang Peili and Boers-Li Gallery

Anna-Catharina Gebbers

is a curator at the Nationalgalerie im Hamburger Bahnhof – Museum für Gegenwart – Berlin, where she has curated exhibitions like *Making Paradise: Places of Longing from Paul Gauguin* (in collaboration with Grace Samboh and Enin Supriyanto) for *Hello World: Revising a Collection* (2018); *moving is in every direction: Environments – Installations – Narrative Spaces* (2017); Anne Imhof, *Forever Rage* (2015) and *Angst II* (2016); Julian Rosefeldt, *Manifesto* (2016). Her curation includes *Christoph Schlingensief* (with Klaus Biesenbach and Susanne Pfeffer), KW Institute for Contemporary Art, Berlin (2013), MoMA PS1, New York (2014), and exhibitions with artists like Kader Attia, Félix González-Torres, Thomas Schütte, Santiago Sierra, and Nora Turato. She is editor at *polar – Politik, Theorie, Alltag*.

Victor Wang 王宗孚

is an associate curator at Performa, New York, and editor of the publication *Performance Histories from East Asia 1960s–90s* (2018). Wang curated the first museum survey in China of Richard Tuttle at MWOODS, Beijing (2019); *Afterimage: Dangdai Yishu*, Lisson Gallery, London (2019); as well as the first solo exhibitions in China of the artists Haroon Mirza, Sifang Art Museum, Nanjing (2019), Michael Dean, ShanghART Gallery, Shanghai (2018), Katja Novitskova, Cc Foundation, Shanghai (2017), Jac Leirner, Museum of Contemporary Art, Pavilion, Shanghai (2016), Neïl Beloufa, chi K11 art museum, Shanghai (2016); and also *XUZHEN Supermarket* and *Zhongguo 2185*, Sadie Coles HQ, London (2016).

Yang Beichen 杨北辰

is a curator and researcher of film and contemporary art. He teaches film and media theory at the Central Academy of Drama and is a guest researcher at the New Century Art Foundation, Beijing. For many years, he was a senior editor at *Artforum China*. His curation includes *WANG BING: Experience and Poverty*, Magician Space, Beijing (2017), *New Metallurgists*, Julia Stoschek Collection, Düsseldorf (2018), *LIU CHUANG: Earthbound Cosmology*, Qiao Space, Shanghai (2019). He has contributed critical essays for the catalogues of artists such as Cao Fei, Laure Prouvost, Omer Fast, and HO Tzu Nyen. His current research focuses on the theory of contemporary Moving Image art, Media Archaeology, and New Materialism.

Pi Li 皮力

is the Sigg Senior Curator of M+, a visual culture museum in Hong Kong. He previously served as the deputy executive director of the art administration department at the Central Academy of Fine Arts (CAFA, 2001–12), and as co-founder and director of Boers-Li Gallery (2005–12), initially called Universal Studios-Beijing, Beijing. Pi Li's curation includes *Right is Wrong: Four Decades of Chinese Art from the M+ Sigg Collection*, Whitworth Gallery, Manchester (2015), Bildmuseet, Umea (2014); *Under Construction*, Tokyo Opera Museum (2002); *Moist: Asia-Pacific Media Art*, Beijing Millennium Monument Art Museum (2002); *Fantasy Zone*, Beijing Modern Art Center (2002); Art Museum of Dong A Daily (2001); *Image is Power*, He Xiangning Art Museum, Shenzhen (2002). He was curator at *Media City Seoul* (2006); *Alors, la Chine?*, Centre Georges Pompidou (2003); and the Shanghai Biennial (2002). Publications include *Farewell to Moralism* (2018) and *From Action to Concept* (2015).

Curators / Co-Curators / Curatorial Advisor

Kuratorin / Co-Kuratoren / Kuratorischer Berater

Anna-Catharina Gebbers

ist Kuratorin an der Nationalgalerie im Hamburger Bahnhof – Museum für Gegenwart – Berlin, wo sie Ausstellungen kuratierte wie *Making Paradise: Places of Longing from Paul Gauguin* (in Zusammenarbeit mit Grace Samboh und Enin Supriyanto) für *Hello World. Revision einer Sammlung* (2018); *moving is in every direction: Environments – Installationen – Narrative Räume* (2017); Anne Imhof, *Forever Rage* (2015), und *Angst II* (2016); Julian Rosefeldt, *Manifesto* (2016). Zu ihren weiteren Ausstellungen zählt *Christoph Schlingensief* (mit Klaus Biesenbach und Susanne Pfeffer), KW Institute for Contemporary Art, Berlin (2013), MoMA PS1, New York (2014), sowie Projekte mit Künstlern wie Kader Attia, Félix González-Torres, Thomas Schütte, Santiago Sierra, Milica Tomić. Gebbers ist zudem Redakteurin von *polar – Politik, Theorie, Alltag.*

Victor Wang 王宗孚

ist Associate Curator der Performa, New York, und Herausgeber der Publikation *Performance Histories from East Asia 1960s – 90s* (2018). Wang kuratierte die in China erste Museumsschau von Richard Tuttle bei MWOODS, Peking (2019); *Afterimage: Dangdai Yishu*, Lisson Gallery, London (2019); sowie die in China ersten Einzelausstellungen der Künstler Haroon Mirza, Sifang Art Museum, Nanjing (2019), Michael Dean, ShanghART Gallery, Schanghai (2018), Katja Novitskova, Cc Foundation, Schanghai (2017), Jac Leirner, Museum of Contemporary Art, Pavilion, Schanghai (2016), Neïl Beloufa, chi K11 art museum, Schanghai (2016); sowie *XUZHEN-Supermarkt* und *Zhongguo 2185*, Sadie Coles HQ, London (2016).

Yang Beichen 杨北辰

ist Kurator und Forscher für Film und zeitgenössische Kunst. Er unterrichtet Film- und Medientheorie an der Central Academy of Drama und ist Gastforscher an der New Century Art Foundation, Peking. Er war viele Jahre leitender Redakteur bei *Artforum China*. Seine Kuration umfasst *WANG BING: Experience and Poverty*, Magician Space, Beijing (2017), *New Metallurgists*, Julia Stoschek Collection, Düsseldorf (2018), *LIU CHUANG: Earthbound Cosmology*, Qiao Space, Schanghai (2019). Er hat kritische Essays für die Kataloge von Künstlern wie Cao Fei, Laure Prouvost, Omer Fast und Ho Tzu Nyen verfasst. Seine aktuellen Forschungsschwerpunkte sind die Theorie der zeitgenössischen Bewegtbildkunst, die Medienarchäologie und der Neue Materialismus.

Pi Li 皮力

ist Sigg Senior Curator am M+, einem Museum für visuelle Kultur in Hongkong. Zuvor war er Mitbegründer und Direktor der Boers-Li Gallery (2005-2012), ursprünglich Universal Studios-Peking, Peking und stellvertretender Geschäftsführer der Abteilung für Kunstverwaltung an der Central Academy of Fine Arts (CAFA, 2001-2012). Pi Lis Ausstellungen umfassen *Right is Wrong: Four Decades of Chinese Art from the M+ Sigg Collection*, Whitworth Gallery, Manchester (2015), Bildmuseet, Umea (2014); *Under Construction*, Tokyo Opera Museum (2002); *Moist: Asia-Pacific Media Art*, Beijing Millennium Monument Art Museum (2002); *Fantasy Zone*, Beijing Modern Art Center (2002), *Art Museum of Dong A Daily* (2001); *Image is Power*, He Xiangning Art Museum, Shenzhen (2002). Er gehörte zum kuratorischen Team von *Media City Seoul* (2006); *Alors, la Chine?*, Centre Georges Pompidou (2003); der Schanghai Biennale 2002. Zu seinen Publikationen gehören *Farewell to Moralism* (2018); *From Action to Concept* (2015).

Diese Publikation erscheint anlässlich der Ausstellung / This publication was published to accompany the exhibition

Micro Era.
Medienkunst aus China
Micro Era.
Media Art from China
微纪元。中国媒体艺术

Kulturforum
05.09.2019 - 26.01.2020

Direktor der / Director of the Nationalgalerie
Udo Kittelmann

Leiterin / Head of Hamburger Bahnhof – Museum für Gegenwart – Berlin
Gabriele Knapstein

Präsidentin der / President of the Gesellschaft für Deutsch-Chinesischen kulturellen Austausch e.V.
Yu Zhang (张彧)

AUSSTELLUNG
EXHIBITION

Kuratiert von
Curated by
Anna-Catharina Gebbers

Ko-Kuratiert von
Co-Curated by
Victor Wang 王宗孚
Yang Beichen 杨北辰

Kuratorischer Berater
Curatorial Advisor
Pi Li 皮力

Kuratorische Assistenz
Curatorial Assistance
Alexander Wilmschen

Projektkoordination
Project Coordinator
Angelika Jaros GeKA e.V.
Li Ying 李蕊 GeKA e.V.

Registrarin
Registrar
Susanne Anger

Sekretariat
Office Manager
Katherine Israel-Koedel

Kommunikation
Communication
Fabian Fröhlich
Fiona Geuß
Mechthild Kronenberg
Manja Weinert

Projektbezogene Pressearbeit / Project-Related Communication
ARTPRESS – Ute Weingarten

Kunstvermittlung
Education
Claudia Ehgartner
Renée und / and Thomas Rapedius

Referat Forschung, Ausstellungen, Projekte / Research Department, Exhibitions, Projects, Staatliche Museen zu Berlin
Maren Eichhorn
Jörg Völlnagel

Ausstellungsarchitektur
Exhibition Architecture, Art Handling
Rommel Artservice

Medientechnik
Audio Visual Equipment
EIDOTECH GmbH

Visuelle Kommunikation
Visual Communication
StudioKrimm

Praktikantinnen
Interns
Merle Hildebrandt
Franca Spengler
Liann Berktold
Ines Gerber
Lu Zhao 赵璐

Haustechniker
Technicians
Mario Wannagat
Reiner Reis

Hausmeister
Caretakers
André Ewert
Heiko Wagner

Eine Sonderausstellung der Nationalgalerie der Staatlichen Museen zu Berlin und der Gesellschaft für Deutsch-Chinesischen kulturellen Austausch e.V. (GeKA e.V. 德中文化交流基金会) aus Anlass des 25-jährigen Jubiläums der Städtepartnerschaft zwischen Berlin und Peking. / A special exhibition of the Nationalgalerie – Staatliche Museen zu Berlin and the Gesellschaft für Deutsch-Chinesischen kulturellen Austausch e.V. (GeKA e.V. 德中文化交流基金会), on the occasion of the 25th anniversary city partnership between Berlin and Beijing.

www.smb.museum
www.geka-ev.de

Colophon

Impressum

PUBLIKATION
CATALOGUE

Herausgeber
Editors
Anna-Catharina Gebbers,
Udo Kittelmann, Nationalgalerie, Staatliche Museen zu Berlin
Yu Zhang (张彧), Gesellschaft für Deutsch-Chinesischen kulturellen Austausch e. V. (GeKA e. V. 德中文化交流基金会)

Redaktion
Editorial Staff
Anna-Catharina Gebbers
Angelika Jaros

Autoren
Authors
Anna-Catharina Gebbers
Pi Li 皮力
Victor Wang 王宗孚
Yang Beichen 杨北辰

Lektorat
Copyediting
Christiane Weidemann (DE)
Dawn Michelle d'Atri (EN)
Anna-Catharina Gebbers
Angelika Jaros

Übersetzungen
Translations
Ida Yang (CN)
Lixin Jiang (CN)
Amy Klement (EN)
Johanna Gewehr (DE)

Publikationskoordination für die Museen
Publication Coordination for the Museums
Sigrid Wollmeiner

Abbildungen
Images
Cao Yueyang
Studio Cao Fei
Jia Wei
Mei Shuhan
Alexander Wilmschen
Yin Yadi
Ida Yang
Zhang Hongpu

Gestaltung
Design
StudioKrimm

Lithografie
Lithography
StudioKrimm

Projektmanagement
Project Management, Kerber Verlag
Claudia Voigtländer

Herstellung
Production, Kerber Verlag
Jens Bartneck

Die Deutsche Nationalbibliothek verzeichnet diese Publikation in der Deutschen Nationalbibliografie; detaillierte bibliografische Daten sind im Internet über http://dnb.dnb.de abrufbar.
The Deutsche Nationalbibliothek lists this publication in the Deutsche Nationalbibliografie; detailed bibliographic data are available on the Internet at http://dnb.dnb.de.

Gesamtherstellung und Vertrieb / Printed and published by:
Kerber Verlag, Bielefeld
Windelsbleicher Str. 166–170
33659 Bielefeld
Germany
Tel. +49 (0) 5 21/9 50 08-10
Fax +49 (0) 5 21/9 50 08-88
info@kerberverlag.com

Kerber, US Distribution
ARTBOOK | D.A.P.
75 Broad Street, Suite 630
New York, NY 10004
Tel. +1 (212) 627-1999
Fax +1 (212) 627-9484

Kerber-Publikationen werden weltweit in führenden Buchhandlungen und Museumsshops angeboten (Vertrieb in Europa, Asien, Nord- und Südamerika). / Kerber publications are available in selected bookstores and museum shops worldwide (distributed in Europe, Asia, South and North America).

ISBN 978-3-7356-0620-4
www.kerberverlag.com

Printed in Germany

LEIHGEBER
LENDERS

Boers-Li Gallery
Cao Fei
Fang Di
Lu Yang
Société Berlin
Vanguard Gallery
Zhang Peili

BILDNACHWEIS
PICTURE CREDITS

Essay Die Entwicklung der Videokunst / The Evolution of Video Art in China: S. / pp. 11–12 Courtesy of Zhang Peili and Boers-Li Gallery, S. / p. 13 Courtesy of Zhang Peili, S. / pp. 14–17 Courtesy of Cao Fei, Vitamin Space, and Sprüth Magers, S. / pp. 20, 23 Courtesy of Lu Yang and Société, S. / p. 26 Courtesy of Fang Di and Vanguard Gallery
Essay Cao Fei: S. / pp. 30–32, 35–49 Courtesy of Cao Fei, Vitamin Space, and Sprüth Magers,
Essay Fang Di: S. / pp. 50–52, 55–69 Courtesy of Fang Di and Vanguard Gallery
Essay Lu Yang: S. / pp. 70–75, 78–79 Courtesy of Lu Yang and Société
Essay Zhang Peili: S. / pp. 90–93, S. / pp. 96–107 Courtesy of Zhang Peili and Boers-Li Gallery, S. / p. 109 Courtesy of Zhang Peili and Boers-Li Gallery, S. / p. 94 Courtesy of Zhang Peili
Umschlag hinten innen: Courtesy of Anna-Catharina Gebbers, Studio Cao Fei, Victor Wang, Alexander Wilmschen, Ida Yang

Colophon

Ein Projekt von / A project by

Nationalgalerie
Staatliche Museen zu Berlin

德中文化交流基金会
Gesellschaft für Deutsch-Chinesischen kulturellen Austausch e.V. (GeKA e.V.)

Gefördert durch / Promoted by

LOTTO STIFTUNG BERLIN

Medienpartner / Media Partners

Deutschlandfunk Kultur

Unterstützt von / Supported by

STRÖER

Aus Anlass des 25-jährigen Jubiläums der Städtepartnerschaft zwischen Berlin und Peking / On the occasion of the 25th anniversary of the city partnership between Berlin and Beijing

Der Regierende Bürgermeister von Berlin Senatskanzlei | be Berlin